THE AUTOMOBILE BOOK

The Carsy Centre
Canterbury College
New Dover Road
Canterbury, Kent CT1 3AJ

CLASS No. ....

BOOK No. 156 998

LOAN PERIOD ....

SHELF ....

D0312110

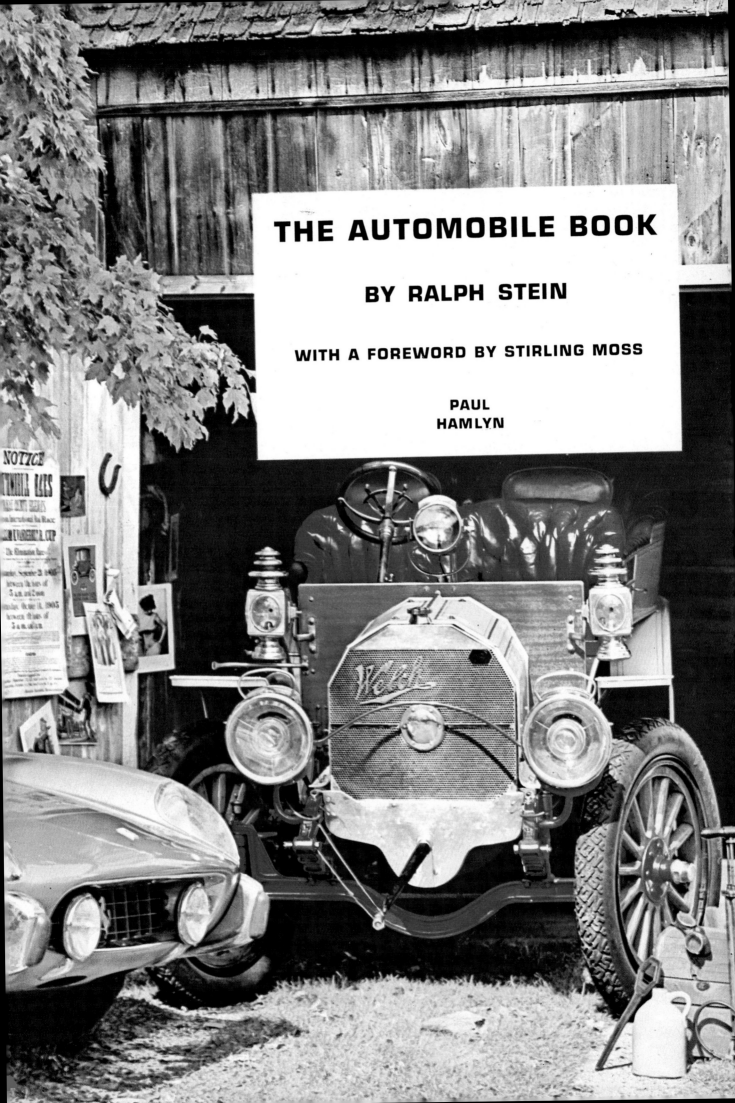

THE AUTOMOBILE BOOK

BY RALPH STEIN

WITH A FOREWORD BY STIRLING MOSS

PAUL
HAMLYN

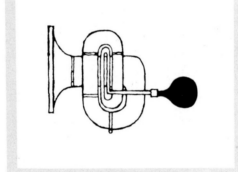

Published by
Paul Hamlyn Ltd
Drury House · Russell Street ·
London WC 2
First published 1962
Revised edition 1964
Second revised edition 1966
© 1961 by Golden Pleasure Books Ltd
Printed in Italy by
O.G.A.M. Verona

CONTENTS

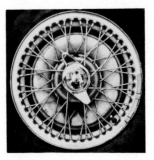

FOREWORD

THE AUTOMOBILE BOOK is one of the most beautifully produced books I have ever seen; the colour photographs alone are superb. But this is no mere picture book. Ralph Stein's writing is both interesting and amusing, and I have learned a lot from it. From steam cars to dream cars, from the first internal combustion engine to the Wankel, he seems to have covered just about everything. I'm glad to see that there is plenty on racing, and racing car design and up-to-date reports on mass-production in the automobile industry, in Britain and Europe as well as in the United States.

The section on old cars reminds me that I once drove a 1904 Cadillac on the London-to-Brighton run. This is a typically British affair, held every November to commemorate the abolition, in 1896, of the law that all self-propelled vehicles must be preceded by a man carrying a red flag. Only cars built before 1905 are eligible, but every year more than 200 set out on the 53-mile run – and most of them get there sooner or later. Thousands of people line the route, and hundreds of modern cars get in the way of the old-timers on their journey out of London and over the hills to the sea. The crowd, in fact, is probably greater than for any other motoring event—Indianapolis and the German Grand Prix included—which gives some idea of the enthusiasm which veteran cars arouse.

In the chapter on post-war racing I find many of the cars I have driven in my sixteen years of competition—Cooper, Keift, HWM, Jaguar, ERA, Maserati, Mercedes-Benz, Aston Martin, Vanwall, BRM, Lotus and others. I started in a little Cooper with a 500c.c. JAP engine mounted at the rear. Then came the Formula Two HWM, with its 2-litre, four-cylinder Alta engine, the Jaguar XK120 with which I won the 1951 Tourist Trophy in pouring rain, and my first real Grand Prix car—a Maserati. I won my first World Championship race, the 1955 British Grand Prix, in a Mercedes-Benz, but it was not until two years later that I achieved my great ambition of winning the event in a British car—the Vanwall. In 1958 I managed to win the Argentine Grand Prix in a 2-litre Cooper-Climax, the car which started the trend towards rear-engined layout by winning most of the races in 1959 and 1960. Later I drove a Lotus—not for the factory team but for my friend "Rob" Walker, a real enthusiast who owns several vintage cars—including a straight-eight Delage—as well as modern racing machinery.

I did not like the 1½-litre Formula One. The cars were too easy to drive and lacked most of the excitement of the old 2½-litres—even though they were already faster on the majority of circuits, thanks mainly to improvements in suspension and tyres. With the new 3-litre Formula One starting in 1966 we can expect a return to much more spectacular racing.

Over the years racing has done a lot to improve everyday cars. It was a big incentive in the early days, when racing cars and touring cars were identical, and even now passenger cars are benefiting from lessons learned on the circuits. Disc brakes, for instance, were first fitted on a racing car only twelve years ago—yet now we take them for granted. I'm not suggesting that disc brakes—or any other part—would not have been introduced if there had been no racing, but it certainly speeds development.

My first car was an Austin Seven, which I learned to drive on my father's farm long before I was old enough to have a licence. Then came a Morgan, an MG TB and a BMW 328, which I sold to pay for my first Cooper. Over the years I have owned cars of all sorts, from a Facel Vega to a BMW Isetta. Today I have a Mini-Cooper and a Lotus Elite, both of which are ideal, in their different ways, for British roads. But for really long journeys I can think of nothing better than a high-powered car with automatic transmission—yes, automatic transmission; I had all the gear-changing I needed when I was racing—power steering, power brakes, air-conditioning and electrically operated windows. It is probably because such cars are so good, so reliable and so easy to drive that more and more people are becoming interested in the rarer and more exotic machinery so beautifully portrayed in this book.

PREFACE

This is a book for people who like the motor car. Any kind of motor car. New cars, old cars, sports cars, steam cars, good cars, even bad cars.

These are the years of the renaissance of the motor car. After decades of disinterest, the rebirth of excitement about automobiles has not only brought forth new and wondrous road vehicles and new clubs devoted to motor sport or the collecting of antiques, but has set people to reading (and writing) about anything and everything to do with cars.

For years, during the 1920's and 1930's, it was hard to find much to read about cars. Those few of us who were daft about automobiles depended on magazines like the British *Autocar* and *Motor*. For information about sporting and racing cars we read *Motor Sport*, also from England. To satisfy our craving for books we found it necessary to go to the Public Library and read what was published between 1900 and 1914—years when cars still engrossed people enough to be written about.

One evening in about 1932, as my brother and I sat enchanted over a dusty volume of the *British Motor* of the Twenties, a young man next to us nudged me. He held up a dog-eared snapshot of a Morgan Three-Wheeler, and motioned towards the door of the reading room. We went outside to talk cars for the next few hours.

No, he didn't own a Three-Wheeler, but he *did* own a 1914 Stutz Bearcat, and his name was Smith Hempstone Oliver. Finding someone who had even *heard* about sports cars in those benighted times was a memorable event. Within the next few days we sampled his Stutz, he our Alfa Romeo. Years later, Oliver became Curator of Land Transportation at the Smithsonian Institution.

Nowadays, happily, there is a wealth of stuff to read: books devoted exclusively to racing cars and racing drivers, to antique cars, to sports cars, books full of mathematical formulae about cylinder heads, books specialising in the cabals of roll centres and slip angles. I love them all. Many people who palpitate with enthusiasm about the innermost minutiae of motor cars love them, too.

But this book is not specialised. It covers a long period and a large canvas, and the brush strokes are necessarily broad. Yet not so broad, I hope, that the car lover who is intrigued by interesting detail will not find enough of it here to pique his curiosity. And I am sure everyone will enjoy the pictures, many of which were especially taken for this book.

Starting with the earliest vehicles, which were not yet cars but were at least horseless, I have endeavoured to evoke the romantic aspects of the earliest steam coaches and the first faltering excursions of the motor car on the public highway. I have tried to recall some of the fierceness of racing, from the early, dusty days to the present. I have even hazarded a strained look at the future.

Many people have helped me with this task. Briggs S. Cunningham allowed Tom Burnside to photograph his notable collection of vintage sporting machinery. Henry Austin Clark, Jr., who owns the Long Island Automotive Museum, opened his bulging files of photographs and other material to us and gave much valuable counsel. In Paris, M. Charles Dollfus allowed us to use material from his extraordinary collection of steam-coach prints; and we are also indebted to Philippe Saalburg for his efforts in tracking down material in France. L. Scott Bailey, Ralph Buckley, René Dreyfus, Jerry Foley and Bob Grier, among many others, helped us photographically. Publications helped us, too: *Autosport*, *The Autocar*, *The Motor* in London; *Road and Track* and *Car and Driver* in the States. We owe thanks also to the Smithsonian Institution, the Henry Ford Museum, the Conservatoire National des Arts et Métiers in Paris, and the Radio Times Picture Library in London, as well as to those car manufacturers who aided us with photographs and information. There are others, I am sure, whom I have neglected to mention here, but whose names will occur to me, conscience-stricken, later. I thank them, too.

"Tumbrils' End" Westbrook, Conn.   R. S.

The Editors would also like to express their thanks to all those who have helped in the preparation of this new edition, not least to Bernard Jourdes, Maurice Perimond and Emilio Ronchini who took special photographs: to M. Jacques Rousseau and to l'Association des Amis de l'Histoire de l'automobile, Musée de Montlhéry, M. Malartre at the Musée National de l'automobile, Château de Rochetaillée, the Marquis de Goulaine, M. René Bolloré, M. Max Terrien at the Musée de la Voiture de Compiègnes, M. Morchet at the Musée du Mans, and to Mr. Peter Roberts in London. They are particularly grateful to the Museo dell'Automobile Carlo Biscaretti di Ruffia of Turin for kind permission to photograph rare models owned by them.

Good Ales

LONDON AND BATH

G.MORTON, Del!

Published by Tho.s M

The Guide or Engineer is seated in front, having a lever rod from the two guide wheels to turn & direct the Carr hind part of the Coach contains the machinery for producing the Steam, on a novel & secure principle, which is con contains about 60 Gallons of water, is placed under the body of the Coach & is its full length & breadth ___ the Cha

THE FIRE
CHARIOTS

Haymarket. London.

PYALL. Sculp.

nother at his right hand connecting with the main Steam Pipe by which he regulates the motion of the Vehicle — the
Pipes to the Cylinders beneath & by its action on the hind wheels sets the Carriage in motion — The Tank which

As far as we know, Nicolas Joseph Cugnot, a French army engineer, was the first man to sit behind the controls of a self-propelled road vehicle. Remember this the next time you are stuck in traffic. There, far down the road, at the very head of the line, in space and time, sits M. Cugnot.

Cugnot designed his steam carriage for hauling field artillery. It was constructed in 1769 by a man named Brézin, but the King's Minister of War, apparently not too satisfied with his first machine, ordered another one built at the royal arsenal. It is this second machine (of 1771) that you can see if you should go to the *Conservatoire National des Arts et Métiers* in Paris.

French politics during the dizzy reign of Louis XV and the Seven Years' War prevented this second machine from being run, but Cugnot's first machine did run, and conflicting reports say that it was capable of carrying four passengers at two to six miles an hour. Its steam-making capabilities were not much; every fifteen minutes it had to stop and boil water.

Cugnot's car was a three-wheeler with a chassis built of heavy timbers. Its great pear-shaped copper boiler and the two monstrous cylinders of 50 litres capacity to which it fed steam, plus the primitive driving mechanism, all hung from and turned with the single front wheel that steered the beast. It evidently didn't steer too well, nor was its stopping power very good, for it is said that Cugnot once knocked over the wall of the courtyard where it was being tested and another time upset it on a Paris street.

Certainly there had been earlier attempts to improve upon the horse. Eccentric European monarchs in the sixteenth century even resorted to faking horseless carriages by putting some of their hapless subjects to work on treadmills inside elaborately carved and gilded structures on wheels. About 1600, Prince Maurice of Nassau had built for himself, by one Simon Stevin, a four-wheeled, two-masted affair to sail on the beach near Scheveningen, Holland. It was big enough to carry his entourage of twenty-eight frightened Dutchmen plus a possibly even more frightened Spanish admiral, Mendoza by name, who was at the time the good Prince's prisoner of war. An early automotive expert of the time, named Howell, wrote in a road-test report: "This engine that hath wheels and sails, will hold above twenty people,

and goes with the wind, being drawn or mov'd by nothing else, and will run, the wind being good, and the sails hois'd up, above fifteen miles an hour upon the even hard sands."

In the late 1700's steam power began to change the world. It powered the industrial revolution of the nineteenth century and the new ships and railways that would shrink the globe. But after Cugnot's brief success in Paris, it was not to be France that would lead the way to mechanical road locomotion. France was too busy with other interesting projects, like storming the Bastille and getting rid of the Bourbon kings. The tumbrils had no engines. For years afterwards the French were too involved with Napoleon to do much about steam wagons. Come to think of it, however, Napoleon, although he didn't dream of it, did do quite a lot toward helping the French become the motoring pioneers of a century later. He built their wonderful road system.

It was in England (although God knows they were busy enough themselves with rebellious American colonials and later with Bonaparte) that the idea of hooking a steam cylinder to a wheel next appeared.

In 1784, in Redruth, a village in Cornwall, William Murdock built a small, three-wheeled, non-passenger-carrying model, which ran away from him after dark one night, throwing out sparks and making an unholy row. It is said to be the first self-powered vehicle to terrify a pedestrian – the village parson, who must have thought that Beelzebub himself was abroad on the roads. But Murdock did not continue his experiments with road vehicles for long. His chief was the great James Watt, who, jealous of his assistant, gave him so much other work to do that he had no time for such frivolities as horseless steam carriages.

About this same time, Richard Trevithick, another English steam engineer, was also working on a model steam carriage — which was really the first locomotive too — and by 1801 he had become so successful with it that he started with his cousin, Andrew Vivian, the construction of a full-size machine. Describing a trial trip on Christmas Eve of that year, a witness said that Trevithick drove his machine up a hill half a mile, carrying eight people "faster than a man could walk." But Trevithick could get no one interested enough to invest money in development and finally scrapped the machine, selling its engine to a man who used it to power a mill.

In the United States in 1805, Oliver Evans, a mechanic born in Newport, Delaware, built his famous amphibious steam-powered dredge, the Orukter Amphibolus, which waddled from the workshop in which he built it, through the streets of Philadelphia, and into the Schuylkill River under its own power.

Preceding pages: Goldsworthy Gurney's Steam Carriage of 1827-28. This machine could carry twenty-one passengers at speeds upwards of 15 m.p.h. If you look closely, just in front of the rear wheels, you can see the "legs" Gurney fitted "to help upon hills".

N. Cugnot's Steam Tractor of 1771 (upper left), second model by the man credited with building the first self-propelled vehicle, is now in the Conservatoire National des Arts et Métiers. Two 50-litre cylinders, its boiler, and its primitive drive mechanism (upper right) all turned with the single front wheel. Steering was obviously almost impossible. An early print (centre, right) purports to portray the world's first car accident when Cugnot's machine struck a courtyard wall. Stephen Farffler (centre, left) employs a more primitive method of propulsion in his one-man power sports-wagen of 1670. Albrecht Dürer's engraving (lower right) shows a mechanical carriage built for Emperor Maximilian I, in 1520.

Steam locomotion was a subject for hilarity and sarcasm in the 1820's. The satirical English cartoon on the right takes a dim view of the future of such transport, investing the movement with a boisterous, chaotic character, and presenting the vehicles in ridiculous, fanciful forms. The machines which took to the English roads in this period were gaily painted and Gargantuan. Typical was F. Hill's passenger-carrying steam carriage of 1839 (below). The huge boiler on the back is reminiscent of those seen on early locomotives and required just as much tending. Also notable is the similarity of the suspension of this machine to the type used on railway carriages. Murdock's model steam carriage of 1784 (bottom, right) is a non-passenger-carrying device and can now be seen at the Science Museum in London.

It was scarcely a steam car, for it weighed some twenty tons, and in addition to wheels it was festooned with chain buckets, digging devices, and paddles to move it through the water. Still, it *was* a self-propelled vehicle and as such a biological ancestor of the motor car.

Men in places as far apart as Hartford, Connecticut, and Prague, and Halifax, Nova Scotia, were building steam carriages. But suddenly in England in the 1820's there was a boom in such road locomotives, a boom — oddly enough — caused by horse-drawn coaches. For coaching had increased tremendously in England owing to the new need for mobility in its rapidly expanding economy after the Napoleonic Wars. And more coaching meant that better roads were needed. Two road-building geniuses, Telford and Macadam, whose name still clings to our tar-surfaced roads today, revolutionised methods of highway construction and within a short time England had wonderful roads eminently suitable for mechanical transport, steam transport.

Starting in the 1820's, there took to the roads of England as wild looking, gaily painted, and oddly designed a lot of vehicles as has ever existed. It seemed for a while that every engineer in Britain was designing boilers and furnaces and running gear for the new steam carriages. These were not for the use of individual owners, however. These were giant pantechnicons, as big as modern motor coaches, to carry paying passengers.

Burstall & Hill, Maceroni & Squire, James & Anderson, and Scott Russell were just a few of the many engineers at work. And David Gordon. We must not forget Gordon, for he was the genius who, convinced that mere wheels could not propel his carriage, fitted it with six steam-powered, jointed legs and feet to push it along.

Even the great Goldsworthy Gurney, whose steam buses were later among the most successful, fitted his first machine in 1827 with similar steam-driven legs, "to help when starting up and upon hills." This first carriage of Gurney's was capable of carrying twenty-

one passengers. It had a water-tube boiler and was fitted with separators to ensure dry steam for the cylinders. This machine was often seen chuffing about in the London area and was capable, when everything was working efficiently, of reaching 15 miles an hour.

As if it weren't dangerous enough just to ride in these carriages with their primitive boilers, shaky steering, and laughable brakes, the passengers had to be continually on guard against angry citizens. Filson Young, in his book, *The Complete Motorist* (London, 1904), tells of one of Gurney's trial trips:

"On one journey which he made to Bath with a number of guests, his carriage was attacked at Melksham where there happened to be a fair. The people formed such a dense mass that it was impossible to move the carriage through them; the crowd, being mainly composed of agricultural labourers, considered all machinery directly injurious to their interests, and with a cry of 'Down with all machinery', they set upon the carriage and its occupants, seriously injuring Mr. Gurney and his assistant engineer, who had to be taken to Bath in an unconscious condition."

The "assistant engineer" was what we would call the fireman. This poor fellow stood on a rear platform in some carriages, or inside, among the hot fireboxes, flailing rods, and leaping chains in others, shovelling coal and coke (liquid petroleum fuels were some forty years in the future), greasing the machinery with a brush dipped in lard or in palm oil and apprehensively checking the safety valve.

A daring entrepreneur of the time, Sir Charles Dance, bought three of Gurney's coaches and operated a sort of bus service between Gloucester and Cheltenham for four months from February to June, 1831, during which time he made no less than 396 trips and travelled 3,644 miles.

But it was Walter Hancock who was the most successful builder of steam carriages. He built nine machines with wonderful names: Infant, Autopsy, Automaton, Era, and the like. In 1834, from mid-August until November, he ran the Autopsy and the Era between the City, Moorgate, and Paddington, carrying in all some 4,000 passengers. He was perhaps the first builder to use high-pressure steam. Where others were satisfied to use it at, say, fifty pounds per square inch, Hancock used over two hundred pounds. This could sometimes be a disadvantage. W. Worby Beaumont reports drily about Hancock's Enterprise of 1832: "The engine attendant had fastened the safety valve lever down with copper wire, and had started the engines and blower while the coach was standing. The effect of the forced draught was that intended, but the steam not being used as fast as made, nor free to escape at the safety valve, it got out elsewhere, and at the inquest which followed, the evidence was more complimentary to the boiler than to its attendant."

There is but one other recorded case of such a mishap, for although it must have been miserably

The charming qualities of early steam diligences and the character of their inventors, who left little to chance, is shown by the illustration of Gordon's steam carriage of 1824 (top, left). Gordon, unwilling to believe that his road locomotive could climb hills or even start from rest without wheelspin, designed a delightful system of mechanical legs to help his creation along. Above are part of the fleet of steam carriages built by Walter Hancock. He made nine in all and engaged in a successful passenger-carrying service for several months — from August to November, 1834 — transporting approximately 4,000 passengers during that period. The Enterprise (below) was involved in one of the few serious accidents suffered by the company. Her engine attendant fastened the safety valve closed with a piece of copper wire while the coach was standing at rest, then developed a fine head of steam in the boiler, which blew up with interesting results.

H.Alken's Illustration of Modern Prophecy, or Novelty for the Year 1829.

I say Fellow, give my Buggy a charge of Coke, your Charcoal is so D__d dear.

THE PROGRESS OF STEAM.

London, Pub.d Jan.y 1828. by S.&J.Fuller, 34, Rathbone Place.

Two men were required to operate these private steam road-carriages — one to steer and another to feed the fire and tend the boiler. Such especially-built contrivances were restricted to a few wealthy and daring gentlemen. The one on the left was built by Thomas Rickett for the Marquis of Stafford in 1858 in England. The one on the far left was built by Cecil Rhodes, also in England, but the lucky owner remains unknown. The fanciful French design (right) is almost prophetic of the tail-finned extravagances of Detroit. Two cartoonists of the 1820's (below) poke fun at the future of such vehicles. H. Alken (lower left) forsees the advent of service stations and "fuel wars" to cut prices, while the illustrator on the right sums up his feelings about mechanical locomotion with his nonsensical teapot fitted with wheels.

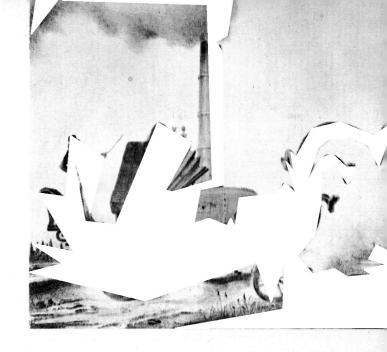

WALKING BY STEAM.   RIDING BY STEAM.   FLYING BY STEAM.

Note ...In the Ladies Vehicle the Steam is made with a strong infusion of Gunpowder Tea   (LOCOMOTION.)   For an explanation of the Machinery see the next Number of the Edinburg Review.

THE GREATEST
MECHANICAL
EXHIBITION
IN THE WORLD.

THE
STEAM
BUGGY!

Pronounced by scientific men to be the most wonderful invention of modern times. It can be driven, with two persons in it, 150 miles a day, upon common roads. It is light and strong, and can be managed better than any horse, and can be driven faster than any person dare to ride. Will match it against any trotting horse in the world.

THE ONLY
Steam Velocipede
IN THE WORLD.

Pronounced a perfect triumph in mechanism. It can be driven up any hill, and will out speed any horse in the world.

TO BE SEEN AT
600 BROADWAY.

ADMISSION . . . . 25 Cents.

uncomfortable, the steam carriage does not seem to have been generally dangerous. In 1834, one of Scott Russell's machines, running between Glasgow and Paisley, burst its boiler and killed three people.

But it was not its dangerous aspects or its discomfort that pushed the steam carriage off the roads of England. It was, rather, the ferocious antagonism of the new railways and the coaching interests, and the savage tolls levied against them. For example, between Prescot and Liverpool, where a four-horse coach would pay 4s., a steam carriage would pay £2-8-0. Bucolic locals vented their spleen against the new machines by continual sabotage. For instance, Summers and Ogle's eighteen-passenger carriage of 1831 (which, by the way, could better 30 m.p.h.), originally had six-foot driving wheels. But these were reduced to five feet six inches after hirelings of the anti-steam-carriage faction sawed the spokes three inches from the rim, so that the wheels fractured and gave way on the road.

The steam carriages were not entirely blameless either, for they blew sparks and smoke into farmyards, and the noise of their passing must have been frightful. Nor was a little device like that fitted to one of Hancock's machines likely to engender the friendship of other road users. This feature was a trap door under the fire-box which slid open to deposit the ashes or, if the operator wished, even the whole fire on to the road.

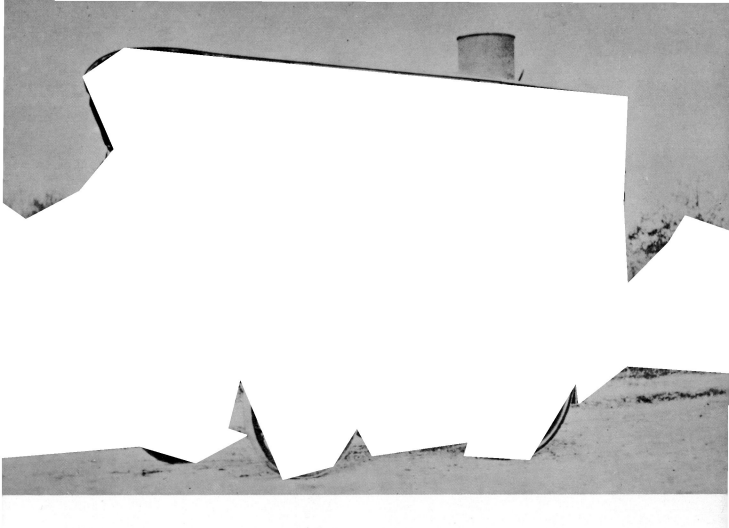

In 1831, a committee had held hearings and reported to the Houses of Parliament in favour of steam coaches and a reduction in tolls, but it was to no avail. The powerful forces against steam on the roads finally won and by 1840 the steam carriages had almost disappeared from the king's highway. Not one of them was preserved. A pity. What a prize one would be today for an antique-car restorer.

In England, a few hardy types persisted in building road steamers for individuals, notably Thomas Rickett of Buckingham, who made them for eccentric milords like the Marquis of Stafford (in 1858) and the Earl of Caithness (in 1860). But in 1865 came the notorious "Red Flag Act" which lasted until 1896. This ridiculous ordinance prevented any self-powered vehicle from travelling faster than four miles an hour in the country, or two miles an hour in towns. And in both instances a man was to walk ahead of such a machine, carrying a red flag.

So, although the British had been the first to operate self-propelled vehicles successfully, they took to the roads only by stealth until 1896. Other men in other countries would develop the motor car.

For a time they continued to concern themselves with steam. In the United States, Richard Dudgeon built steam vehicles not too different from those of Rickett: small, horizontally-boilered locomotives, coal-fired, with seats arranged about the boiler, just the thing for a ride on a hot summer's day. Dudgeon

Built shortly after 1875 by Amédée Bollée senior, this bulky steam-driven vehicle (opposite page) belonged for a long time to the Marquis de Broc, the "châtelain" of Parigné-le-Polin near Mans. For a quarter of a century this large brake could be seen travelling round the roads of the Sarthe district. It carries the arms of its owner and now, in its restored state, it is one of the most remarkable items in the collection of the Compiègne Museum. "L'Obéissante" (above) was Amédée Bollée senior's steam omnibus. He built it in 1873. It was one of the first vehicles to have pivoting front wheels (Lankensperger steering). The front wheels were independently sprung, and each rear wheel was driven individually by its own two-cylinder, "V" engine. The boiler was coal-fired. It weighed 8,000 pounds and its 20 h.p. engines propelled it at 25 m.p.h. Left: is a handbill advertising Sylvester Roper's steam vehicles.

built his first machine in 1853, but a late Dudgeon steamer of about 1867 still exists in the museum of the Veteran Motor Car Club of America in Brookline, Massachusetts.

In 1869, Sylvester H. Roper, of Roxbury, built a steam velocipede which astounded the peasantry at country fairs in New England. A later four-wheeled steam carriage of Roper's can be seen today in the Henry Ford Museum in Dearborn, Michigan.

In 1884, Lucius D. Copeland fitted a "Penny-farthing" bicycle with a beautifully delicate and light steam engine and then went on to fit a three-wheeled car in the same manner. He even formed a company to market his vehicles — the Moto-cycle

PHAETON MOTO-CYCLE

WEIGHT, 220 POUNDS.
SPEED, 10 MILES PER HOUR.
POWER, 2 HORSE.

MOTO-CYCLE MANUFACTURING COMPANY,

J. E. WATKINS, PRESIDENT,
W. H. TRAVIS, SECRETARY,
E. F. SMITH, TREASURER.

1529 Arch Street, Philadelphia, Pa.

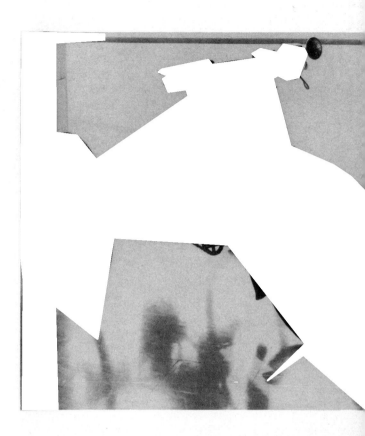

Manufacturing Company of Philadelphia — but without success. As Richard Dudgeon had earlier complained, people were not yet ready for personal mechanical vehicles. The poor could not afford them and the status symbol of the rich was still the varnished and shining open carriage, in charge of a cockaded coachman driving a matched pair of blooded horses.

In France, Amédée Bollée, the elder, was building successful steamers (his L'Obéissante of 1873 is still preserved in France), as were the Count de Dion (in 1887) and Léon Serpollet, who in 1890 was among the first to use liquid fuel in a flash-steam boiler. Serpollet was destined to keep steam important well into the twentieth century, though he died in 1907.

In any case, although steam cars would be built in America until the 1920's, the age of the road locomotive was ending. The petrol-driven car was almost ready to appear.

Yet even the first crude motor cars could never have appeared on the roads of Europe and America without a host of inventions, discoveries, and new techniques, which were the fruits of the nineteenth century's mechanical investigations. A few of the

Lucius D. Copeland (left) sits aboard his wonderful steam tricycle outside the Smithsonian Institution in 1888. Copeland, unlike so many of his predecessors, succeeded in building marvellously light and delicate steam engines, one of which still exists in the Arizona Museum. The circular advertising his vehicle (above, left) was distributed by the Northrop Manufacturing Company of Camden, New Jersey, which formed the Moto-Cycle Manufacturing Company to market the Copeland design. But, alas, without success. This de Dion Bouton petroleum tricycle (above) is of French origin, although it was used in Italy. It was built in 1899 and had a one-cylinder engine, with bore and stroke of 66 x 77 cm., a capacity of 240 c.c. and developed 1 h.p. It is thought that Ettore Bugatti made one of his first motorised expeditions on a vehicle of this type.

more important were:

1. The ability to bore an (almost) truly round hole or turn an (almost) truly round shaft.

2. Metals with predictable and uniform properties.

3. Petroleum (for lubrication and fuel).

4. The vulcanising of rubber and the invention of the rubber tyre.

5. The application of electricity (the battery, the induction coil).

6. The Lankensperger (or Ackermann) steering

system, whereby each front wheel turns on its own pivot, or king-pin, as opposed to the method of pivoting the whole front axle at its centre, as on a horse-drawn carriage.

7. The differential gear.

8. The internal combustion engine—of course!

Who invented the internal combustion engine? Who first put the fire inside a cylinder and used its expansive force to drive a piston directly, instead of using the fire first to boil water and make steam, and then to pipe the steam to the cylinder to move the piston?

There were many, each of them making advances—and mistakes—from which others learned. The first people to put the fire inside the cylinder seem to have used too much fire. They tried gunpowder—with uncomfortable results. It wasn't until combustible gases became available that combustion inside a cylinder was possible. In 1804, a Swiss, Isaac De Rivaz, succeeded in building an internal combustion engine of sorts, using hydrogen. In fact, he even mounted it on a wheeled chassis which is said to have moved. Although De Rivaz was granted a patent for this vehicle on January 30, 1807, he did not succeed in developing his invention.

In 1860, in France, however, J. J. Etienne Lenoir

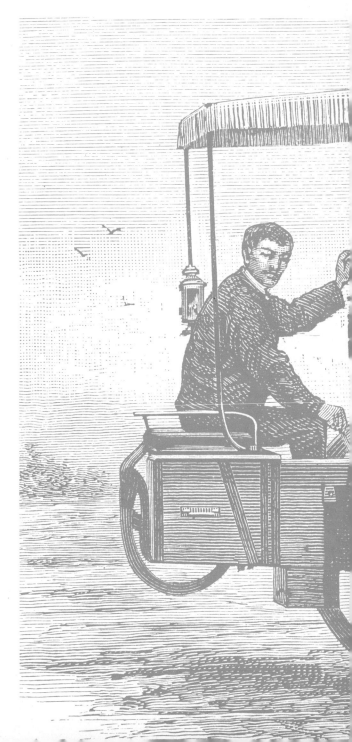

Before setting forth on a run from Paris to Lyons in 1890, Léon Serpollet (above) poses for a moment with his friend, Ernest Archdeacon. Serpollet's machine, like that of his American contemporary, Lucius Copeland, was light and handy compared to the cumbersome road vehicles of the day. Messieurs de Dion, Bouton, and Trepardoux (right) are transported by a far more weighty conveyance. However, this steam phaeton was built in 1885, pre-dating the Serpollet machine. Count Albert de Dion, a wealthy boulevardier, became interested in the Eighties in building a "horseless". To this end he enlisted the services of two penurious model makers, Bouton and Trepardoux. Trepardoux left, but the firm of de Dion et Bouton, after building many types of steam vehicles, went on to fame as one of the great petrol-driven motor manufacturers, thanks to their extraordinarily lightweight engines.

built what must be considered the first practical gas engine. He used illuminating gas for fuel and an electric spark from a Ruhmkorff coil for ignition. This first engine of Lenoir's was not much smaller than a bungalow and about as light. Lenoir is said to have experimented with liquid fuels, too, and even to have installed one of his later engines in a road vehicle he drove in the environs of Paris as early as May, 1862. He also used it to run a motor-boat at about the time the *Monitor* and the *Merrimac* were fighting it out at Hampton Roads. These later experiments came to naught, but Lenoir must be acknowledged the creator of the first internal combustion engine that really worked. Further, Lenoir's efforts attracted other inventors to the possibilities of internal combustion. In 1862, the Frenchman, Alphonse Beau de Rochas patented, but never built, a four-cycle engine. In 1878, N. A. Otto, in the town of Deutz, Germany, actually constructed a four-cycle engine that is the direct ancestor of the engine in the car you are driving today. Otto never tried to put one of his engines in a vehicle. He and his partner, Langen, were interested in stationary engines, not horseless carriages. One of their employees, Gottlieb Daimler, was, however, interested in horseless carriages.

The first petrol-driven car is popping and grinding

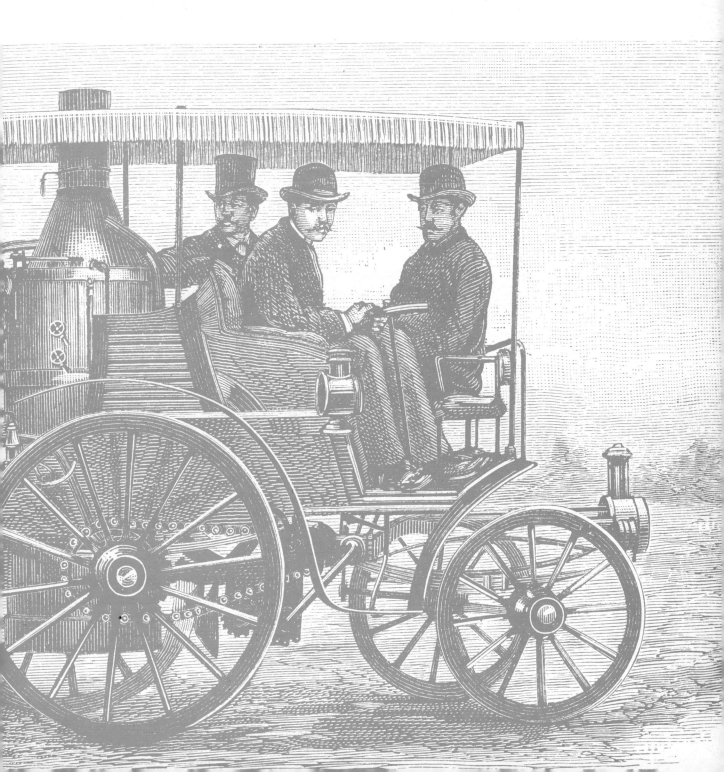

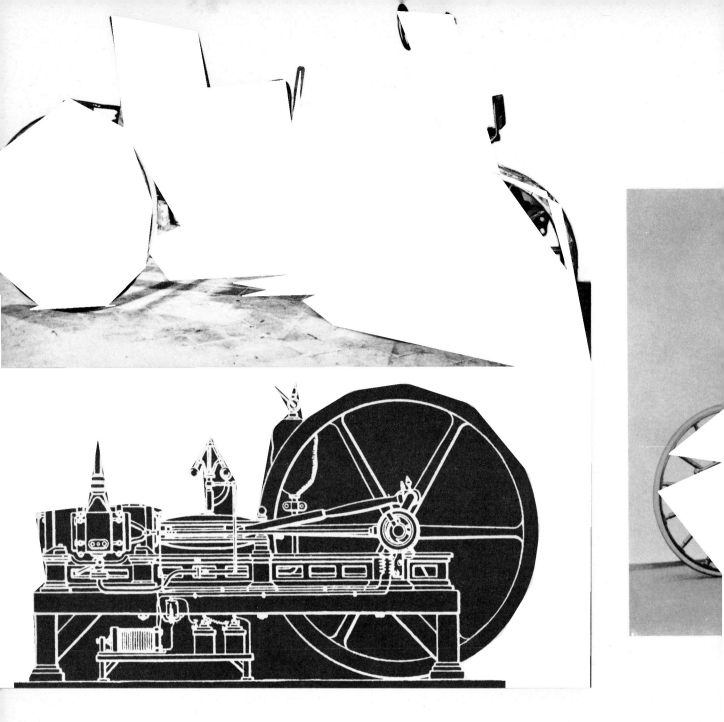

just around the corner now. Who is in the driver's seat? Is it that erratic genius, Siegfried Marcus? The work of Marcus was until recent years so unrecognised that the 1946 edition of the Encyclopaedia Britannica even spells his name wrong. It calls him Narkus. He was born in Malchin, Germany, in 1831, and from the age of twelve, when he was apprenticed to a machinist, until he died, poor and worn out by sickness in 1898, he lived and worked in a frenzy of engineering excitement. He restlessly dabbled in chemistry, electricity, even dentistry. He once pulled out one of his own teeth, but in his excitement made a great wound in his cheek; he treated that himself, too. When he was seventeen he was hired by the then newly organised firm of Siemens and Halske, for whom, two years later, he invented an electrical relay system for telegraphy. When he was twenty he left them and went to Vienna. There he worked for the court mechanic,

the Imperial Medical Academy, and the Royal Chemical Laboratory. In 1860, when he was twenty-nine, he rented some rooms at 107 Mariahilferstrasse, Vienna, and set up his own engineering laboratory. Here he secretively worked on all manner of inventions, in his own dilettante way, seldom finishing anything once he was satisfied it could work.

He was fascinated by the idea of electric lighting and got the idea that perhaps benzene vapour ignited by an electric spark would make a beautiful light. It didn't. It made a beautiful explosion. From there he jumped to the idea that a benzene-vapour explosion in a cylinder might make an engine run.

By 1865, he was driving a car—a hand-cart powered by a two-cycle engine coupled directly to the rear wheels, *sans* clutch. It was necessary to lift the rear wheels off the ground to start the engine; when they were dropped the hand-cart took off. Lacking a

Siegfried Marcus may have invented the world's first petrol-driven car. He built his first car in 1865, his second (upper left) in 1874. The first man to build a "usable" gas engine was Etienne Lenoir, who as early as 1860 used "cooking gas" to run his engine (below). This Benz "Comfortable" (left) was built between 1894 and 1897, with a rear engine, and is provided with two excellent seats. These vehicles were imported into France by Emile Roger who modified the model slightly and popularised the "Roger Benz", in which he participated in the famous Paris-Rouen run (1894).

clutch, it also had no brakes. But it ran well enough to suit Marcus, and he therefore abandoned it. Anyhow, what sense was there in using benzene imported in bottles from Germany at three marks a litre!

For the next ten years or so, Marcus turned to other ideas and projects and even prospered a little. He tutored the Austrian Crown Prince in science, installed an electric-bell system in the royal palace (during which he horrified the courtiers and amused the Empress by leaping on the silken royal bed to mark the spot on the wall for the button) and was even grudgingly recognised by the Royal Academy of Sciences.

In 1874, he was involved with motor cars again. This time he made three cars—one in his own shop, the other two were done by an outside firm under his direction. One of these still exists in the *Technisches Museum* of Vienna, and is still capable of running

under its own power. This car has a single cylinder four-stroke engine (very likely built before Otto's) with low-tension magneto ignition and a carburettor fitted with an internal revolving brush to assist vaporisation of the fuel. It is of 1,570 c.c. and develops ¾ h.p., which is capable of driving the car at about four miles an hour. The chassis is of wood, has half-elliptic springs, a steering wheel, iron tyres, a steel-cone clutch, but no gear lever (for the simple reason that it has but one speed).

Marcus had a car, all right. He called it a *Strassenwagen*. Anyone but he would have worked to get support to go on and improve it, to build more and better cars. But the police fussed about the noise and Marcus was bored with his new gadget, anyhow, so he just said the hell with it and went on to other, more exciting experiments.

In 1924, the Viennese put up a statue to Marcus,

31

and the *Technisches Museum* exhibited his car and even had a booklet about the inventor available until 1938, when Hitler's troops marched in. The Germans tried to destroy the car, but the museum people had hidden it. The Nazis did manage to burn most of the booklets. They didn't like people thinking that a Jew might have invented the motor car before Gottlieb Daimler and Carl Benz.

The Nazis, as usual, were being wrong-headed. Marcus's accomplishment did not detract from the glory Gottlieb Daimler and Carl Benz had so right-fully earned. For while Marcus had drifted away from his idea, Daimler and Benz nourished and developed their weakling, putt-putting, single-cylindered brain children. From them, directly, grew the giant motor industry of our day.

In 1885, when Daimler and Benz, each unknown to the other, first wheeled internal combustion-engined vehicles out of their workshops, Europe was just about ready for the motor car. People—at least the upper classes—felt secure and prosperous. The long peace after the Napoleonic Wars had been broken but once

by the Franco-Prussian War. In half a century, the railways had changed from a frightening new means of rapid travel for the adventurous to a commonplace which spread its tracks across the continents. Every town had its factories and foundries. Now, too, people were just about to get their first taste of really fast personal travel on the newly invented safety bicycle.

Gottlieb Daimler was fifty-one by the time he had his first roadworthy machine running. He had spent most of his working life with engines, first with steam, which convinced him that for many purposes the

It was the efforts of Carl Benz and Gottlieb Daimler which made commercially practicable, petrol-engined motor vehicles possible. Daimler constructed a "motor-cycle" in 1885 with a single-cylinder engine using "hot-tube" ignition. The photograph (top) shows a reproduction of the original machine. In that same year, 1885 — and quite unknown to Daimler — Carl Benz, as fascinated as his countryman by the prospects of internal combustion, powered his three-wheeled design (left) with a one-cylinder engine which employed an electric ignition system. Within a decade, Benz had developed his primitive design into a highly saleable carriage, such as the 1898 Benz (above).

steam engine was outmoded, and then, in 1872, with gas engines as technical director of the Deutz Engine Works owned by Otto and Langen. Otto and Langen were well satisfied with the ponderous, slow-speed, stationary gas engines they built, but Daimler was not, although he had made many improvements in them. Daimler's dream was a light, high-speed engine that could be run on benzene (*not* named after Carl Benz, by the way). In 1882, after much argument with Otto and Langer, Daimler left, taking with him Wilhelm Maybach, who had worked closely with him, and opened his own experimental shop in Cannstatt. By 1883, Daimler had perfected his system of hot-tube ignition, based on earlier experiments by a man named Funk, and soon afterwards he had a neat, compact, high-speed (750 r.p.m.) engine. This is as good a place as any to explain hot-tube ignition.

Nowadays an electric spark ignites the charge in the cylinder. Lenoir also used an electric spark, but his apparatus was huge and clumsy. Otto's engine used an open gas flame which was exposed to a gas-air mixture at just the right instant by a sliding valve which then clapped shut again. Daimler's device was a small platinum tube which screwed into the side of the cylinder much like a modern sparking-plug. A Bunsen burner, fed from its own little tank of benzene or petrol, heated this tube red hot. When the rising piston compressed the mixture in the cylinder, some of it rushed into the tube and was ignited. Simple! I once saw the late Joe Tracy—of Vanderbilt Cup fame—experimenting with hot-tube ignition on a Bollée tri-car. It worked pretty well. Of course, he had to light the burner with a match before cranking the engine. And there were other nuisances, such as having the burners blow out in a high wind or the whole business catch fire if the car upset. But Tracy showed me how it was even possible to vary the ignition timing by changing the position of the flame along the tube. The further away from the cylinder, the later the timing.

In 1885, Daimler installed one of his engines in a bicycle of his own design—a primitive motor-cycle of wood, with iron-shod tyres and outrigger wheels. A great leather saddle covered the single cylinder of the ½ h.p. engine. The benzene tank for the burner was practically in the rider's back pocket, while the burner itself warmed the crook of his right knee.

But the thing ran. On November 10, 1885, Daimler's son, Paul, drove it the three kilometres from Cannstatt to Unterturkheim and back. Later, when Lake Cannstatt froze over, this early motor-bike, fitted with studs on its rear wheel and a sort of ski in front, amazed the local skaters as it did figures-of-eight on the ice.

Emile Levassor was the first designer to put the engine in front. Behind it, logically, he placed the clutch and gearbox. By so doing he set a fashion which persists into our time. The diagram (upper right) from Worby Beaumont's "Motor Vehicles and Motors" (1902) shows Levassor's Daimler-engined car of 1894. This Panhard et Levassor of 1891 (lower right) driven by a 2-cylinder V-type Daimler engine, is justifiably considered as the first French petroleum car sold to a client. The Panhard Levassor of 1895 (top of the page) is fitted with what must be one of the very first attempts at closed coachwork. The Renault below it, built in 1900, five years later, doesn't show any great advance in the art of building saloon bodies.

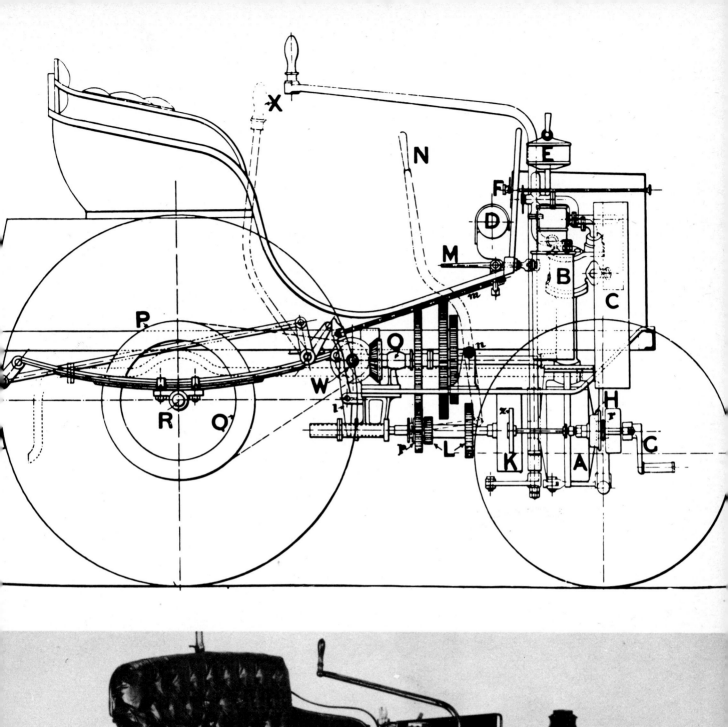

Daimler was really more interested in engines than in motor cars. He installed them in boats, in tram-cars, and even in a dirigible built by a local genius. Certainly he saw that his engines would be wonderful for propelling road vehicles, but, at first, he looked upon them as accessories people might buy and install, instead of the horse, on the family carriage. He tried it himself in 1886 and Daimler's first four-wheeled car was no more than a glorified horse carriage with an engine sticking up out of the rear floor. Nor did he use swivelling front wheels to steer. The whole front axle still swung on a centre pivot. Still, this car ran pleasantly enough, attaining some 10 m.p.h. from its 1½ h.p. engine which drove the rear wheels by means of belts. There was no differential and the two speeds were selected by tightening and loosening the belts.

Daimler rapidly improved his cars, but it was his engines, exported to and licensed in other countries, especially France, that gave motoring its great push forward.

At about the same time that Daimler's son was riding his father's motor-cycle, Carl Benz was trying out his first car, a spidery three-wheeler. Benz, like Daimler, was fascinated by small internal combustion engines, but while Daimler had been an important engineer, employed by a successful gas-engine company, Benz was starting small engine factories,

going bankrupt, taking in partners with capital, and being cheated by financial backers. Eventually, with new backers, he founded a company styling itself Benz & Cie., in Mannheim, to manufacture stationary gas engines using an electric ignition system he had devised. It was almost exactly like the one we use today, with storage battery, coil, and sparking-plug. Business was fine, but Benz had the urge to build a car using one of his small engines and in the spring of 1885 he succeeded.

Benz's car was three-wheeled. He had either not heard about Lankensperger steering, or perhaps considered it too fussy to build. Rightly, he dismissed the horse-carriage steering that had satisfied Daimler. The car had a single-cylinder, ¾ h.p. (at 250-300 r.p.m.), water-cooled engine in the rear. The connecting-rod stuck nakedly out of the horizontally-mounted cylinder and drove, by way of a similarly unenclosed crankshaft, a huge, horizontal, spoked fly-wheel which had to be pulled around to start the engine. Like Daimler's machine—which, of course, he hadn't seen —it was driven with belts and pulleys. But unlike Daimler, he devised a differential of his own for the rear axle.

To the detriment of his gas-engine business, Benz kept fussing and fiddling with his baby and constantly improving it. And running down his battery, too. At night he'd lug the battery home and hook it

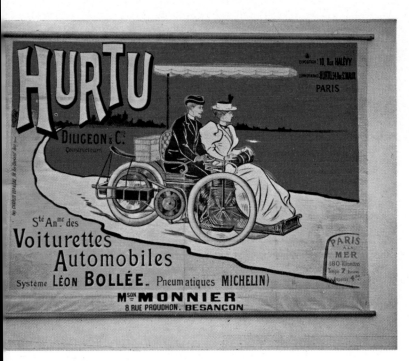

America's first mass-produced car was the Curved Dash Olds of 1901 (above, a 1902 model). Built by Ransom E. Olds (whose initials also formed the name of a car), it had a rugged simplicity typical of American cars of that period. Powered by a single-cylinder, 5 h.p. engine, it was capable of 20 m.p.h. Note the tiller for steering. Comparatively sophisticated machines like the Peugeot quadricycles of 1893 (far left) and 1896 (left centre) were already gaily chuffing down the grands boulevards of Paris when American machines were still in their early, experimental stages. Note the front seat in the 1896 car, which could make a bumper of your mother-in-law. On the left is a poster for the Hurtu Tri-car, another European marque.

37

Above is one of the very first cars built at Tours in 1897 by Emile Delahaye, before he moved to the Rue de Banquier in Paris. This 3-seater had a horizontal rear motor. It was first designed with handlebar steering and was given a steering-wheel in 1898. A typical "horseless" of 1895 stands on the right. This German-built Lutzmann had a 4 h.p. single-cylindered engine in the rear and a belt clutch like a modern lawn-mower. Seated in it are H. J. Lawson and early motorist J. A. Koosey. Lawson later tried to form a monopoly of the infant British industry. The Duryea brothers' car of 1903 (below) was the first successful American car.

up to a generator driven by the foot-treadle of his wife's sewing machine. So, while Herr Benz studied blueprints under the gaslight, Frau Benz pumped away for hours to charge the battery for tomorrow's experiments. It was Frau Benz, also, who went on one of the first long trips in a motor car. At five o'clock one morning, while Benz lay fast asleep, she took her two older boys and set off in the car (a slightly later model) from Mannheim to Pforzheim. Eugen, the eldest, steered. On hills they all got out and pushed. But they made it. The first person to pilot a car on a longish road journey was a middle-aged German hausfrau!

Although at first Benz had a terrible time selling his cars, the time came when he couldn't make them fast enough. For the first fifteen years of motoring Benz did very well. But he was inclined to be stubborn and, although his later cars had four wheels, he still clung to his belt drive and his slow-speed rear engines. It was not until 1903, when he hired a Frenchman named Marius Barbarou, who designed a front-engined car for him, that Benz began to catch up

with the automotive parade he had done so much to start.

It was the French who made the petrol-driven car popular. De Dion, Bollée and Serpollet had done wonders with steam cars, but it was not until the French got their hands on Daimler's (and Maybach's) wonderful engine that their car industry blossomed. And no one had more to do with that than Emile Levassor. Levassor was a partner of René Panhard in the firm of Panhard & Levassor, who in those days were in the business of making band-saws. Daimler and Levassor had a mutual friend, Edouard Sarazin, a Belgian who had acquired the rights to sell Daimler's engines in France. Sarazin talked Levassor into making them there as well, and when he died, Mme Sarazin not only continued the business arrangement with Levassor, but eventually married him—complete with the licence to build Daimler engines. In this way the firm of Panhard & Levassor entered the car-manufacturing field.

Naturally, Levassor had seen the latest model of Daimler's car, which had been built for the Paris Exhibition of 1889. He was unimpressed by the quadricycle, which looked like two bicycles side-by-side with the passengers and machinery slung between them, but he was much taken by its motive power: a two-cylinder, 15-degree V-engine which turned at what was considered in those days to be the very high speed of 750 r.p.m.

When Levassor designed his own car, it was the archetype of almost every machine which would be built for the next fifty years. Levassor put the engine in the front. Behind it he put a clutch and behind that the gearbox. Between the rear wheels was a differential.

At last the car as we know it today had appeared. France was ready. And no wonder, for the French loved cars and France was the one country in Europe with long, straight, smooth Napoleonic roads. It also had a logical officialdom that wasn't against everything new (as were the British) and an upper class with plenty of money to spend.

The Panhard & Levassor was not the only car buzzing along the *grands boulevards*. Peugeot, a

manufacturer of coffee grinders and bicycles, soon brought out his own model—also with Daimler engines, under licence from Levassor. French-licensed Benz cars (the Roger-Benz and the Hurtu-Benz) were popular, as were the Bollée and the de Dion-Bouton. And there were the Renault Brothers too.

Eventually, the British woke up. Daimler had licensed his engines to the company which still uses his name, and Frederick Lanchester was building the first petrol-engined, four-wheeled cars made in England.

Almost immediately, American millionaires began importing the fashionable new toys from Europe. But tinkerers in Connecticut and machinists from the railroad shops in the Midwest were but vaguely aware of this latest craze of Newport society. They weren't part of Newport. They were hammering and filing away at their own kinds of horseless carriages. Hiram Percy Maxim, Ransom E. Olds, Elwood Haynes, the Apperson brothers, H. Ford, the Duryea brothers—any of these or a score of others could have been first, but in 1893 Frank Duryea drove the first petrol-powered American car in Springfield, Massachusetts.

In design it was years behind the Europeans. They were already building cars. This was still a buggy with an engine attached to it. But while the European car would for years be the plaything of the privileged, this piece of machinery was the true precursor of the typically tough, solid American car.

Preceding pages: In this 1901 Columbia, Hiram Percy Maxim, following the lead of Emile Levassor, placed the engine
at the front. Mounted on springs, it jiggled nervously as it
ran. This Columbia was also the first American car to sport
a steering wheel instead of a tiller. Built by the Pope Manufacturing Company, of Hartford, Connecticut, its design
was well ahead of most other American cars. On the left:
the Léon Bollée tri-car of 1897. This engaging little beast
was the sports car of its day. Its air-cooled, hot-tube-
ignited, 3 h.p. engine could make it scoot along at over
30 m.p.h. No wonder young sportsmen like C. S. Rolls, later
of Rolls-Royce, here seen at the midship controls, loved
driving it. Bottom: An 1896 veteran Delahaye. The French
Delahaye of this period was inspired by the Benz. Note the
radiator made of bent tubing. The 1901 two-cylinder Autocar (below) was built in Ardmore, Pennsylvania. These
cars already had drive and left-hand steering (by tiller).

THE YEARS OF
FULFILMENT

During the 1890's America's towns were tied to each other by the railroad, not the highway. At the edges of the cities the pavements suddenly disappeared and gave way to mere scratches across the landscape. These were the roads. Elongated mud-holes in winter, dusty, sandy tracks lacking sign-posts in summer, they were used mainly by farmers to haul their produce to the towns or to take their families to the village church on Sundays in the family buggy. Unhappily, the village doctor used these miserable byways, too, as he forced his horse and buggy towards some winter midnight's childbirth.

The farmer would have snorted with derision had anyone told him that the new-fangled horseless carriage was about to change his life, that he was about to be rescued from his kerosene-lit isolation.

But the village doctor could hardly wait. He wanted a motor car more than almost anything else in the world. The townsman, too, wanted a car. The bicycle had on Sundays freed him from the trolley car. With his friends of the bicycle club or with his girl friend aboard a tandem, he had discovered a new way of personal travel outside the iron-bound routes of the transport companies. Cycling was delightful, but he wanted a motor to keep his legs from getting so tired. And then, of course, there were the

Preceding pages: This Welch touring car of 1907 was a typical, high-priced ($5,500) luxury car of its time. Its seven-passenger "Roi des Belges" coachwork was upholstered in diamond-pleated leather, and it was possible to buy a "hard-top" to keep its passengers cosy behind plate glass in wintry weather. Built in Pontiac, Michigan, the Welch had a four-cylinder, 50 h.p. engine, and a multiple-clutch transmission. In the early 1900's, when the American motorist ventured into the countryside, he was entirely on his own. Paved roads were luxuries of the future. There were no petrol stations, motels, or even milestones. Help was always distant. Those who owned these early machines had to be dedicated, willing to suffer for their sport, unafraid to dirty their hands in caring for their cars' innards. The owner of the 1904 White Steamer (below) has run into luck and found a source of water to refill his car's thirsty flash steam boiler.

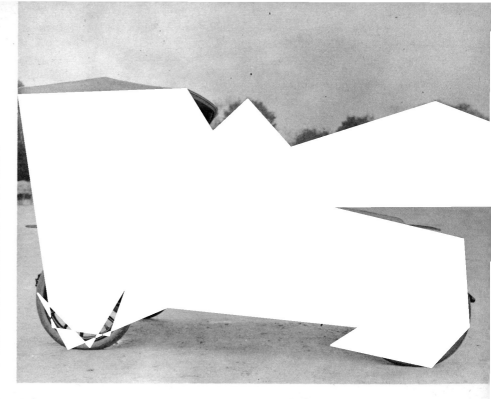

Bearing a strong resemblance to a handsome buggy, the 1905 Pierce Stanhope (left) was also sometimes known as the "doctor's car". It was powered by a one-cylinder, French, de Dion engine. Its gear lever was attached to the steering column. As an added attraction, the Pierce had a fold-away front seat that stowed neatly beneath its dummy hood. Another device of the times was used in the 1903 Model A Ford (lower left). A tonneau to hold two more passengers could be fitted to its rear deck. Right: This double phaeton with side entrance, mounted on a long Renault-Frères chassis with a 4-cylinder, 14 h.p. engine, dated from 1905, marks the beginning of the great French firm's history. The radiator is behind the engine and not on the sides of the bonnet.

rich; they just had to have a motor car. Didn't the papers say Mrs. Vanderbilt had one?

The car of the Nineties was a horror on wheels. The brave eccentric who owned one happily put up with its crankiness if the beastly thing would only run. It was unbelievably difficult to operate and control, and when it wouldn't run nobody knew how to fix it.

By 1914 the motor car was, in almost every respect as good as the cars on the roads today—and in some ways it was better. In those few years since the Nineties the car advanced more than at any time before or since.

Let us pretend that it is, say, April of 1898 and that you are a small-town American. Last autumn you started your campaign to convince your wife that a horseless carriage was exactly what you needed:

"Look how much we'll save on oats for the mare. An automotor (even the word 'automobile' wasn't common usage yet) doesn't eat when it isn't actually running," you said, "and there isn't all that cleaning up after it, or harnessing, or those bills from the veterinarian."

Your logic finally prevails and on this fine spring morning there stands before your house a sparkling, black horseless carriage, cautiously towed by a horse, from the freight station.

Your new car is a pretty little thing not too different in appearance from the buggy in your stable. It has a patent leather dashboard and patent leather mudguards over its tall, nickel-plated wire wheels and rides on sausage-thin pneumatic tyres. Its 5-h.p., one-cylinder engine is cleverly hidden under the seat, but unlike a buggy it has a tiller on top of a column sticking out of the floor. Also affixed to the column

are some little handles and knobs. A few pedals grow out of the floor, too. It doesn't, naturally, have any shafts for a horse but, strangely, it has a whip socket. Furthermore, a metal bar a yard long is hinged below the chassis, its free end pointing rearwards. This is a sprag, which can be quickly let down to dig into the road should the brakes fail and the car start rolling backwards down a hill.

You'll have to teach yourself to drive it; nobody in town can show you how. Nobody has even seen a horseless carriage, let alone driven one. But luckily an instruction book has come with the machine.

"Charge the tanks with water and gasoline," it reads, "and make sure that the crankcase is filled with lubricating oil."

The water part is easy, but you rush your son down to the paint store on the corner for the gasoline, which he brings back in gallon bottles. Meanwhile you have crawled under the car to, as the book says, "open the pet-cock in the side of the crankcase and watch for some oil to drip out." It drips; you have enough oil. You also check various grease cups on the chassis; they have been filled at the factory.

Now to start the engine!

Luckily, this car of yours has electric ignition, unlike some of the old-fashioned machines which used a hot tube. "Set the spark back to preclude breaking your wrist," says the book. "Also put the gears into their neutral position by means of the lever on the steering column; then set the brakes."

You insert the plug which turns on the ignition.

"Now vigorously turn the handle which protrudes from the right side of the body and the engine will start," says the book optimistically.

You do this. Nothing happens.

Before the days of the sports car, it was not unusual for wealthy young gentlemen to take to the road in out-and-out racing cars, like this 1902, 40 h.p. Mors (below, left). The huge sprocket upon which the chain runs shows that it is a racing machine. Note, however, that it was equipped with a headlamp for night driving. Charles S. Rolls, who is here shown at the controls, was still several years away from his epic collaboration with Henry Royce. The 1907 Cadillac (left and above) was the model that would make Henry M. Leland famous. It was similar to those which were torn to bits, scrambled, then reassembled to show how well its parts interchanged. It had a single-cylinder, 9 h.p. engine and a planetary transmission.

You do this some more. Much more. Still nothing happens. Your wife, your son, your neighbours stand around expressionless as you crank. Nothing. A man driving a wagon goes by. "Get a horse," he yells. It's a brand new expression he's picked up from a drover in the next town where there is also a motor car.

You crank some more.

Suddenly, happily, the engine is running. Everybody has backed away from your car which is vibrating like a mechanical jelly. Everything shakes, the mudguards, the kerosene lamps. You yell, "She runs, she runs," but no one can hear you over the wild barking of the exhaust and the howling of gears.

Fearfully, you mount to the seat, release the hand brake and step on the clutch pedal which also applies the foot brake. You put the gear lever into its lowest speed and very s-l-o-w-l-y, as the book advises, let out the clutch! With a neck-snapping jerk you're going down the street at four miles an hour. To slow down you fiddle with the spark control or slip the clutch. To speed up you must go into a higher gear.

Control of engine speed by means of a foot throttle—or even a hand throttle—is still in the future. True, one of the pedals on the floor is called an accelerator, but that is only for momentarily cutting out a governor which keeps the speed of the engine down to 750 r.p.m. A higher speed will certainly break something. As the book says: "Continued use of the accelerator will cause the engine to 'run away' and seriously damage it." But today you are satisfied to go chuffing around the houses in your low gear. When you've learned better how to control that tricky tiller, so you don't swerve from one side of the road to the other, there will be time enough to learn about changing gears.

Within the week you succeed in changing the gears, but it is a noisy, crunchy, operation, since it is difficult to slow the engine down in neutral no matter how much you set back the spark control. But it is worth the risk, for, while you could do but four m.p.h. in first gear, you find that you can go up to nine m.p.h. in second, and a thrilling 17 m.p.h. in top.

This photograph (right) taken in the Ile-de-France in 1906 by Monsieur Henri Depasse, the first Ford importer in France, shows in the foreground a vehicle said to be a K type Ford. Note the two-seater runabout coachwork. The Earl of Dudley's 1902 Panhard-Levassor stands on the far right. This expensive Edwardian had a rear entrance to the tonneau which spread voluptuously out over the rear mudguards, and a typical gilled-tube radiator. Compare its suave design with that of the crude two-cylinder Winton (bottom, right) in which H. Nelson Jackson crossed the North American continent in 1903. Jackson's trip took sixty-three days.

But things aren't really going smoothly between you and your car. Your wife doesn't think you should have paid out that hard-earned $900 on it. Especially since you spend as much time under it as in it. For one thing, there's that awful vibration that keeps shaking bits loose. You're forever tightening loose nuts, if you're lucky enough to find them still on their bolts. Otherwise you have to put a new one on from that big tool-box you carry about with you. Another thing that gives you trouble is road dirt getting into moving parts. The exposed gears, for instance, just grind themselves away in a paste of grit and grease and road filth, and the factory takes ages to send new ones, which you have learned to put in by yourself. Tyres last no time at all. Your hands become a bleeding mess from continually tearing tyres off the rims to patch them or to throw them away and put on new ones. Nor has the car been able to take you on those wonderful little trips into the country that you promised the family. At the edge of town the paved roads suddenly end. And you find that your 7 h.p. are not enough to push those thin tyres through hub-deep sand or mud.

Did you give up motor cars? You did not! In spite of your dear wife, you bought another car, a better car. Cars had to get better fast in those days. Or the new little companies that rushed into the business of making them would go right out of business. Which most of them did, anyhow.

Doctors were the first people to buy cars in any quantity. Brave men, they tried every type: electrics, steamers, and "hydro-carbon wagons." At first the steam cars were more popular. Electrics were too slow and petrol-driven cars too complicated and mysterious for the steam-oriented men of the nineteenth century.

Early car magazines, such as *The Horseless Age*, are filled with accounts of the experiences of motorists, most of them doctors. In the issue of November 6, 1901, there are a pair of typical accounts:

"After having used horses in my medical practice for ten years I became interested in the automobile as doing away with the great expense of keeping teams, the bother and disagreeable features of drivers, etc. I subscribed for the three leading automobile journals, sent for a catalogue of every vehicle I saw advertised, attended every automobile show I could get to, and finally pinned my faith to steam as the best power for my business. The first of April finally saw me in possession of a steam carriage of the latest construction. Ready for anything and on the point of selling my teams—so sure was I that the automobile was the proper means of locomotion for a doctor. My experience with steam had all been on paper, my knowledge of it being derived entirely from catalogues and journals. So after fixing up after a fashion I started out and ran quite a distance very successfully. Then, wishing to appear before my family as a full-blown chauffeur, I started for my residence, just in front of which I began to smell gasoline for five minutes. Without stopping to think, I pulled out a match and attempted to relight the fire. Piff! Bang! And the whole thing was ablaze. I retained presence of mind enough to turn off the main gasoline supply and to throw out the cushions and throw mud and dirty water from the street at it until I had subdued the flames, but my $800 auto looked like a bad case of delirium tremens: the paint was scorched and the machine covered with mud, my clothing was dirty and soiled and my reputation as an expert shattered the first day among all the neighbours, who, as usual, witnessed the accident.

The car at the top is not a phaeton without its team or a horseless carriage of the Nineties, but a Kiblinger auto buggy built in 1907. It had tiller steering and a two-cylinder engine, and was perfect for farmers, who needed plenty of road clearance. Built in a different idiom is the four-cylinder 1910 Buick (left). Above: The engine of the 1907 Welch. This car had an overhead camshaft engine with hemispherical combustion chambers as early as 1904. It was unique in its day.

"This first experience rather put a damper on my enthusiasm, at least for two or three days, but when the machine had been washed up it looked somewhat better, and after much persuasion I induced my wife to accompany me on a short spin. After we had ridden out about a mile I suddenly missed the water. The fusible plug blew out and my boiler was burned. Now I was simply going to shine! I explained how this could easily be overcome, for (according to the catalogue) all that is necessary is to insert a key where the fusible plug was, pump up the water by hand, and go rejoicing on your way. Spreading a robe on the ground I proceeded to put my printed instructions into practice; but, alas! I found the key would not fit in the opening, as the babbit metal stuck to the sides and the tubes were leaking badly. So with fingers burned and clothes soiled and disordered I was again towed home in disgrace, and here I learned my two first lessons in automobiling: First, don't believe over one-half you read in the printed catalogue; second, never wear a silk hat, frock coat and white linen on an auto trip; they don't look well after an accident."

Another cautiously enthusiastic doctor wrote:

"Many object to the steam type of machine on the ground that there are so many important things to keep in mind. I personally think this is one of the advantages, for it gives one a great deal of personal satisfaction to master a beautiful piece of mechanism and keeps the faculties alert while utilising the same. We do not go fishing for pleasure with a net, and spirited horses are still in demand. As I have never had two machines at one time I cannot really decide on my preference for use. I intend to have both styles next year, and shall be curious to find out which one I really get the most use out of. I am sure the beginner will usually have more luck with the steam machine, for its main points can be appreciated in fifteen minutes' time. I have seen an expert work on a gasoline machine all day, and then after it got to running be unable to tell which of his various adjustments had accomplished the end in view. There is no question that the gasoline machine is far ahead as to economy of fuel, though the repairs of batteries and cost of oil used are somewhat amazing.

At a time when most machines still steered from the right, Autocar already had moved the tiller to the left. Its position is clearly visible in this 1903, two-cylinder model (below). It was a neat car with a rear entrance and a gigantic "glass front" which ran from the dashboard to the top.

This light Darracq of 1904 won fame more than fifty years after it was first built, when it became the heroine of the British film "Genevieve", based on the famous London-to-Brighton Run. Right: One of the first models built by Fiat shortly after the firm was founded in 1899. This car could have an engine of either 4 or 6 h.p. according to whether it was used to seat 2 passengers or 4.

The usual repair shop would hardly care to tackle the mechanism of a gasoline engine, and if the carriage is purchased from a manufacturer some hundreds of miles away the element of time and expense involved is rather appalling. Another trouble with the heavy gasoline machines is the very weight which enables them to obtain the big speeds and be properly steered. Many of them cannot be pulled by a single horse and offer a severe strain to the ordinary harness. If one gets down into a ditch it is practically impossible to do anything without the assistance of quite a gang of men."

But the doctors never did go back to the horse and buggy, and it was their example, perhaps more than anything else, that encouraged the more progressive small-town types and farmers to think about owning a horseless carriage.

In 1900, Americans bought 4,192 motor cars. By then the American motorist had a choice of makes. Some were destined to become famous; some to last even until our day: Oldsmobile, Packard, Winton, Autocar, Peerless, and a dozen makes of steamers and electrics.

Elegant and wealthy Easterners sneered at native machinery. They imported Panhards and Mercedes and almost until World War I would continue to look down their noses at even the best American cars. But these American machines had something. They were cheaper and, if cruder, they had a certain agricultural simplicity which made every blacksmith a motor mechanic. Furthermore, they were light and not quite so likely to subside into the inevitable knee-deep mud as the heavier, more luxurious European machines. True, Europe, especially France, made light cars, too, like the Decauville and the de Dion-Bouton. But the American machines of the early 1900's had another advantage which made them singularly suitable over here. They had a four-foot eight-inch tread and would fit the ruts made by farm wagons. (Roman chariots made four-foot eight-inch ruts, too). European cars running over decent roads had no trouble with ruts and were narrower.

One of these new American vehicles, the Curved Dash Oldsmobile, first of a famous line, was a simple enough machine and is fun to drive even today, as I discovered when I recently went out in one owned by a friend. It is perhaps the shortest car I've ever ridden in. Its wheelbase is a mere sixty-seven inches, although its tread is a full fifty-six inches wide. It has one long spring on each side with the front axle attached to the forward shackles, while the rear axle is gripped by the rearward ends. Additionally, a small transverse, full-elliptic spring keeps the front axle from getting too lively. Mounted on this grasshopper-like structure is a pair of seats with a box behind, while the famous curved dash curls toward one's ankles. From the floor a graceful tiller arches towards the driver's hand.

The machinery, consisting of a single cylinder of about 1,500 c.c., which turns a huge flywheel, a planetary two-speed transmission, and the single chain drive to the rear axle, is all nicely hidden under the seat and the box.

My friend cranked for a few turns and I was surprised at how easily the engine started and how quietly it ran. There was only a subdued puffing

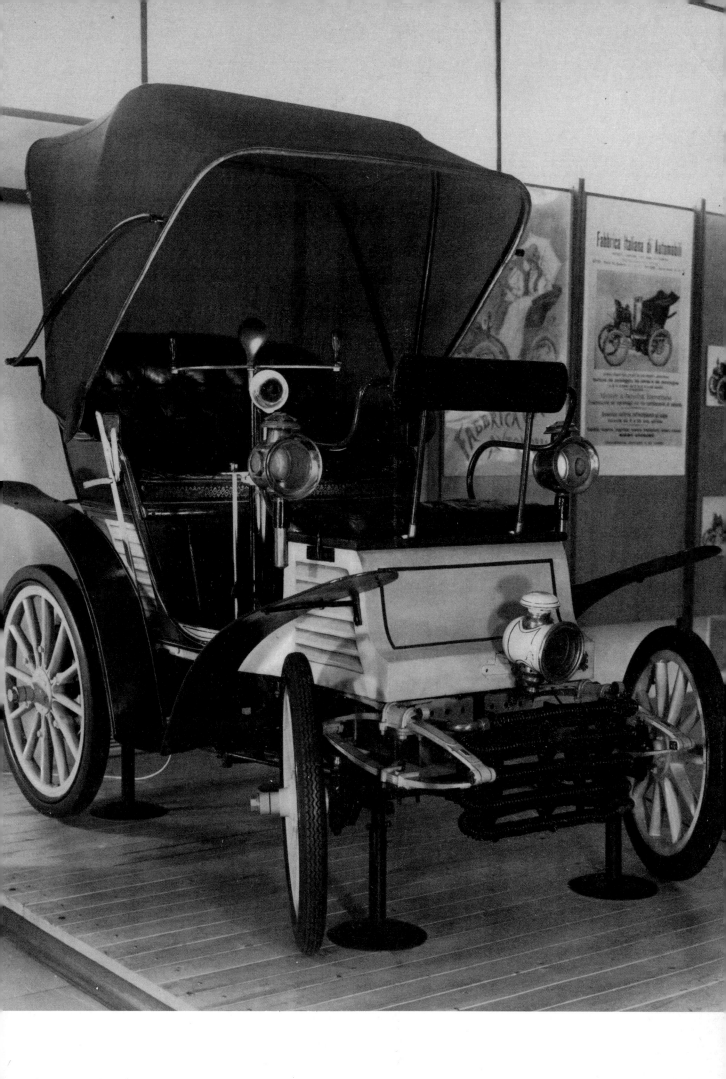

In 1910, when most big cars were doing, say, 60 m.p.h., the Simplex "Speed Car" (left) was booming along at better than 80. Its four-cylinder, T-head engine, although rated at 50 h.p., developed considerably more power. It was to be expected, therefore, that this muscular Simplex, and its bigger brother, the 90 h.p. model, were favourites among America's wealthy young sporting set. These Simplexes, among the last American machines to be chain driven, were built on Manhattan Island itself and were tested on the then open roads of Long Island. The cheap and popular four-cylinder 1911 Hupmobile (right) was exactly the opposite kind of car. Henry Ford's six-cylinder Model K of 1907 (lower left) was one of the few high-priced cars to bear his name.

sound from the exhaust and the vibration was just about enough to set the brass kerosene side-lamps gently jiggling.

If you've ever climbed aboard a light buggy, you'll know the feeling as I set foot on the running-board of the Olds. There was no denying its springy horse-carriage ancestry. On the road the absence of any structure in front made for slight unease at first as the road surface seemed to streak right beneath me. There was no problem with wind, nor did I feel the need for goggles as I have in windscreenless cars of just a few years later. For flat-out on a level road we couldn't have been doing more than 20 m.p.h. The slightest rise meant shifting down to the lower of the two gears and just crawling while the engine behind gave vocal notice that it was working. But remember, the Oldsmobile was only a 5-h.p. car.

Until about 1904 the Oldsmobile was typical of American cars. Most of them (except perhaps Hiram Maxim's Pope-built Columbia) had a one- or two-cylinder engine under the seat, a planetary transmission, single-chain drive, and a rudimentary cooling system utilising a few yards of finned pipe as a radiator, which hung almost anywhere on the car where there was room.

Except for individual idiosyncrasies on the part of their builders—like Alexander Winton's compressed-air system of governing engine speed—the Cadillac, the Ford, the Pope Hartford, the Packard, and a dozen others were all built in the same American idiom, although some of them had wheel steering instead of a tiller.

But times were good in the early 1900's—until 1907, anyhow. People wanted cars big enough to carry the whole family, cars that looked like those fancy foreign machines New York swells owned. They could, very early, have bought a detachable tonneau, which device, containing some back seats, was fastened on aft of the usual two front buggy seats and into which the passengers inserted themselves by way of a high and tiny back door. Once in, they sat facing each other, knees touching, while their feet were entangled in a greasy stew of tools, chains, punctured tyres, cans of oil, and filthy rags.

The earlier European cars had offered their rear passengers no better amenities, rear entrances being necessary until wheelbases grew longer and the sprocket and chain moved far enough back so that a side door became feasible.

By 1904 or so, European machines, led by Mercedes, already had honeycomb radiators, gate gear levers, four-cylinder engines up front, good acetylene headlamps and, above all, comfortable, commodious, side-entrance *Roi des Belges* coachwork. This type of tulip-shaped body, with its after quarters swelling voluptuously out above the rear wheels, was named after that which the King of Belgium had built to be mounted on his "Sixty" Mercedes in 1901. He was said to have been given this idea by his great and good friend, the actress Cleo de Mérode, who, hearing that he was having a car body built, pushed together two of the lavishly upholstered armchairs in her boudoir and suggested that the body be based on their combined shape.

George Baldwin Selden, of Rochester, New York, was a sharp young lawyer far-sighted enough to realise that some day somebody would build and try to sell a petrol-driven car. When that day came he wanted to hold the patents on it. He got his idea after seeing a Brayton stationary engine at the Philadelphia Centennial in 1876. By 1877, he had come up with an idea for a car, a crude vehicle in which a Brayton engine, the gearbox, and the clutch were attached to the front axle and turned with the front wheels. Crude as his proposal was, the U.S. Patent Office allowed him to file it in 1879. But Selden was too canny to allow the Patent Office to grant him a patent. He didn't want a patent, which was valid for only seventeen years, until somebody started building cars. He kept his application alive by changes and legalisms until 1895, when he finally permitted the papers to be issued.

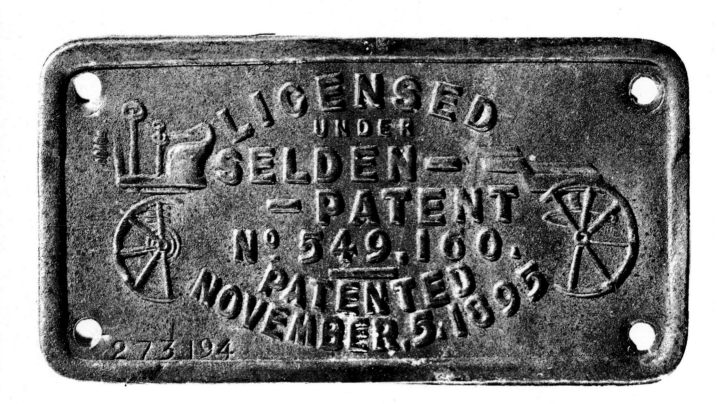

At about that time, Colonel Albert A. Pope, the bicycle tycoon who had had Hiram Percy Maxim design and build various electric and petrol-cars for him, learned with horror that somebody besides himself had a right to monopolise the budding petrol-car industry. The good Colonel, therefore, rounded up some of the millionaires who were his pals and partners in an outfit called the Electric Vehicle Company and got Selden to join them in a cosy plan to control the petrol-car industry.

To this end they formed the Association of Licensed Automobile Manufacturers. If you wanted to sell cars, you paid these gentry five per cent of the retail price — of which percentage Selden got a tidy share — and got a Selden-patent plaque to stick on your product. If you wouldn't play, they sued you and also threatened to sue anybody who bought an "unlicensed" car.

Most manufacturers fell for this, but Henry Ford told the A.L.A.M. to go to hell.

After years of legal pettifogging, Ford won. In 1911, when the patent had almost expired, the courts decided that Selden's patent applied only to vehicles driven by the Brayton engine. The car shown here was built in 1905 to prove to the courts that a Selden machine would actually go. Fourteen hundred feet was the farthest it ever ran.

By 1907, the *Roi des Belges* type of touring body on a chassis long enough to accommodate it was commonplace not only in Europe, but in America as well. And now, too, tall structures of bevelled glass and wood rose over the back portions of the body to enclose the passengers in luxurious silken privacy and to protect them from the weather. By now, too, the four-cylinder engine sitting up in front behind a brass-bound radiator was usual even in cheap cars. In England, Napier and Rolls-Royce were already building six-cylinder-engined cars of a magnificence which has never been surpassed. In the United States Packard, Peerless, and Pierce, the great "three P's" were making superlative cars, hardly inferior to the best Europeans and better suited to American conditions. For although American roads were getting slightly better, they still were rough and rutted enough to require a simpler, more rugged type of car with a higher ground clearance than the European machines.

I drive a lesser-known make of this period, a Welch made in Pontiac, Michigan—a car which cost $5,500, a fortune in its day. It is quite a large machine with a wheelbase of 128 inches and weighing some 4,000 pounds ready for the road. Its four-cylinder engine develops about 50 h.p. at 1,500 r.p.m., but is somewhat unusual for its day in having an overhead-camshaft and hemispherical combustion chambers. Its transmission, however, although no longer of the planetary type common five years earlier, is not yet the sliding-gear selective gearbox for which Mercedes had set the fashion. The Welch gears are in constant mesh, but rotating freely on their shaft until the one the driver wishes to use is locked to its shaft by means of a multi-plate, steel-and-bronze clutch which is selected by a long, bronze hand lever. There is, of course, a separate clutch for each of the three speeds, but no foot-operated declutching mechanism.

On the road it is a delight. Seated behind the mahogany-rimmed steering wheel on the end of its brass column, the driver has an almost dangerous feeling of omnipotence. He feels superior to anything on the road beneath him. Yes, beneath him, for the roofs of modern cars are at the level of his knees. Once in high gear the sound of the slow-turning engine is left behind and the car glides along quite as silently as any modern machine, with an easy, springy motion from its full-elliptic rear suspension—helped, no doubt, by its great, three-foot diameter wheels which don't fall into every little hole in the road as modern, caster-sized wheels do.

To a modern driver, the Welch's steering would feel odd. The diameter of its steering wheel is small and even a tiny movement puts the car into a terrifying swoop. The steering transmits a considerable amount of movement from the front wheels, and gripping the wheel hard enough to make the knuckles white does not control it. So the driver must allow the wheel to jiggle gently in his hands, taking firm measures only when disaster is imminent.

But it wasn't all roses for the motorists of 1907. They struggled with unreliable tyres and an afternoon's trip almost always meant that there would be some bother with patches and pumping. If the casing was damaged as well as the tube, there was a little leather corset in the tool kit that could be laced to the wheel over the wound. Dust was the terrible enemy. Every car trailed a great cloud of it, part of which was sucked forward to settle on the muffled and duster-clad unfortunates in the tonneau. Blindly passing another car in its almost opaque dust cloud was no joke. By modern standards the two-wheel brakes were laughable, but the roads were free of the suicidal traffic of today. They didn't need the neck-snapping brakes we must have to stay alive.

The first cars lit their way with candles in coach lamps. Next came paraffin lamps, feeble but better. In the early 1900's acetylene lamps came into use, with each lamp containing its own means of making gas from carbide and water. By 1907 the acetylene generators lived on the running-boards, and copper tubing carried the gas to the lamps. About this time, too, it became popular to buy compressed acetylene gas in cylinders, which were less of a nuisance than generators. Since they had to be filled with water and lumps of calcium carbide, the generators, like the self-generating headlamps before them, required constant cleaning out.

These match-lit gas lights were not too bad considering the lack of traffic and the low speeds of cars at night. In fact, people even complained of being blinded by what we would consider dim light, giving headlamp manufacturers a chance to market dimming devices—little shields which were pivoted to hide the fearsome glare of the gas flame.

In 1907 the bottom dropped out of the market for expensive cars when the United States suffered a financial panic and depression that would not be equalled for twenty-two years. Still, unlike 1929, production went up from 43,000 cars in 1907 to 63,500 cars in 1908. The cheaper, mass-produced car was beginning to rear its ugly little hood.

Most people believe that Henry Ford was the first man to think of mass production; some are even convinced that he invented the motor car. Ford was perhaps the first to adopt assembly line production to cars, but assembly line production required interchangeable parts so precisely made that any part of

Shown above is a little private bus on a chassis by Amédée Bollée junior, dating from 1901-2. This commercial vehicle was very advanced from a technical point of view — note the appearance of wheels of equal size at the front and rear. When loaded, this car could achieve 25 m.p.h. The lower picture shows a Herald limousine tourer, built in 1905. This car was equipped with a 4-cylinder engine fitted with a Herald carburettor. The designer had grouped the controls at the centre of the steering-wheel. Very much under the influence of Mercedes, the 1905 Fiat (right) used a honeycomb radiator almost identical in shape to that of the German marque. F.I.A.T. also produced a 60 h.p., six-cylinder version similar to the four-cylinder model. A major difference between the two models was an early self-starting device which worked by compressed air. Only the six-cylinder car offered this innovation.

any car of the same model would fit any of its mass-produced brothers.

The first man to have this revolutionary concept of interchangeable parts for mass production was Eli Whitney, of Connecticut, inventor of the cotton gin. He first used his idea in 1798 to make muskets for the United States Government. He first tooled up, made dies, jigs, and then put each man in his small factory to work on one specialised bit of each gun.

The idea of interchangeable parts took hold in New England and by the mid-nineteenth century factories were turning out everything from watches to sewing machines by assembly line methods. And

it was a Vermont Yankee named Henry M. Leland who first applied real standards of precision and interchangeability to car manufacturing in quantity. Born in 1843, he had worked during the Civil War for the Springfield Arsenal and later for Colt's Patent Firearms Manufacturing Company, where guns were made according to Whitney's ideas. After the war, he went to Detroit where, with a partner named Faulconor, he built Oldsmobile engines. In 1902 he became one of the organisers of the Cadillac Automobile Company and in 1908 he showed the world what true interchangeability of parts meant.

He sent three Cadillacs to Brooklands in England.

There, officials of the Royal Automobile Club had the cars disassembled and their parts scrambled like so much scrap iron. Then Cadillac mechanics, using hand tools only, rebuilt this clutter of metal into three Cadillacs. Officials of the R.A.C. then had the cars driven for 500 miles on the track. The cars behaved perfectly. The amazed and delighted British awarded Cadillac the Thomas Dewar Trophy for the outstanding motoring feat of that year.

By the time of the World War, the motor car had almost ceased to be an instrument of adventure and a mark of wealth; true, Henry Ford had much to do with this. By 1914 he was selling 248,307 cars a

year at the fantastically low price of $490 for a tourer.

But it wasn't only interchangeable parts, mass production, and low prices that made the motor car the household object it is today. It was the woman driver. Certainly there had been lady drivers from the very beginning, even lady racing drivers like Mme. Du Gast, who had driven in the great Paris-Madrid race of 1903, or Mrs. Joan Newton Cuneo, who drove in the Glidden Tours. And, of course, lady drivers sat behind most of the tillers of the crawling electric cars that were blocking traffic on the shopping streets of every American city. But women stayed out of the driver's seats of petrol cars for a very obvious reason. Hand cranking an engine was just too hard and dangerous a job for them.

Manufacturers had from the beginning come up with all kinds of laughable devices to eliminate the starting handle. One consisted of a giant spring which was attached to the engine where the crank normally lived. This spring was wound up by the engine while it ran. Theoretically, the next time you wanted to start the engine, you had but to release a lever and, presto, the unwinding spring would whir it into life. Unfortunately if your engine was suffering a slight malaise your spring would unwind itself to no avail, and you'd had it, sister! Pushing the car was your only remedy.

Another crank-eliminator offered by some manufacturers, including Delaunay-Belleville, also stored the power of the engine, but in the form of compressed air and a cat's cradle of piping to the cylinders. The driver opened a valve and air rushed in to the cylinders and rotated the engine. If it felt like it, it started. The Winton, from 1907 on, had saved exhaust gas under pressure to start its engine, and the Prest-O-Lite Company, which was supplying tanks of acetylene for lighting, tried for a while to sell a mad system of piping and valves which would

Above left is the ingenious and advanced Lanchester of 1903. With its two-cylinder opposed engine and twin crank-shafts, it successfully eliminated the bone-shaking vibration which was the bane of early motor cars. It had an epicycle transmission and a worm-drive rear axle. The Stevens Duryea (upper right), also built in America in 1908, was another fine car of the day. It was one of the first machines equipped with an all-aluminium body. Its engine had six cylinders instead of the more usual four. It sold for $3,500 and was marketed just in time to ride the crest of a new enthusiasm for giant six-cylinder engines. The movement had begun in 1907 and was led by Napier and Rolls-Royce. A favourite gimmick to gain publicity for such cars was to run them tremendous distances with their transmissions locked in high gear to show that their power was sufficient to preclude changing gears. The 1907 French Darracq (right), also with a six-cylinder engine, is a portrait in Edwardian elegance before a Motor Club run to Brighton.

fill the cylinders with acetylene gas whose explosion, it was hoped, would start the engine.

In 1912, Cadillac offered an electric self-starter and electric lights. A lady could now start a car just by touching a button with the toe of her high-button shoe. In America, at least, the rough, tough open car built for male drivers was doomed. Henceforward, women would have as much, if not more, to say than men about the kind of car that would be built. From now on cars would be glass-enclosed rooms on wheels, softly sprung to insulate ladies' delicate bottoms from the realities of rough roads. And steering would become lower geared to make it easier for women to turn and park.

But it took years to complete the undoing of the motor car. A quality car of 1913 or 1914 was still a delicious mechanism to take out on the road.

By 1914, a Sunday afternoon's excursion in the family car was no longer the near-desperate adventure of ten years before. Roads were much improved, tyres were better, and with the advent of the quick demountable rim, hardly more difficult to change than they are today. Mechanically, a high-grade car was as reliable as a contemporary car. Engines were more flexible, and gear changing was necessary only for hills and starting from rest. The six-cylinder engine was a commonplace on higher-priced cars. A

V-8—copied from de Dion in France—was available on the 1914 Cadillac and a year later Packard came out with its famous twelve-cylinder Twin-Six.

The Locomobile catalogue of 1912 gives a mouth-watering glimpse of the wonderful construction and luxury a man could buy in those spacious days: "The rear seat cushion and back in our six-cylinder models are provided with upholstering *ten inches thick.* . . . This detail alone permits any one regardless of age, figure, or constitution to enjoy the same

Below: This 1911 Léon Bollée "double saloon" with twin-block 4-cylinder engine was one of the first machines to have "inside drive". Ventilation was studied with special care, so was the comfort of the passengers. It has been completely restored and put up a brilliant performance in the International Rally between Lyons and Le Mans. This very fine example of a 16-18 h.p. Panhard et Levassor car (upper right) dates from 1908. The luxurious limousine coachwork, designed in the most elegant proportions, earned the car the name of "La Marquise". Graced with the charming name of "Palombella" this 35/40 h.p. Itala of 1909 (lower right) belonged to the Queen Mother Margherita of Savoy. Its 7,400 c.c. engine developed sufficient power to drive this immaculate black limousine at 43 m.p.h.

restful ease when riding in the car as when seated in the most luxurious library chair. . . . The Locomobile crankcase is *government bronze.* . . . The crankshaft has seven main bearings, one between each connecting rod. . . ." But there is a disturbing note too: "Passengers are seated low in the car, giving a sense of security," says the catalogue. The days when a motorist sat on a car rather than in it were ending. The delights of sitting high and mighty with a commanding view of the countryside were nearly gone. Since around 1910 there had been front doors, too. The occupants of a motor car were destined to be enveloped by more and more sheet-metal bodywork until a nadir would be reached in the Thirties, when they would see the passing world through glass slits in tank-like bodies.

However, almost all cars of this period still had the one serious flaw that would make them useless on the roads of our era: two-wheel brakes. Fast—70 or better for powerful types—a joy to handle, they took forever to come to a stop. Argyll in Scotland and Isotta-Fraschini in Italy already had early forms of four-wheel brakes, but not until after the World War would most cars have an anchor on each wheel.

Not everybody wanted a car capable of carrying the whole family. Young bloods wanted machines that were more like the racing cars of the day: rakish two-seaters with bodywork consisting of bucket seats with a bolster-shaped fuel tank and a pile of spare tyres behind them. Light and windscreenless, these first sports cars (although the term didn't come into general use until many years later, in England) were fast, surprisingly stable and manoeuvrable, and a joy to drive. Almost every manufacturer built cars that looked like this, but only a few built cars that had the exhilarating performance to match their looks: Stutz and Mercer, Marmon, Lozier, and Simplex.

I had a wonderful ride in a Simplex "Speed Car" once, a 50 h.p. model of 1912. For some reason, which I cannot remember, it had been necessary to follow in a Rolls-Royce a friend of mine, Austin Clark, who owned this machine. We were on an open stretch of the Montauk Highway on Long

Famous English racing driver Charles Jarrott (left) takes his 1908 Crossley across the channel to motor in France. This car was not dissimilar from staff cars of the same marque used by the British Army in World War I. It had a 4½-litre engine of some 50 h.p. Before the first World War, the 1913 model (top) was among the most powerful and greatly desired American sporting machines. The 50 h.p. Lozier engines were remarkable among the domestic machines for having roller-bearing crankshafts in their six-cylinder engines. Above: When Mr. Theodore Roosevelt, President of the United States, paid an official visit to the Elysée Palace in 1907 he travelled in a "coupé de ville" by Delaunay-Belleville, a marque celebrated for its meticulously constructed 4 and 6-cylinder models. The absence of windscreen and headlamps indicates the shortness of the journeys undertaken.

Island and to my surprise I had found that I had to do 80 even to keep the Simplex in sight. When we reached our destination I climbed out of the Rolls and expressed my amazement at the manner of the Simplex's going.

"Want to drive it?" asked my friend.

"Oh, no—thanks. I might bend it," I said insincerely as I moved to climb behind the wheel.

Clark turned the ignition switch, then walked up front, and after one quick, practised flick of the crank, aided by a decompression device, he had the engine singing its healthy basso-profundo song. An

open cut-out contributed to this, of course. Clark climbed in on my left and handed me a pair of goggles. We were sitting in minuscule, leather-upholstered, bucket seats set low on the chassis, with our legs stretched out toward a mahogany dashboard so distant that I could read neither the speedometer nor the fuel-pressure gauge mounted upon it. There was, of course, no windscreen. I could see before me a great, red, kennel-shaped hood, a pair of brass headlamps, and the front mudguards. I could also see both front wheels. (Visibility was hardly a problem in those days.) I must have looked worried as I

The tradition of the "big Renaults" dates back to 1911, when the famous 6-cylinder "40 h.p." model first appeared. It lasted nearly twenty years. The picture (above) gives some idea of the dimensions of its very long chassis. Right: The loftily-built Stoddard Dayton of 1910.

sat there gripping the mahogany steering wheel on the end of its impossibly long, brass tube.

"Go ahead. Put her in gear and let's go," said Clark callously. "She has four speeds, you know. When you want to stop, put on the hand and the foot brake at once."

This really gave me pause, but I grasped the outside gear lever and put it into the first speed notch in the big brass gate, let in the clutch, and we were off. I was hardly giving her any gas at all with the foot throttle (there's another on the steering column), but even in first gear, the Simplex seemed to surge

The six-cylinder, 50 h.p. Napier (seen below) in 1912 was the rival of the other great British-built, six-cylinder car, the Rolls-Royce. The Napier's engine was so long that it was necessary to extend the hood ungracefully forward beyond the axle. Note that its radiator is wider than the hood.

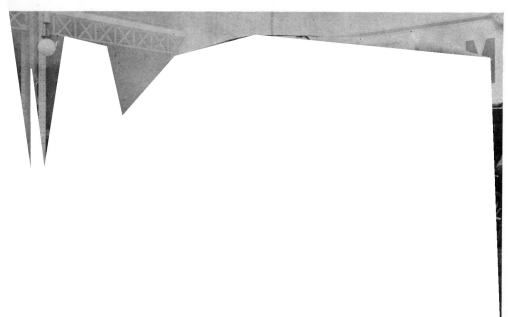

An extravagance of Latin magnificence — the 50 h.p. Itala (left) was constructed for the Queen of Italy in 1906. Note the three rows of richly upholstered seats for her court, and the bucket seat over the tool box — for the King. Before 1912, when electric lighting brought vast changes to motor history, the car gloried in its sparkling brass gaslights, bulb horns, and other gleaming accoutrements. People who didn't have chauffeurs or diligent wives to polish these decorative — but necessary — accessories, welcomed the coming of nickel and, eventually, chromium.

away. I shifted, double-clutching, into second. "No need to double-clutch on upward shifts," Clark shouted into my ear. He was right. On these early gearboxes with their big, coarse teeth transmitting power from low-speed engines, gear changing is far easier than on cars of twenty years later.

I was in third gear now and we were flying. The engine just burbled and didn't seem to be working at all. But there was noise all right from the big chains driving the rear wheels. In the tradition of the early Mercedes, which it resembled more than somewhat, this Simplex was one of the last of the chain-driven monsters, like the Mack trucks of my youth.

I put my foot down as we charged along. "Ha!" I thought, "I bet Clark thought I couldn't drive this beast of his."

But Clark deflated me. "Shift," he screamed in my ear, "Shift into high." The Simplex surged ahead. Never has a car felt so fast to me. A modern sports car at 120 seems dull by comparison. My cheeks were pulled out in the gale. My hair was being yanked by the wind. The back of my jacket was a balloon trying to lift me out of my seat.

"Turn left at the next cross-roads," Clark bellowed.

I stamped on the foot brake, shifted into third, pulled at the hand brake—Clark was right; the brakes were lousy—I was still going far too fast to make that corner! Foolishly I wrenched the wheel hard left. The big Simplex just sailed around, no squeal, no sway, no sweat!

Sobered, I drove slowly back to Clark's place. "Sorry I drove so fast," I said trying to forestall any sharp remarks about my high-speed cornering. "Not at all," said the ever-polite Clark. "But you don't have to slow down that much for a turn."

Even before the war in 1914, the United States was building more cars than all of the countries in Europe combined. By 1920, the United States was making, with a few exceptions, 2,000,000 of the stodgiest, most uninteresting cars the world had ever seen. When Europe got back on its feet we would see exciting motor cars again, but meantime most Americans lost interest in them except as prosaic means of transport. It would be thirty years before Americans really fell in love with cars again.

Famous to almost every American is the name "Stutz Bearcat". The 1914 version (above) had a four-cylinder, T-head engine which could develop some 60 h.p. and, although it weighed about 4,000 pounds, it was capable of 80 m.p.h. The car sold for $2,000. In those days, the Stutz and the Mercer owners were great rivals on the road and off. The Stutz owners composed and chanted this measure: "There never was a worser car than a Mercer". Not to be outdone, the Mercer contingent countered: "You have to be nuts to drive a Stutz".

This 1908 Mercedes tourer limousine (above) had
an extraordinarily long chassis and was equipped
with a 6-cylinder engine developing 70 h.p. Note
that the rear accommodation included no less than
3 side windows, while the front part is provided
with curved windows with no central column between them. The whole thing is designed with the
greatest contempt for aerodynamics, but is not
lacking in dignity. In the 1916 Locomobile "Spor-
tif" (below) the line from radiator cap to tail is
unbroken.

EARLY RACES

AND RALLIES

The earliest racing was done in France and it began almost as soon as the machines were invented. Théry, aboard the Richard-Brasier (preceding pages) leaves his competitors in a cloud of dust as he hurries home to win the 1905 race for the Gordon-Bennett Cup. The first official car competition was organised by "Le Petit Journal" of Paris in 1894 and ran from Paris to Rouen. Some of the competing cars are left to right from top: A Panhard-Levassor two-seater and a sister Panhard model, two early Peugeots, the de Dion-Bouton Steam Tractor — seen again at right with a carriage attached, trailer-fashion — and M. Maurice de Blant's nine-passenger steam omnibus.

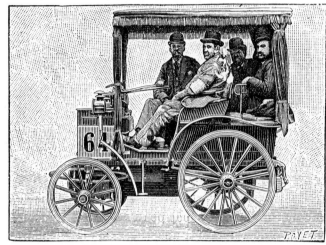

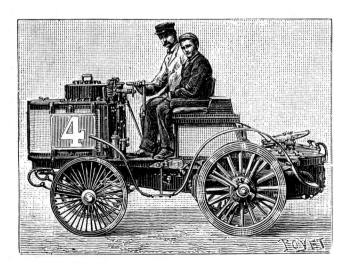

No sooner did an early builder of a "horseless" succeed in actually making it run, no matter how painfully and haltingly, than he looked around for other such machines against which he might pit his darling in a contest of speed.

It was, naturally, in France that motor racing first started, for only there did enough machines exist; only there, in any case, were the roads good enough. Motor racing has always done much to develop the speed, road holding, and stamina of cars, and it was these races, perhaps, that did as much as anything else to enable France to lead the world in *l'automobilisme* in this period.

The first such contest, the Paris-Rouen Trial of 1894, was not strictly a race, for as the organisers, *Le Petit Journal* of Paris, pointed out, the winning car would be that which was "without danger, easily handled and of low running cost." One-hundred-and-two entries were received, but each entry had to undergo a preliminary trial to prove that it could do fifty kilometres in three hours. This was later altered to four hours when the competitors claimed that ten miles an hour was a dangerously high speed. Considering the odd vehicles that were entered, who could blame them? For some of these early sporting gentlemen spurned such prosaic means of propulsion as steam, electricity, or petrol. One, Monsieur Rousselet of Paris, insisted that his *voiture* ran by gravity. A Monsieur Victor Popp contemplated running under compressed air, and a Monsieur Laval entered a machine he called a Baricycle that "moved by the weight of the passengers." Others had such delightful propellants as "a system of pendulums," "automatic," and "combination of animate and mechanical motor". On July 22, 1894, nineteen cars, the very first group of racing cars ever to leave a starting line, departed the Porte Maillot in Paris for Rouen, 126 kilometres away, accompanied by an industrious reporter from Mr. James Gordon Bennett's *New York Herald* aboard a bicycle.

The start was not without incident. For a Monsieur Etienne Le Blant, described at the time as "a person of good intentions but insufficient motoring experience," ran a big steam van belonging to the Parisian shop *La Belle Jardiniere* up on the pavement, demolishing a bench and frightening the whiskers off a Monsieur Cassignol, the official observer riding with him. His more experienced brother, Maurice Le Blant, had entered a nine-passenger omnibus which was to perform a most useful service during the run; it picked up the crews of such cars as became disabled. At one point the Maurice Le Blant steamer itself got stuck among the loose stones of a road under construction and forty or fifty of the wildly enthusiastic spectators started hauling on ropes to drag the fuming monster clear. Suddenly its wheels became unstuck and the machine bounded away amid a shower of stones and fleeing rescuers.

But Maurice Le Blant's steamer finished in the money, anyhow. *Le Petit Journal* announced on July 24, 1894:

FIRST PRIZE 5000 FRANCS
Awarded equally to Messrs. Panhard and Levassor, of Ivry, Seine, and Les fils de Peugeot Frères, of Valentigny, Doubs, "both employing the petrol motor invented by Herr Daimler, of Wurtemburg."

SECOND PRIZE 2000 FRANCS
Awarded to Messrs. de Dion, Bouton et Cie., "for their interesting steam tractor which draws a carriage like a horse, and develops (though with a powerful engine it must be admitted) a speed absolutely beyond comparison, especially uphill."

THIRD PRIZE 1500 FRANCS
Awarded to M. Maurice Le Blant, of Paris, "for his nine-seated car on the Serpollet system."

For the 78.75 miles from Paris to Rouen, the de Dion had averaged 11.6 miles per hour. (Although fastest, it did not comply with regulations, since it carried a steam engineer in addition to the driver). The fastest Peugeot (five finished) averaged 11.5 m.p.h.; the fastest Panhard (four finished) 11.1 m.p.h. Le Blant's steam bus averaged 7.3 m.p.h.; even his clumsy brother averaged 6.9 m.p.h.

They could hardly wait, these Frenchmen, to do it again in 1895. But this time it would be a proper race, from Paris to Bordeaux and back to Paris, an astronomical distance for those days of 732 miles. Drivers could be changed en route; repairs made only by such means as could be carried on the car. Nothing outside was to be procured except, as the regulations said, "entertainment for man and machine".

Manuel Roble's impressionistic aquatint (preceding pages) was engraved after the 1903 Paris-Madrid Race, the last of such country-to-country competitions. Marcel Renault (above, before the race) was among the many drivers and spectators who were killed. Lady-driver Mme. du Gast (upper left) appears confident at the controls of her de Dietrich. She and the chevalier René de Knyff in a 90 h.p. Panhard Levassor (bottom, left) were among the other competitors in that fatal 1903 run. A year earlier, de Knyff's mount was the 75 h.p. model Panhard (centre, left).

At noon on June 11, 1895, twenty-two racers started from the Place d'Armes at Versailles: thirteen petrol cars, six steamers, one electric (a Jeantaud), and two motor tricycles.

Troubles started early, as Mr. Gerald Rose recounts in his monumental *Record of Motor Racing*, published in 1909: "It appears that one of the big ends [of a Bollée steam bus] heated and M. Bollée wrapped a pad of wet rags round it during a stoppage for supplies. Unfortunately, the pad was forgotten, and, on re-starting, the rags were drawn into the machinery and played havoc with the engine..."

It is the great Emile Levassor's run that still excites us most after sixty-odd years. Levassor knew he couldn't win from the start. Only four-passenger cars were qualified for prizes. Levassor's was a solid-tyred two-seater of his own make, a Panhard with a 2-cylinder, 4-h.p. Phénix engine of 1,206 c.c., which ran at 750 r.p.m.

Not long after leaving Versailles, Levassor succeeded in passing the fast steam cars that had been sent off ahead of him. By the time he reached Ruffec, the town where a relief driver was waiting, he was well in the lead, even though he had by then driven for over six hours in darkness, his road ahead lit only by guttering candle lamps. At Ruffec, his relief was still abed. Rather than waste time waiting for him to rise and dress, Levassor drove on to Bordeaux.

It was easier now. In that latitude the summer sun rises early. By 10:30 in the morning Levassor was in Bordeaux making his turn back to Paris, fighting his way through streets crammed with excitedly cheering Bordelais. He had reached Bordeaux in the impressive time of twenty-two hours.

This time his man in Ruffec was all set to take his seat on the Panhard. Levassor waved him off and pushed on for Paris non-stop except for halts to take on fuel and perhaps a quick drink. Not long after noon on June 13, Levassor pulled up at the Porte Maillot, two days and forty-eight minutes after he had set out for Bordeaux.

In an account printed in the "North American Review" in September, 1899, the Marquis De Chasseloup-Laubat, himself a formidable early motoring enthusiast, wrote of Levassor:

"M. Levassor remained on his machine about fifty-three hours, and nearly forty-nine of these on the run. Yet he did not appear to be over-fatigued; he wrote his signature at the finish with a firm hand; we had lunch together at Gillet's, at the Porte Maillot; he was quite calm; he took with relish a cup of bouillon, a couple of poached eggs, and two glasses of champagne; but he said that racing at night was dangerous, adding that having won [?] he had the right to say such a race was not to be run another time at night.

"The general mean of his velocity was 14.91 miles an hour; the maximum was eighteen-and-a-half miles an hour between Orleans and Tours."

Of the twenty-two machines that started, nine finished. Among these only one was a steamer. Five steamers had fallen out, as had the Jeantaud electric. Second and third places had been taken by Peugeots, respectively, six hours and eleven hours behind Levassor's Panhard. It was one of the Peugeots that actually collected first prize, for it was a four-seater.

In 1894, right after the Paris-Rouen trial, a bright young newspaperman named Francis Upham Adams, who worked for the *Chicago Times-Herald*, sold his boss, H. H. Kohlsatt, the publisher, the idea of running a motor car race. Adams must have been a great salesman for he got Kohlsatt to put up $5,000 as a purse, with $2,000 for the winner.

Applications poured in, almost ninety of them, from every cross-roads mechanic who ever dreamed of building a horseless carriage. *Two* entries were even received from a place called Pine Bluff, Arkansas. But as race day approached, Adams and Kohlsatt came to the horrifying realisation that most of the cars entered were still but dizzy dreams in the heads of their inventors. The race, originally set for the Fourth of July, 1895, was postponed and postponed again, finally to Thanksgiving Day, while the oppositon papers in Chicago, which had jeered at the venture from the beginning, howled with glee.

To stir up some interest in the race as the months went by, Adams announced a prize contest for a new name other than "horseless carriage" for the new mechanical marvel.

When Thanksgiving Day dawned there were eight inches of snow and slush on the ground, and even getting to the starting line at the Midway Plaisance was quite a feat. The cars that ploughed their way to the start were: an Electrobat electric built by Morris and Salom, a Duryea petrol machine, two Benz petrol machines, a Roger-Benz petrol machine entered by R. H. Macy, and a Sturges electric.

At 8:55, the Duryea got the flag and slithered off with Frank Duryea at the helm and an umpire in the seat beside him. The other machines were sent off at one-minute intervals, most of them requiring a push by the happy spectators before their macaroni-thin tyres could get a grip on the slushy snow.

Meanwhile, Frank Duryea's brother, Charles, took a train to the Loop where he had a light horse-drawn sleigh waiting. Driving this he met his brother by taking a short-cut to Van Buren Street where he fell in behind him.

The course followed the lake shore to Evansville where, after a control check, it was to return via Roscoe and through Humboldt Park to the start. The gasoline wagon, as the Duryeas called it, ran well until it crossed the Rush Street Bridge. There the steering gear suddenly let go, but Frank managed to stop without hitting anything.

Frank couldn't fix the broken part with the tools he had on the car; he needed a workshop. Charles, in the sleigh, charged around frantically until he found one open on the holiday. There Frank mended the part, but he had lost fifty-five minutes. Macy's Roger-Benz was now thirty-five minutes ahead of him.

Deep snow now slowed the car down, and Charles in the sleigh got bored and hungry. He stopped for a leisurely lunch for himself and oats for the horses, while poor Frank went ahead through the slush on an empty stomach. Charles took a short cut and caught Frank, who was now back in the lead. This business of Charles stopping for refreshment and then taking short cuts to meet his brother went on for a while, until Frank finally failed to show up at a relay station where Charles was waiting.

Frank had not only lost his way, but had broken down with ignition trouble. By the time Charles, who had been dashing up and down back streets, found him, Frank was squatting over a little charcoal fire heating an electrical part, so that he might bend it enough to refit it.

Early racing was a spectacle of monstrous cars and super-human driving. Drivers struggled with mechanical troubles and unreliable tyres. Christian Werner (below) changes a tyre on his Mercedes during the Gordon-Bennett Race in 1905. Villemain (centre) on a Clement-Bayard, corners in the 1906 French Grand Prix. A 120 h.p. Panhard Levassor (bottom) shows Henri Farman up. In the 1903 Paris-Madrid, he drove a 90 h.p. model (left). Mme, du Gast (far left) checks her route-card box before a race. Charles Jarrott — well known to early racing fans — poses (above) in his Gordon-Bennett Napier.

Even though he had lost a whole hour this time, Frank Duryea was still in the lead, and though he had further mechanical trouble—a chipped tooth wedged in the gears—his drive back was almost a lark. (We hope Charles got him a sandwich on the way). It was a holiday, remember, and the Duryea, its noisy engine popping and its warning bell ringing, was followed through the darkening November afternoon by a cavalcade of cheering young bloods and their girls in sleighs to the finishing line at 7:18 p.m. It had covered the fifty-four-mile course in eight hours and twenty-three minutes.

The only other car to finish was a Benz entered by Oscar Müller, but Müller wasn't at the tiller. Overwrought and dead tired, he had collapsed. Charles King, his umpire, who would later make a great name for himself in the motoring world, brought the Benz to the finishing line at 8:53.

The contest for a new name for horseless carriages? The name that won was "motocycle".

Now began a golden time of road racing from town to town, country to country. Bewhiskered, begoggled giants, (the like of whom disappeared, perhaps forever, at Verdun or on the Marne), raised clouds of choking dust on the high-roads of Europe as they raced their monstrous, almost unmanageable machines from Paris to Amsterdam, Paris to Berlin, Paris to Vienna, and, finally, tragically, from Paris to Bordeaux towards Madrid. Soon, too, the world would see the Vanderbilt Cup races in America and the beginnings of the French Grand Prix.

Typical of these almost legendary country-to-country contests was the Paris-Vienna Race of 1902. In the six short years since Levassor's epic run on his Panhard in 1895, racing cars had chaged out of all recognition. Where Levassor's machine was in no way different from the touring cars of its day, the machines of 1902 had, during the frenzy for motor racing which suddenly gripped Europe, developed into road monsters almost utterly useless for touring purposes. Where Levassor's Panhard had developed

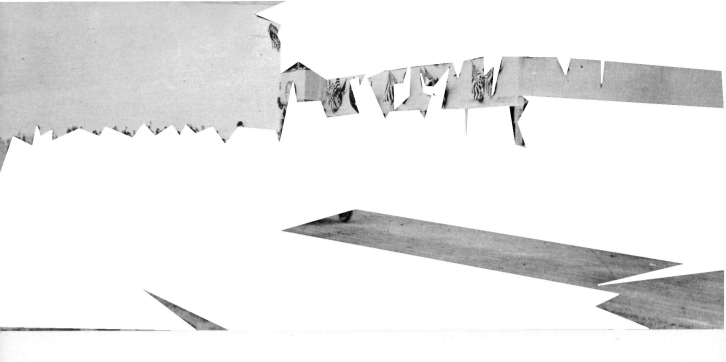

Once as popular as the World Series, the Vanderbilt Cup Race was great annual road event. Important foreign drivers brought their European machines to the United States each year to pit them against the best drivers and cars America had to offer. In 1908, it was "Old 16" (pages 84-85) that took the cup for the Americans. George Robertson drove the 120 h.p. 1906 Locomobile racer home. Crossing the finishing line (above), he seems far ahead of the field.

4 h.p., some of the Panhards in the Paris-Vienna were of no less than 70 h.p.! To develop such power in those days, their four-cylinder engines had to be, by our standards, gigantic, with cylinders of 160×170 mm. and a total capacity of 13.7 litres. These huge and heavy engines were mounted in wood-framed chassis, hardly strong enough to bear their great weight, let alone the racking strains of racing over the rough road across the Alps to Vienna. Nor was it only the Panhards that had such over-powered light chassis. The Mors cars had 60-h.p. engines, the Mercedes 40 h.p.

The 615.4-mile Paris-Vienna race started on June 26, 1902. Before dawn, the competitors were sent off at two-minute intervals. The race was divided into classes: heavy cars, light cars (under 24 h.p.), voiturettes (under 12 h.p.), and even a class of motorcycles and tricycles.

The scene at the start, at Champigny, on the outskirts of Paris, must have been fantastic. Thousands of spectators had come on foot, by car and carriage, but weirdest of all were the endless lines of thousands of bicyclists lighting their way with, among other things, Japanese paper lanterns bobbing and dancing in the moonlight. At the roadside, stands had been set up where the excitable mob could buy everything from croissants to champagne, bicycle clips, and petrol. Drivers were hard put to force their way through the jam. They blew exhaust whistles, rang bells, and even used sirens, still legal on private cars in those

days. To add to this delightful French uproar, an outfit called the Vincennes Motor Corps showed up en masse to bellow out songs calculated to encourage one of their number who was starting in the race.

First off was Girardot, on a 60-h.p. C.G.V. After him went Fournier on a Mors; S. F. Edge, the publicity-conscious Englishman who was later to promote Napiers and A.C.'s, on a Napier, and then the brown-bearded René De Knyff, on a big Panhard.

A special train was waiting to take those spectators who wanted to see the racers arrive at the Belfort control. And they were delighted to see Fournier, followed by a great cloud of dust, come alongside and then pass the fast express as if it were welded to the tracks. For Fournier was really moving on his 60-h.p. Mors, *averaging* over 70 m.p.h. for the first fifty miles out of Paris. But, near Chaumont, some 125 miles from the start, the train passed Fournier. He was out with a broken gearbox. But he wasn't the only one. Before Belfort, near the Swiss border, was reached at the end of the first day's run (and where the cars would be put in a locked parking area overnight), the roadside was strewn with sick and smashed cars, including Girardot's C.G.V.

The real racing didn't begin again until the cars had passed out of the territory of the suspicious Swiss, who permitted the cars to pass—but not to race—through their country. The crossing of the 6,000-foot Arlberg Pass in Austria is typical of the special kind of hell those early racers endured.

To quote Gerald Rose's *Record of Motor Racing*:

"The pass was nearly 6,000 feet above sea-level, and shortly before the competitors were due the roads were almost impassable from snow. And such roads! Hardly more than tracks in some cases, winding along precipices with nothing but boundary stones between the road and the drop beyond, crossing torrents on improvised bridges made of a few planks, climbing hills of extraordinary steepness with descents on the other side of equally terrifying appearance, with the constant fear of the precipice before the eyes of the driver should he miss his corner at the bottom. Small wonder that the competitors imagined at times that they had mistaken the road, and were only reassured by the constantly recurring flagmen. Up the drivers went, climbing to the clouds through the snow-covered passes, with nerves strained to the utmost by the unknown peril behind every bend in the road. Max, whose escape is now historic, missed his corner and charged a boundary stone; seats broke loose, and Max and his mechanic were thrown clear while the car went over the edge. Max climbed down a little way to see what had become of the car, and, reappearing just as Baras came up, gave the latter the impression that he had followed the car to its resting-place on a ledge a hundred feet down, and had climbed up unhurt; a story which Baras subsequently retailed in the controls, to the no small astonishment of his hearers."

Finally, the road behind them strewn all the way back to Paris with wrecked cars, forgotten tools, oil cans, and shreds of tyres, the finishers, covered in white dust, their hands torn and bleeding from constant tyre-changing, limped into Vienna, Amazingly, no fewer than seventy-four cars, including light cars and voiturettes, reached the finish.

The winner of the heavy car class was Henry Farman, on a 70-h.p. Panhard, who finished in 16 hours and 25 minutes. But amazingly, it was one of the light cars, a Renault, driven by Marcel Renault, which did the fastest time and won the race: 15 hours, 46 minutes.

A year later Marcel Renault was to die in the disaster of Paris-Madrid, the last of the country-to-country races. The London newspapers of May 25, 1903, in their sensational fashion called it "The Race to Death". It was, certainly, a nasty mess, and unfortunately some drivers and not a few spectators came to a sticky end. Starting on the very day of the race and continuing into our time, over-blown accounts have exaggerated the carnage and importance of Paris-Madrid which, of course, never reached Madrid. But the fact remains that the French authorities, frightened by the accidents, stopped the race at Bordeaux.

There were two chief reasons for the débâcle. First, the manufacturers, not having learned the lessons of the Paris-Vienna Race, stuffed even bigger, over-powered engines into even more anaemic chassis. Gerald Rose describes these murderous machines as follows:

"Never before or since has the factor of safety in the chassis been so small or the frames so light, and had the race gone through one the rough roads of Spain the number of failures by the way would in all probability have been far higher than in Paris-Vienna The engines also were light in structural details, though the power was high. In some cases the attention paid to the driver's comfort was ludicrously

Preceding pages: Mercedes 4½-litre. See caption page 95. A year after their spectacular victory in the first Grand Prix organised by the A.C.F. and run on the Sarthe circuit, the famous partnership consisting of the driver Szisz and his faithful Renault found themselves in 1907 at the Dieppe Grand Prix; but this time they had to be content with second place, giving way to Felice Nazzaro on his very powerful Fiat.

Ernest Henry revolutionised racing-car design with his 1912 Peugeot. (Right, a 1913 model.) The world's first twin-overhead-camshaft engine (above) with which he powered them has been the model for most racing engines since then. Georges Boillot battled the German Mercedes team in the 1914 Grand Prix in such a car.

small, and one man was expected to take his car to Madrid, over roads known to be very rough beyond the frontier, seated on a board covered with a skin rug. Some of the cars were radically altered in design, and others, like the huge Gobron-Brillies, were far bigger than anything hitherto built. Most were riddled with holes, every possible part being lightened to the utmost extent. Piston walls were drilled out, beadings were taken off seats, bolts were chipped and filed away, frames and levers were slotted until they became a mere network of metal."

No wonder the cars spread themselves and their drivers all over the highway after even a minor jolt, especially when you consider their speed. Louis Renault, for example, on his 30-h.p. car, was timed between Bonneval and Chartres at nearly 90!

The other big reason for the horror of Paris-Madrid was the suicidal tendency of the spectators. Some 3,000,000 of them, pumped up into a fever of excitement by the newspapers, swamped the efforts of the French army to keep them out of the road. The tremendous speed of the cars was something their horse-and-buggy-age brains just could not conceive. They stood in the middle of the road, opening a narrow path as an 80-m.p.h. car roared straight at them and closing in behind it again. The ones that didn't move fast enough either forced the driver into the ditch or got themselves killed.

No one has ever found out how many people lost their lives that day, but the man who was considered the winner of the shambles was Gabriel, on a 70-h.p. Mors, who averaged 65.3 m.p.h. for the 342-mile run to Bordeaux.

The French Government wouldn't even allow the racing cars to leave Bordeaux under their own power. Horses dragged them to the railway station and they went back to Paris in goods vans.

Of all the wild and glorious racing in these past sixty years none has such an aura of romance attached to it as the series of races for the Vanderbilt Cup on Long Island, New York.

William K. Vanderbilt, Jr., whose name you'll find not only in early, musty, social registers, but also in those heroic lists of entries for the great European road races, offered the Cup. To encourage the building of American racing machines, he said. But we suspect that at least part of his reason was to transplant some of the foreign excitement to the dirt roads near the Gold Coast of Long Island, where he and

his millionaire friends had their country seats.

He succeeded only too well!

The 30,000 spectators who showed up at 6 a.m. on that dark Saturday morning of October 8, 1904, had but a vague idea of what high-speed motor racing was all about. They were stunned by the crash and roar of the flame-spitting engines as the drivers, many of them from Europe, came up to the starting line. But they weren't, it seems, stunned enough to keep off the road after the cars took off. Only the yells of "Car coming, car coming" sent them diving for the ditches as a car shot past, leaping and swaying. Not that they hadn't been warned.

The crowd had a great time, with just enough gore and bent machinery to please everybody. Five Mercedes had entered. One driven by George Arents, Jr., an American, blew out a tyre near Elmont, caught the rim in trolley-car tracks, slewed around and toppled over, killing Arent's riding mechanic. Another Mercedes *mécanicien* crawled under his car to fix

something just as its impatient and bemused driver drove off—with effects deleterious to the mechanic.

A big, 75-h.p. Smith and Mabley Simplex, driven by Frank Croker, had its chassis so drilled and cut for lightness that it gradually buckled and twisted. Before long the onlookers were treated to the rare sight of a four-wheeled car leaving a triple track in the dust. Joe Tracy driving a stripped-down American touring car, a 35-h.p. Royal Tourist, broke a pin in his universal joint, but far from giving up, headed for a local machine shop where he made himself a new one. This did him no good; his engine disintegrated and he had to give up. Webb, on a Pope-Toledo, suddenly found himself without steering and entwined himself around a tree. After 6 hours and 56 minutes, a 90-h.p. Panhard driven by George Heath, an American, came in first over the 284.4 mile course. Albert Clement on an 80-h.p. Clement-Bayard was second. Before Herbert Lytle, who was lying third on a 24-h.p. Pope-Toledo, could cross the finishing line, the uncontrollable mob swarmed out on the road and the race had to be stopped to avoid carnage.

The 1905 race was an even wilder affair. This time the top drivers of Europe showed up, including Szisz on a 90-h.p. Renault; Camille Jenatzy, the "Red Devil", on a 120-h.p. Mercedes, Felice Nazzaro on a Fiat, and the fabulous young Italian, Vincenzo Lancia, also on a Fiat. Facing them was a newly formidable group of American drivers, including Joe Tracy on a 90-h.p. Locomobile.

The crowds were quite as crazy and disorderly as in 1904. One bunch from Bridgeport, Connecticut, where Tracy's Locomobile was built, anxious to cheer their home-town product, chartered the paddle-wheel steamer, *Isabel*, to take them across the Sound to Oyster Bay. But never giving a thought to the problem of getting to the race course from Oyster Bay, they finally arrived just about when the race was ended. At that they didn't do much worse than some of the people who tried to get there by car.

Vincenzo Lancia was naturally the mob's hero. Only twenty-five years old, big and bull-like, he was given to bellowing snatches of grand opera between swigs of champagne. He drove his 110-h.p. Fiat with maniacal dash, averaging 72 m.p.h. for the first 100 miles of the race.

He was leading the race, when he pulled in at his supply depot on Willis Avenue for fuel. Just as he was leaving, Walter Christie on the front-drive car

he had designed came snaking down the road. Lancia, impatient, took a chance and shot out in front of Christie. The Christie didn't give way, rammed the Fiat, and went end over end, smashing itself into scrap iron and hurling Christie's mechanic's body through a wild parabola into a field. Christie himself was only slightly hurt and lived to develop the famous Christie tank for the army, about which there was so much talk in the Thirties.

Lancia was lucky not to be lynched by the same mob that had so recently been cheering him. It took him an hour to repair the smashed rear wheels of the Fiat. Where he had been in first place, he was now sixth. He finally finished a poor fourth.

There were plenty of other frightful incidents to delight the spectators, but one of the craziest concerned Lytle on a Pope-Toledo. On a rough piece of road through a wooded area, his mechanic was bounced out of his seat into the brush. Lytle didn't slow down, but picked up a replacement mechanic at his pit. However, Vanderbilt and a doctor did head into the woods to find and repair the mechanic.

Hemery, on a 80-h.p. French Darracq, won the 283-mile race at 61.5 m.p.h. Heath on a Panhard was second, and Tracy was third on the Locomobile.

For the 1906 race, the course included some fancy new turns, on a somewhat different route, including the murderous hills at Roslyn and Manhasset on Northern Boulevard. The European aces—Lancia, Nazzaro, Clement, Wagner—all entered again, and

Joe Tracy had a brand new Locomobile.

The Vanderbilt Cup, at least around New York had become more popular than the World Series. Before daylight on that misty, rainy October 8, some 350,000 people had lined up around the course. One newpaper said that $50,000,000 worth of cars were parked or trying to park near the course by starting time at 6:15 a.m. Some of them had taken half the night to get there, driving headlight to tail-light, by way of the Brooklyn Bridge and the East River ferries and through the streets of Brooklyn. The Vanderbilt Cup had a certain aura of class. There was even a successful musical called "The Vanderbilt Cup" running on Broadway, and it was the thing to have a fancy party at the Waldorf or Rector's before setting out in a big touring car, well-laden with hampers of lobster and pheasant, plus cases of champagne. Some manufacturers set up parking areas for cars of their own make, but the Long Island yokels still made a quick profit fantastically over-charging New Yorkers who wanted to park in their front yards. There were the usual alarms and excursions, but only one death. Elliot Shepard, W. K. Vanderbilt's cousin, on a Hotchkiss, went into the crowd at Krug's Corner where 20,000 people had set themselves up as targets.

The French won again: Wagner was first on a Darracq, Lancia second on a Fiat, and Duray third on a de Dietrich. Joe Tracy came in tenth on the Locomobile, although he had done the fastest lap at a dazzling 67.6 m.p.h.

There was no race in 1907; nobody could devise a way to control the suicidal mobs.

Meanwhile, Vanderbilt and a syndicate of his influential friends were busily building a private road, the Long Island Motor Parkway, which ran from the dismal outskirts of Queens County, New York, to Lake Ronkonkoma. For a dollar anybody could use it as his private, fenced-in speedway. By the time I was old enough to drive on it in the early Thirties, it already seemed a narrow, twisty, old-fashioned road.

But in 1908 it was considered an ultra-modern super-highway. The 1908 race included almost ten miles of this road in every lap of 23.46 miles. The crowd was as unruly as ever, and even came armed with wire cutters for snipping holes in the new fencing.

This time the 120 h.p. Locomobile won the race, but George Robertson was driving, not Joe Tracy. This car—"Old 16"—now belongs to the famous motoring artist, Peter Helck, and in 1954, during a fifty-year celebration of the race, I had the luck to follow it in an antique car around what was left of the 1904 Course, now partly covered with a cancerous growth of ranch-houses, shopping centres, and pizzerias.

Robertson, an elderly man, drove the Locomobile again and, to the discomfiture of the local cops, had

Pages 88-90: During the French Grand Prix of 1914, on the eve of the Great War, few spectators could doubt, from their militarily precise strategy, that the Germans were out to win. The 4½-litre Mercedes with its single-overhead-camshaft engine is similar to the big white car that Lautenschlager rode to victory that day (left). The unlucky hero of the A.C.F. Grand Prix of 1914, run on the Lyon-Givors circuit, was the great French driver Georges Boillot, driving a 4,500 c.c. 4-cylinder Peugeot. After staying stubbornly in the lead for 19 laps out of 20 the French champion had to give way before the team of three German Mercedes, for his car broke down and proved beyond repair.

GRAND PRIX de l'A.C.F.
CIRCUIT de LYON   LA PEUGEOT de BOILLOT

Continental road races and rallies like the Herkomer and the Prinz Heinrich ran over public roads not usually cleared of normal traffic. Road races of those days not only battled dust and farm wagons on the highways, but they never knew when a slow goods train might block their path.

a grand time. They couldn't even catch him to threaten him with a ticket, except when traffic held him up as he roared into the main street of Hempstead. The rest of the procession of gaudy antique cars wheezed along miles behind.

The Vanderbilt Cup was run again on Long Island in 1909 and 1910, and won both times by an American-built Alco driven by Harry Grant. The crowds were as huge and as bent on self-destruction as ever. When you speak to old-timers who saw the races they speak with awe of the half-million spectators, the score of injured (mostly trampled by the hysterical mob), and the four dead (two killed in the race, two in traffic). But it is the 1908 race somehow that lives as a fond memory; 1910 was *too* bloodthirsty, too much of a wild and hopelessly uncontrollable mob scene.

The race left the Island after 1910 and took to the hinterlands—Milwaukee, Santa Monica, Savannah, San Francisco. It was never the same again. The days of the monsters were almost over.

After the hue and cry raised in 1903 by the much-publicised horrors of Paris-Madrid, the Gordon-Bennett Races, which until then had been a poor relation, became the chief event in European racing. Run on closed-road circuits, protected by police and soldiers, the organisers were able to promote the happy fiction that they were, somehow, safer.

S. F. Edge, as we have seen, won on his Napier in

1902. Therefore, under the rules, the 1903 race was to be on British soil. The race was run in Ireland, road racing being prohibited in England. (Evidently Irish spectators were considered more expendable than Englishmen).

The Germans won this one, Camille Jenatzy, on a Mercedes coming in first. In 1904, it was won at Hamburg in Germany by Théry on a Richard-Brasier. The next year Théry on the Richard-Brasier won again.

But in spite of their wins, the French were getting fed up. "We're the leading motoring country," they fumed, "and yet we can't enter more than the same three regulation cars that any backward little motoring country can. It's unfair."

After much argument, the French prevailed. The Gordon-Bennett faded away, and in 1906 the French Grand Prix (*Le Grand Prix de l'Automobile Club de France*) took its place. This first Grand Prix was run at Le Mans, but not over the same circuit as the famous Le Mans Sports Car Races of our day.

It was won by Szisz on a mammoth-engined Renault of no less than 12,970 c.c., at 63 m.p.h. for the 770-mile race. If you think this was a big engine, consider the cubic capacity of the 130-h.p., four-cylinder Panhard in the same race: 18,146 c.c. Each *cylinder* was bigger than the entire V-8 engine of many family cars today.

Imagine what it must have been like to handle

such nose-heavy brutes at high speed. And they did reach high speeds. The Renault was timed over a kilometre at a staggering 92.2 m.p.h.!

But the drivers had other troubles during those scorchingly hot days of June 26 and 27, 1906. The rules said that the drivers and their riding mechanics had to make their own repairs and tyre changes. The heat and the speed caused their tyres practically to melt and many a crew changed a full set of tyres ten or twelve times—no fun in those days of non-detachable wheels. They sliced the used tyre away from the wheel with knives, frantically tearing at the remaining shreds with their fingers, refitted the new tyre, struggled with the security bolts, then in the broiling sun pumped it up and restarted the engine. (Think of the horror of restarting an 18-litre engine by hand). A lap later they might have to do the same thing all over again, unless they stopped sooner because they'd left a tyre-lever between the tube and the casing. One of the reasons Renault won this race was due to their use of the newly invented demountable rims, which saved time and labour.

Dust had long been a terror during races. To pass, a driver plunged blindly into the dust cloud raised by the car ahead without knowing whether the road went straight on or not. At least one driver who set his course in an earlier race by cleverly following the tops of the telegraph poles came to grief when the road curved and the line of poles didn't. For this first Grand Prix, the organisers had thought to lay the dust by tarring the road, but the sun soon turned the tar to liquid, almost blinding the hapless drivers.

For a few more years these dinosaurs among motor cars pitted their huge and foolish engines against each other in the French Grand Prix. In 1907 the organisers, in an effort to stop the crazy trend towards even larger power plants, ruled that the cars had to get along on one gallon of petrol for 9.4 miles, but to no avail. Racing at Dieppe this time, a 16-litre Fiat—Nazzaro driving—was the winner, averaging 70.5 m.p.h. for 477 miles. Nobody ran out of petrol.

The next year, bore size was limited to 155 mm. for four-cylinder engines and 127 mm. for six-cylinder engines. But the effort was vain. To get around this, most competitors merely made their cylinders longer. Lautenschlager won with a Mercedes at 69 m.p.h.

From all this you might get the idea that the French Grand Prix was the only race in the world. True, it was far and away the most important, but there were other great races too: the Targa-Florio in Italy, the Kaiserpreis in Germany, and, of course, innumerable races like the Coupe de l'Auto, sponsored by *l'Auto*, the sporting paper, for the smaller, lighter cars which were soon to slay the giants.

The French Grand Prix wasn't run in 1909, 1910, and 1911. The big-bellied monsters had almost done themselves in. So expensive were they to build and prepare, and so out of touch with the realities of motoring, that they caused the Grand Prix, which depended on them, to sicken and almost die for want of entries.

In 1912 the giant racers ran again at Dieppe, but this time there were among them three machines that were to end their reign. These were the Peugeots designed by the Swiss, Ernest Henry, abetted by two famous drivers, Georges Boillot and Paul Zucarelli—the latter a notable conductor of Hispano-Suizas in the Coupe de l'Auto Races.

The Peugeots, mere striplings among Goliaths like Bruce Brown's gigantic 15-litre Fiat and the 15-litre Lorraine-Dietrich, were a mere 7.6 litres, but they had engines whose design has been the basis of almost every successful high-performance machine built in the last fifty years. Here, for the first time were twin-overhead camshafts, operating four inclined valves per hemispherically headed cylinder.

George Boillot, on one of the Peugeots, won the race at 68.45 m.p.h. The other two Peugeots retired with plugged petrol pipes.

The age of the giants was over.

In 1913 and 1914 the twin-overhead-camshaft Peugeots were almost unbeatable. They won the French Grand Prix again and, invading America, Jules Goux won the Indianapolis 500 in 1913 in spite of a reduction of engine size to 5.65 litres.

In 1914 Boillot took second place at the Indianapolis brick-yard, at 80.89 m.p.h., with a startlingly modern 3-litre version of the Peugeot, breaking the lap record at 99.5 m.p.h. (René Thomas, on a Delage, won that year).

For the Grand Prix at Lyon in July, 1914, the blue Peugeots of France went out to do battle with the Mercedes team of 4½-litre cars which was already organised as though for war. The German cars were prepared in secrecy in a village at some distance from the course. A complex strategy was worked out, with one of the German machines being assigned the role of decoy to separate the French cars. Pit work was practised and repractised. The Germans were out to win—and win they did. And they finished in line-ahead formation—first, second, and third; Lautenschlager, Wagner, and Salzer—to a deathly silence from the stands.

A few months after war was declared George Boillot was shot down by a German aeroplane powered by a single-overhead-camshaft engine not unlike the one Lautenschlager had used to vanquish him on the ground.

The first car to go a mile a minute was an electric; the first to go *two* miles a minute was a steamer. In the early years of this century electrics and steamers far outsold the cantankerous petrol-engined cars. The first taxis were electrics. Yet today only a few zealots still fiddle with electric and steam-powered cars.

What were these machines like? Why did they go the way of the Pianola, the Morris chair and other turn-of-the-century gadgets? The electric car is, theoretically, a simple device. It consists merely of a carriage loaded with electric storage batteries connected to an electric motor that turns the wheels. My twelve-year-old boy made one recently out of a twelve-volt starter motor, a couple of six-volt batteries, and a soap-box on wheels.

Actually, an electric was rather more complicated. It had a steering system, chassis, and springing very much like that of a petrol-driven car. And although it had no clutch or gear lever, it had a maze of complex wiring to enable its batteries to be hooked up in various combinations, depending on whether it was starting, climbing a hill, or rolling along at cruising speed.

The electric car was the natural development of that clanking wonder of the early Nineties, the elec-

tric-batteried trolley-car. A crude electric road vehicle using un-rechargeable electric cells had been run by a Scot named Robert Davidson in Aberdeen as early as 1839. But it was the invention of the storage battery by Gaston Planté in 1865, and its perfection by Camille Faure in 1881, that made the electric vehicle possible. By 1888 Fred M. Kimball of Boston had the first American electric car on the road and within ten years the electric was a commercial proposition.

On April 29, 1899, near Achères, outside Paris, Camille Jenatzy, on *La Jamais Contente*, a peculiar electrical contrivance that looked like an aerial bomb on a trailer, set the world's land speed record by covering the flying kilometre at 65.8 m.p.h. This was faster than petrol-engined cars of the time could go, but the record was achieved at some cost.

The trouble with elecrics was that you could, if you wanted to, go quite fast for a very short distance, or very slowly for a slightly longer distance.

This didn't bother those elegant ladies who slipped silently from Le Bon Ton department store to the hairdressers and then, mayhap, to tea in those little glassed-in drawing rooms on wheels that were in their heyday just before World War I. They seldom drove faster than 20 m.p.h. and it didn't matter too much that they could drive no more than fifty miles before they had to get home and have the handyman hook up the battery charger. By morning the batteries were up to running the car again.

It was their batteries that made electric cars such sluggards, for they used much of their power in moving their own great weight. A set of batteries in a fair-sized electric car weighed close to a thousand pounds. They didn't last for the life of the car, either. You had to buy a new set every three years or so.

Camille Jenatzy sits proudly on the world's fastest car of 1899 (preceding pages). "La Jamais Contente", was an electrically-powered vehicle that had rightfully earned its flowery garlands. Driving her, Jenatzy set the world's land speed record at 65.8 m.p.h. for a kilometre.
A Krieger electric "limousine de ville" (above, right) built in 1906. The general design is similar to that of a conventional petrol-driven car, but the bonnet conceals batteries, while the engine is placed close to the wheels that take the drive. The electrics were quiet and reliable cars when petrol-engined buggies were still noisy, cantankerous shakers.

The 1908 Baker (p. 100) exhibits a major disadvantage of the electric: its battery required continual recharging. The Morris and Salom Electric (below) ran on New York City streets in 1896. It was the world's first horseless hansom cab.

Faintly ludicrous, but too mannerly to be laughed at is this 1918 Detroit Electric coupé with curtained windows and tiller steering. It was powered by a nearly indestructible storage battery developed by Thomas A. Edison.

Electrics were wonderfully easy to drive. Most of them had tiller steering with some form of controller, either incorporated in the tiller or close by. A foot pedal applied the brakes and a button on the floor activated the electric bell that politely warned pedestrians of your coming. Brakes were sometimes magnetic. The plushy interiors of electrics were lovely to see. Overstuffed chairs in conversational groupings— it was possible for the driver to sit in the back seat in some machines by means of an extra set of controls —tasselled silk curtains on the windows, flower vases, and window shades made them more like cosy boudoirs than road vehicles.

The manufacturers of electrics were continually trying to show how far they could run on one charge. Sometimes they'd go a hundred miles or more, but only if they kept their speed down to about 12 m.p.h. It was, however, possible to tour for long distances in an electric if you went from charging station to charging station, or if you carried a kit along to charge your batteries from the 550-volt overhead wires of the trolley-car lines which covered the country.

The first taxis in New York were Columbia electrics, hundreds of which appeared in 1900. The batteries for these cars (weighing nearly a ton) lived in a box which could be removed from underneath the car for charging and instantly replaced by a box of freshly charged cells. Of course, the taxi company needed a pit and a sort of hydraulic elevator to do this, but it kept the money-making machines from being laid up. These taxis were not too successful. The thug-like drivers of the day, who make modern cabbies seem almost angelic, just tore the heavy brutes to pieces. The faster, lighter, cheaper petrol taxi soon drove them off the streets.

The self-starter did as much as anything to doom the electric, since the more practical petrol-engined cars now required no hand cranking. And it was the fearsome starting handle as much as anything that had made the electric such a favourite with women.

By the mid-Twenties the electric had almost disappeared. The last survivor, the Detroit Electric, finally bowed to the inevitable and ceased manufacture in 1938.

STEAMERS

To the man of the late nineteenth century, steam was the one truly logical source of power. It ran his railroads; a steam engine powered the wonderful complex of shafting and belts, which ran the machines in the factory that gave him his living, and it even ran the dynamos which produced that strange new force, electricity.

To the practical man, a steam engine was more sensible, somehow, than a petrol engine. A petrol engine was a temperamental mystery. It didn't even seem as if it ought to work. And if it ran badly most mechanics of those days couldn't tell quite why. But there was some sense to a steam engine. If it stopped you could *see* why, and mechanics even in remote country districts had been familiar with steam for fifty years.

Just mention the words "steam car" to almost any man over fifty and he'll start spouting about the Stanley steam car. Although there was a long string of steamer types built before World War I, the name Stanley is the one that sticks in people's minds. Only a few Americans remember the magnificent and popular White Steamer and the toylike and fragile Locomobile.

"Oh, boy," the fifty-year-old chortles. "That Stanley Steamer was the greatest car ever built. Y'know the Stanley people would give you a new car if you just held the throttle open for three minutes. Nobody ever did, though. Those cars went so fast they couldn't be held on the road. Easiest car in the world to drive, though. No clutch, no shift, no nothing. But even so, they made you have a locomotive engineer's licence to drive one. My pop had one for years. I drove it lots of times when I was no more than ten years old. The gas-car 'interests' put 'em out of business."

Ridiculous! I have often heard perorations like this about the Stanley, and in my youth I saw Stanley Steamers in operation—an undertaker in our neighbourhood used a fleet of them for funerals. But until a few years ago I had never ridden in one. Finally, at that time I got a steam-happy friend (all steam enthusiasts are a bit odd) to take me for a ride in one of the many steamers in his collection.

He proudly rolled out a 1913 Model, 20-h.p. Stanley Roadster to show me what steam was all about.

At first glance a steam car looks about like any other motor vehicle. It has four wheels, a hood, a dashboard, seats, a steering wheel. But lift the hood and you'll be surprised to see a big, dirty-white, drum-like affair sitting in a tangle of sloppy plumbing. That's the boiler. Under the boiler, located where the crankcase in any other car would be, is the burner. Two holes in the front of the burner (about where you'd ordinarily stick a crank) give you a fine view of a terrifying mass of roaring blue flame. The holes admit fuel nozzles.

If you want to see the engine, it lives in close proximity to the rear axle and is a two-cylinder affair that looks as if it had been stolen off the side of a locomotive. Since it is covered with a big tin fairing (full of oil in later models), it's pretty hard to see, however. In the back of the car is a big tank full of paraffin. You do, however, carry a little tank of petrol to prime the burner and to keep the pilot light lit. The dashboard is a really fearsome thing, with innumerable little wheels on long stems stuck in among some very unfamiliar-looking dials.

Furthermore, there is no clutch pedal, no gear lever, no accelerator pedal. The pedals on the floor of this one are a reverse pedal, a "hook-up" pedal, and a foot brake. On the steering column is a long throttle lever in about the same position as a modern gear lever, which is the main speed control and the water-control valve. On the floor, slightly aft of where an old-fashioned floor lever would be, is the long handle of a pump. In the old days people were braver than they are now and left the pilot light under the boiler burning all the time, so that there was always some steam up. If your wife suddenly realised that Aunt Minnie's train was due at the station in six minutes, you had but to nip out to the garage, release the hand brake, and without even monkeying with anything so foul as our present day self-starters, you were off to the station. Nowadays Aunt Minnie would walk or have a long, long wait if she had to depend on steam-car transportation, because modern steam enthusiasts usually start with a stone-cold boiler and "steaming up" takes about half an hour. (Some real steam fiends claim they can do it in fifteen minutes; anti-steam characters claim it takes all day).

If you have ever struggled with a paraffin stove or a blow-torch, you know that you have to build up fuel pressure by pumping air into the little fuel tank, and that it helps first to heat the fuel jets with a little alcohol fire, so that the fuel coming from the tank through the jets will be vaporised and yield the necessary hot blue flame. The Stanley burner is not unlike one of these camp stoves, but on a Gargantuan scale. It is necessary first to build up pressure in a little auxiliary paraffin tank (so that the main tank won't be under pressure) and in that little petrol tank on the running-board. The petrol takes the place of the alcohol primer of your camp stove and also feeds the pilot light. On a Stanley, however, it is usual to carry a little tank of acetylene in the tool kit. This has attached to it a short length of rubber hose ending in a nozzle. You open a valve on the tank, light the end of the nozzle, and play this flame over the pilot jet to get it really hot. Then you open the pilot valve a little. Now your pilot light is lit. Next you open the firing-up valve and let some petrol burn on the main burner for half a minute or so to warm *it* up. Now you can open the main fuel valve and paraffin will soon be heating the water in your boiler. If the water in the boiler isn't up to the right level, an automatic valve will shut off the fuel, preventing you from idiotically burning out the boiler. Conversely, if the steam pressure gets too high, another valve ("the steam automatic", the Stanleys called it) automatically shuts off the paraffin.

The drum-like boiler of a Stanley carries the terrifying pressure of 600 pounds per square inch, but none has ever been known to explode. For strength the Stanleys wound it with two layers of piano wire—the way Armstrong's in England wound naval guns. These are fire-tube boilers—as opposed to water-tube boilers in which the water runs in the pipes—and there are as many as 750 tubes in the larger ones. The Stanleys tried to blow up one of their own boilers one day, but even after jamming in 1,500 pounds of pressure nothing happened. At that pressure some of the tubes started to leak, so that it was impossible to get a higher reading. But explode, no! The only time they succeeded was when they left off some of the wire wrapping. Almost blew Boston across Cape Cod Bay!

Once you have made enough steam, you can get behind the wheel and drive. As we climbed up and in,

Three-wheel De Dion and Trépardoux steam-car. A large number of these light vehicles were built between 1885 and 1889 and very fortunately several of them have been preserved and restored. The Trépardoux boiler generated rapid steam-heat and drove a simple engine without condenser. This silent vehicle was extremely adaptable.

my friend pointed to the steam gauge. "Five hundred pounds per square inch. We could run on two hundred if we had to, but we'd have no reserve power." So saying he released the hand brake and a little locking arrangement which kept the hand-throttle lever from being accidentally displaced. Then he slightly moved this lever, which was a long, shiny, nickel-plated affair attached to the steering post, and we moved off up a slight grade. Just like that!

My friend had turned no ignition key, pushed no starter button, had listened to no grinding, no sudden roar of engine. He hadn't stepped on any clutch or changed any gears.

But softly, with a slight, odd creaking from the engine behind us we were off. It was an eerie feeling, coasting up a hill like that with just the merest suggestion of a chuff-chuff. I mentioned the chuff-chuff.

"Oh, we steam people like that, but you can't even hear that much in the latest models."

We were rolling along a fairly twisty, hilly piece of country road now, doing about fifty, slowing for the turns with the rather primitive two-wheel brakes. I was glad we did, too, because the high, fully elliptically-sprung body rolled and bounced like a buggy. No sports car, this.

I still couldn't get over the strange effortlessness of the car's running. So quiet was it that every little squeak of the old bodywork, every little creak of the leather upholstery as we shifted our weight was oddly magnified, as unexpected as people coughing in a library.

To stop for a cross-road, my friend just closed the throttle and stepped on the brake. The engine didn't idle; it stopped dead.

In the early 1900's the White Steamer was the great rival of the Stanley. A 1907 model (left) was the property of President Theodore Roosevelt. White Steamers were made until 1911, when they abandoned steam and commenced the production of petrol-powered cars. The Whites had a wooden chassis frame "amoured" with reinforcing plates of nickel steel. The under-seat, semi-flash boiler of the White could be fired by paraffin. The French engineer Léon Serpollet was one of the most active supporters of the steam-car. In 1902, driving a stream-lined racer called "The Easter Egg" (below) he beat the world speed record by going at 75 m.p.h.

"Your power isn't made in the engine, as in a petrol car," he explained. "It's in the steam you've made and saved up in the boiler, and if you think you have enough, you can just turn off the main fire and go home on the steam you have in reserve, which I think I'll do right now because we've been driving around without licence plates."

He reversed into a drive-way by merely stepping on a reverse pedal which instantly made the engine go backwards without gear-changing or the manipulation of a clutch.

I noticed another pedal and asked about it.

"That's called the hook-up. When you push it part way down it'll stay there until you push it again. It limits the valve opening on the engine and saves steam when you're cruising. At low speeds or in traffic, you can run more smoothly without it."

When we got back I took a closer look at the Stanley's innards. There was a lot more to it than just a burner, a boiler, and an engine.

First, there were the pumps: pumps for air pressure, pumps for water, fuel, cylinder oil. These little pumps are situated under the floor-boards and are mechanically operated from the engine. Then there are gadgets like the superheater; this dries and heats the steam for greater power. And there is the condenser. The 1913 model I rode in had no condenser and it had to stop for water every fifty miles or so (it carried a strainer-ended hose for sucking the stuff up from brooks and horse troughs). But from 1915 on the Stanley had what looked like a normal radiator out in front which condensed the used steam back to water, greatly increasing the range (to 300 miles or more) you could travel before having to make a water stop. All these devices were interconnected by what seemed miles of piping, valves, and joints.

The engine—I examined one removed from a car—was a much simpler device than I had imagined: two cylinders, side by side; simple slide valves, crossheads, eccentric link and crankshaft with a big gear to couple it to the axle, no fly-wheel, and only thirteen moving parts, which were all on ball bearings.

Later models than the one I sampled also had a rather simplified electrical system for lighting and, in later models still, an electric heating device for lighting the pilot from the dashboard.

The twin brothers, F. E. and F. O. Stanley, who invented the Stanley Steamer, were born in Kingfield, Maine, in 1849. Like many farm boys they were tinkerers. More especially they were whittlers— violin whittlers. Until they died they were passionate whittlers of violins, F. O. particularly. If he liked

you, he'd take you into a little room he had fixed up in the factory and proudly show you the latest violin he was working on.

They never had much schooling. One of them went to college for a few weeks, but didn't like it and came home. Oddly enough, they became school teachers, but their real enthusiasm was inventing things. They invented and successfully marketed a home gas generator and X-ray equipment. They manufactured violins. They experimented with photography and came up with the famous Stanley Dry Plate, which they sold to Eastman Kodak for a fabulous sum.

They saw their first car in 1896 at the Brockton Fair and decided that they could do better. Their first steamer appeared in Newton, Massachusetts, in 1897 and an early photograph (made on a Stanley Dry Plate, I'm sure) shows the prim-looking, bearded, bowler-hatted, rug-wrapped brothers sitting in this little machine which caused such a sensation in

On the left are the boiler and the engine of an 1899 Stanley Steamer; the complete car is on the right. The Locomobile Steamer of the next few years was almost identical, since the Stanley brothers sold their rights in this machine to the Locomobile Company in 1899. Later the company split into two groups: Mobile and Locomobile. These cars acquired a reputation for fragility due to the rough treatment their owners gave them on the sandy and rocky roads of their day. Rudyard Kipling in his charming story, "Steam Tactics", which concerned the Locomobile Steamer he owned, has First-Class Engine-Room Artificer Hinchcliffe complain that the machine was as delicate as a "wicker-willow lunch basket" and that the "boiler's only seated on four little paper-clips". Yet, it was on an 1899 Stanley that F.O. Stanley and his wife drove up the ten-mile road to the top of Mount Washington, a feat no car had previously performed. Above is a 10 h.p. 1910 Stanley Roadster.

its day. By 1899 they were making two hundred cars a year and F. O. drove one of the spidery little steam carriages, complete with wife, up the rocky, unpaved carriage road to the top of Mount Washington in two hours and ten minutes.

Everybody wanted to buy a piece of them and, finally, to get rid of a particularly persistent pest, they set an astronomic sum as a selling price for the whole works. Unfortunately, the buyers weren't scared, and the Stanleys found they had sold their business to what became the Locomobile Company.

In two years, unable to keep away from the things, they were back making steam cars, having had to redesign the whole machine in order to circumvent the patents they had sold. The Stanleys were so much better that the Locomobile people gave up in disgust and sold the patents back for a song. No more steamers for them, only petrol cars.

The Stanley brothers hated advertising and seldom in all their years did they pay for it. But publicity from racing success was something different. For their really serious speed tests, they employed the now almost legendary Fred Marriot. For him they built a special racer, something like an inverted canoe, called the Stanley Rocket. She weighed but 1,600 pounds and Marriot broke five world's records at Ormond Beach, Florida, doing 127.6 m.p.h. in 1906!

In 1907 he tried again, pushing the steam pressure up to 1,300 pounds per square inch. The speedometer stood at 197 miles per hour when something went wrong. The car took to the air, bounced, broke up. The boiler shot down the beach for a mile. Marriot flew clear but was badly hurt. Luckily, he lived, but the Stanleys never tried for record speed again.

Using mass-production methods, the Stanley could have made—and sold—more cars. They were always

110

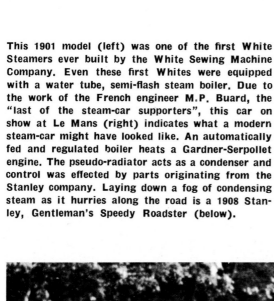

This 1901 model (left) was one of the first White Steamers ever built by the White Sewing Machine Company. Even these first Whites were equipped with a water tube, semi-flash steam boiler. Due to the work of the French engineer M.P. Buard, the "last of the steam-car supporters", this car on show at Le Mans (right) indicates what a modern steam-car might have looked like. An automatically fed and regulated boiler heats a Gardner-Serpollet engine. The pseudo-radiator acts as a condenser and control was effected by parts originating from the Stanley company. Laying down a fog of condensing steam as it hurries along the road is a 1908 Stanley, Gentleman's Speedy Roadster (below).

behind on their orders, especially in the days before the self-starter. But they just didn't care to make cars except by meticulous hand-craft methods. Nor would the Stanley brothers give you a new car if you held the throttle wide open for three minutes. You could hold it open for three hours for all they cared. They never gave anything away.

In 1918, F. E., making a trial in one of his steamers on the Newburyport Pike, ran it off the road rather than run into two farm wagons wich were filling the whole road while their drivers conversed. F. E. died. His brother had no heart left for the steam-car business and pulled out. Others tried to reorganise the company and carry on, but in 1925 the last Stanley Steamer silently left the factory.

With the tremendous success of the early Stanleys, all kinds of steamers were built in competition. Perhaps the most successful of these was the White

Steamer, which used a water-tube boiler on the flash-steam principle. Although it could make steam faster, it did not have the reserve power of the Stanley. The beautiful and complex steam cars built by Abner Doble were perhaps the last and most modern of the steam cars. Starting cold, these could be driven away in half a minute, and everything worked from the dashboard by means of a beautiful electrical system, so that all of the drudgery of firing-up was eliminated. But the Doble cost too much—up to $20,000 or so. The Stanleys had never been priced at more than a tenth as much.

Steam types mutter darkly about the "interests" having done in the steam car. This sounds very dramatic, but just isn't true. Steam cars disappeared because nobody bothered to make them any more, the demand being virtually non-existent and their method of construction utterly uneconomic.

THE GRAND

ES MARQUES

OF THE LONG LINE OF MOTOR CARS THAT HAS TAKEN TO THE ROAD THESE SEVENTY YEARS, A NOBLE FEW STAND FORTH ABOVE THEIR FELLOWS. THEY HAVE GIVEN US JOY. THEY HAVE CHANGED OUR WORLD. LET THE GREAT NAMES HERE SPEAK FOR THEMSELVES.

ROLLS ROYCE

"The engine's sealed up, isn't it?"

"They guarantee 'em for life, don't they?"

"Are the latest models still hand-made?"

For twenty-four years—as long as I've owned Rolls-Royces—I've happily listened to these same questions every time I've stopped the Rolls I was driving long enough to be engaged in even a few moments of conversation. The facts are: Rolls-Royces never had sealed engines, they are not guaranteed for life (but for three years), nor are they hand-made (no car ever is or was).

Nonetheless, these are genuine questions. Whatever people may ask about other machines, in the case of the Rolls they are really telling me, letting me understand that they know as well as I do that the Rolls-Royce is "The Best Car in the World".

But why this awe, why this veneration for the "name"?

It is simply this: The Rolls-Royce is perhaps the finest mechanical artifact that has ever been made, that an individual can own, that he can get his hands on and operate.

A famous and perhaps slightly jealous engineer many years ago cracked that "The Rolls-Royce is the triumph of craftsmanship over design." He meant it as no compliment, but his quip penetrated into the very core of the reason for Rolls-Royce's success for almost sixty years. For every Rolls-Royce has been a triumph of craftsmanship and if its design has often seemed behind the times, it is because flashy mechanical tricks have always had to take second place to the homely virtues of silence, smoothness, and, above all, unbreakability; and the not-so-homely virtue of luxurious travel.

Preceding pages: Delahaye type 145 V-12, a unique model notable for its ultra-luxurious coachwork, adapted by Franay, on an authentic Grand Prix assembly.

A Rolls at 50,000 miles is just nicely broken in. There are Rolls-Royces which have done 500,000 miles and still delight their owners.

The car that more than any other made Rolls-Royce's reputation and is the basis upon which much of Rolls-Royce's present fame still rests was the Silver Ghost of 1907. In a day when cars were expected to be noisy and smoky and unreliable, the Silver Ghost, besides being silent, left no trail of oily smoke. In a day when most cars used a primitive system of external oilers, which sometimes fed the engine too little oil and most times too much, the Ghost had a hollow crankshaft, fed by oil from a pump, like the smokeless car of today.

By 1903, Royce had a successful business building dynamos and electrical cranes, but his annoyance with the Decauville changed that. He knew he could build better cars himself. Within a short time, after driving his mechanics into a state of near desperation from overwork and his demands for perfection, he had several finished cars which satisfied him. These were by no means yet in the class of the Silver Ghost, but by the standards of the day his little two-, three-, and four-cylinder machines were marvels of mechanical excellence.

These cars were brought to the attention of an

aristocratic young man named Charles Rolls. Rolls, the son of a Lord Llangattock (a good thing they didn't name the car after him), was like many of the bloods of his time—crazy about ballooning, aeroplanes (he was killed in one in 1910), and cars—mostly cars. He knew everything there was to know about them, wrote about them and raced them. He was the dealer for Panhard Levassor cars in London when he saw and was entranced by Royce's cars, and almost immediately the firm of Rolls-Royce was born to market them.

Although these early cars were a success in sales and in racing—Rolls won the Tourist Trophy Race in 1905 with a 20 h.p., four-cylinder machine—it was not until 1907 when the first Ghosts were delivered that the name started on its road to greatness.

The Silver Ghost was made from 1907 to 1926, from the Edwardian era through World War I, when it did yeoman service as the chassis for armoured cars, to the Jazz Age and the General Strike. Certainly there were slight changes in the car. Towards the end, some Ghosts even had front-wheel brakes, and a factory in Springfield, Massachusetts, started to manufacture an Americanised version. Basically it was still "The Best Car in the World", but never again would there be such a wide gulf between it and other, less regal machines.

Above: With an 8-cylinder V engine and an automatic transmission, the Rolls-Royce Silver Shadow can do 120 m.p.h. This is the first time that Rolls-Royce have made a monocoque body.

In 1926, to meet the competition of great luxury cars like the Isotta-Fraschini, the 37.2 Hispano-Suiza, and the 6½-litre Bentley, which was already on the stocks, Rolls announced a successor to the Silver Ghost: the New Phantom.

The engine was entirely new. Still a six, with the cylinders cast in pairs of three, it now had overhead valves and was slightly larger (7,668 c.c.). It had slightly more power than the old engine. (Rolls never divulges the horse-powers of its engines, but the Phantom I developed about 100 h.p., not high for some of the weighty arks it was expected to drag around). But unhappily it did not have nearly its sweetness and charm. In general, the Phantom I was rather a lump to drive, especially the Springfield left-hand-drive version, which had a three-speed gearbox.

Within four years Rolls-Royce discontinued the unloved Phantom I. In 1929 the Phantom II was announced, as fine a car as the firm has ever built. The Phantom II's engine was basically the same as that of the earlier car, but minor modifications

115

Preceding pages: A 1932 Phantom II, Continental Rolls-Royce. The original 1907 Silver Ghost (p. 119) can still be viewed in Rolls-Royce's London showroom. The Isle of Man Tourist Trophy Race of 1906 was won by the four-cylinder, 20 h.p. Rolls-Royce (upper left) at an average speed of 39 m.p.h. Edwardian exaggeration: Joseph Cockshoot of Manchester built the body for this 1908 Silver Ghost (upper right). This regal equipage was the first Rolls-Royce in India. Known as the "Pearl of the East", it had a removable top and could be used in open form. The "Silent Sports Car" (right), a 1938, 4½-litre Bentley, was more of a sports car then.

somewhat increased its power to perhaps 125 h.p. Its chassis, however, was entirely new. The heavy torque-tube drive was eliminated and long, supple, half-elliptics replaced the cantilever rear springs which had been a Rolls habit for so long. The frame itself was also considerably stiffened. The car now had superb road holding and steering, and even with the heavy, formal bodies that some of the company's stuffier customers demanded, it would do over 85 m.p.h.

In 1930, to satisfy its less stodgy clients, Rolls introduced what is perhaps the finest sporting luxury car ever built by anybody (except Hispano-Suiza?). This was the "Continental Touring" model built on the "short" 144-inch chassis. (The "long" chassis had a 150-inch wheelbase). It had flatter springs, a higher compression engine (5.25 to 1), and a slightly higher rear-axle ratio. Late models were also fitted with four-speed, synchromesh, close-ratio gearboxes and adjustable shock absorbers.

In 1934, Sir Henry Royce died and in 1936 there appeared the first Rolls-Royce designed without his involvement. This was the fabulous Phantom III,

powered with a marvellous and somewhat complicated V-12 engine of about the same cubic capacity as the earlier engines. And now for the very first time there was a Rolls-Royce with independent front suspension.

The P-III was probably the very last truly great luxury car the world will ever see. Usually fitted with huge palaces of bodies, lined in rare woods, and fitted out with bars and vanity sets, these 100-mile-an-hour giants could be steered over rough, pot-holed roads and through dense traffic with greater precision and comfort than an ordinary small car. It would be nearly impossible to build such a machine today. One of these cars with a good bespoke body cost nearly £4,000 in 1939. With today's high costs for labour and materials £15,000 would hardly give its makers a profit.

Parallel with these "battle-cruiser" Rolls-Royces, there appeared in 1923 a line of smaller machines from which descend the Rolls-Royces and Bentleys of today, up to the appearance, in 1959, of Silver Cloud II.

The first of the "baby" Rolls-Royces was the 20 h.p. model. Its big brother was rated at 40 to 50

h.p. as has been mentioned. Over the years these Twenties grew into 20/25's, 25/30's and just before the war, the Wraith. All of them were in every respect as meticulously made as the larger cars, although a criticism of the earlier smaller machines, especially the Twenty, was that they were painfully underpowered.

Since the war, Rolls has been making cars which are still "The Best Cars in the World". But nowadays, Rolls buys many things from outside suppliers, including steel bodywork which would have been anathema in the old days when the company made chassis exclusively.

Still, despite changes every bit of metal is to Rolls-Royce specification, every component bought from the outside is examined by an army of inspectors using electronic devices. Each engine is run for eight hours on a testing rig fuelled by cooking gas, thirty minutes idling, thirty minutes at medium revolutions, and seven hours at full power. Then every twentieth engine is taken down to its smallest bolt and every single part carefully examined, some under a microscope. And then, if there is some suspicion about any part, every one of the previous twenty engines is torn

apart for examination. Every fiftieth engine goes through an even more stringent trial, running for twenty-four hours. If, upon being stripped down, it still doesn't please the inspectors, the previous fifty engines are torn down. Not only the engine, but every single part of a new Rolls or Bentley is treated with equally cruel suspicion by the testers. It's a wonder any finished cars ever leave the plant.

I was at the Rolls-Royce factory recently watching them build the new V-8 Silver Cloud II and the Bentley. I asked a Rolls engineer how many cars a day were produced.

"Well," he said, "we finished five yesterday, but the blasted testers brought every bloody one back."

Yet all the electronic measuring gadgets and microscopes and listening devices didn't impress me as much as a group of quiet men in a corner of the plant who were doing something with shining sheets of stainless steel. They were making Rolls-Royce radiator shells and they were soldering them together by hand. I wouldn't have been a bit surprised if one of their big, coke-heated, soldering irons had been the self-same one used to solder together the very first radiator shell of the very first Royce car.

119

Above: The author's 1935 Phantom II Continental Rolls-Royce. Its convertible body was built by Henry Binder of Paris.
Below: A 1914 Rolls-Royce Alpine Silver Ghost was especially designed to take milord on the Grand Tour.

HISPANO-SUIZA

Had you been a gay young Continental in the feverish Twenties, a dashing blade who found it absolutely necessary to transport himself and his blonde of the moment from Maxim's in Paris to the gaming tables of Monte Carlo, there would have been only one eminently correct machine for the journey—a Hispano-Suiza.

True, a Bugatti or two on a similar errand might have leaped past you with a sound of tearing calico issuing from its exhaust, but the young man in its cockpit would have had at least part of his mind occupied with things mechanical: for instance, was that No. 1 plug oiling up again? You in the Hispano could keep more of your mind on the delicious creature at your side. As for the English milord in his Silver Ghost Rolls-Royce—a rattle of gravel against the varnish of his elegant Hooper coachwork and you were past him.

The words "Grande Marque" might well have been coined to describe the great Hispanos of the Twenties: the 37.2-h.p. model and the 46-h.p. Boulogne which developed from it.

Mark Birkigt, their designer and, with Royce and Bugatti, one of that great triumvirate of original automotive minds, first showed an awed motoring world his new car in 1919. Not unexpectedly, its engine was based on the highly successful Hispano-Suiza aircraft engines which he had designed and of which some 50,000 had been built to power the French Spads, the English SE-5's and American JN4H's of the First World War. Such famous aviators as René Fonck, Eddie Rickenbacker, and Georges Guynemer had flown behind them to many victories. It was from Capitaine Guynemer's personal blazon that the stork, which graced the radiator caps of post-war Hispanos, was evolved. (The Hispano instruction book, worried lest careless owners harm this stork, warned: "The stork placed on the radiator plug is silver plated. Never brighten it up with copper-cleaning substances.").

The aero-engine had been a V-8 with a single camshaft over each bank, but the new car engine was a 6½-litre six, like one of the banks with two cylinders added. It too had an overhead camshaft. The method of valve adjustment—almost identical to that of the Alfa Romeos of the late Twenties and Thirties—employed gear-toothed steel mushrooms upon which the cams pressed to open the valves. The aluminium cylinder block was merely a cooling chamber into which the outwardly threaded, nitrided steel cylinders were screwed. This "cooling jacket", to quote the instruction book again, "is made corrosion-proof by a special process of enamelling under pressure." The seven-bearing crankshaft which had completely circular webs was made from a single billet of steel weighing some 700 pounds before machining and only about 90 pounds after. I remember a mechanic striking one lightly with a steel rod to let me hear the sweet, bell-like sound it made.

The engine had dual ignition by specially designed coils and distributors, a twin carburettor whose innards could be instantly detached with a lever, and a huge oil filler into which a whole can of oil could be dumped at one swoop. The entire engine was of such wonderfully clean design—all shining black lacquer and bright aluminium—as to make one swoon with covetousness.

The first 37.2's engines turned over quite slowly (aircraft practice again) to deliver their power. At 3,500 r.p.m. the engine generated 135 h.p., but at a mere 2,000 r.p.m., 120 h.p. was produced. This from a compression ratio of but 4½ to 1. So enormous was the torque that in spite of a high rear-axle ratio of 3.37 to 1, it was possible to crawl along at four m.p.h. in high gear!

Power was transmitted through a single-plate clutch (a cone clutch in earlier models) and a short, stiff torque tube to a handsome rear axle (a pity it wasn't visible). The chassis was a conventional design, but quite stiff and light, with half-elliptic

springs. The whole car was light for its size. The chassis weighed a mere 2,500 pounds in road trim.

The four-wheel brakes were operated by a servo-mechanism through a clutch at the side of the gear-box—à la Rolls-Royce—but Birkigt didn't copy it from Royce. Royce was the copy-cat. The finned brake drums were of aluminium with shrunk-in cast-iron liners (such as Buick recently invented). The stopping power was phenomenal. The steering—two-and-a-quarter turns from lock to lock—was light and positive, making Hispano another of those rare big cars which feel small in traffic.

I discovered this (in 1932, I think) when Ray Gil-hooley, who tried to sell us used sporting cars in those days, let me drive a Boulogne he was demon-strating for me. With its 133-inch wheelbase, the car was no baby and as I was driving it down Broadway in New York I gave the taxis swarming around me a wide berth, not engaging in any cut-and-thrust duels with them. My gingerly driving annoyed Gil-hooley, who growled, "Pull over to the curb, I'll show you how to drive this bastard." And he did. With mere flicks of the steering wheel while his foot stayed

well down on the accelerator, he carved up those taxis as they'd seldom been carved before. The big car seemed to bend in its middle and sailed as effort-lessly in and out of the heavy traffic as a telegraph boy on a bicycle.

I didn't buy the Hispano, though. He wanted too much for it—$150!

This Boulogne had a bigger engine than the 37.2. It had a capacity of 8 litres and was known as the 45 h.p. (Both the 37.2 and the 45 were known by their British horsepower ratings). It would do well over 100 m.p.h. The 37.2 would approach 90 m.p.h. or so.

These glorious vehicles were in production for some twelve years, during which time they made some record runs. André Dubonnet, the apéritif manufac-turer, drove the 580 miles from Paris to Nice, carry-ing three passengers and their luggage, in 12 hours 35 minutes. In 1921, he won the Boillot Cup at Bou-logne at an average of 64 m.p.h. for 237 miles. Woolf Barnato, who later controlled Bentley Motors, took several records at Brooklands, doing 300 miles at a brilliant 92.2 m.p.h.

Following pages: 1922 H6B Hispano 6-cylinder Torpedo, bore and stroke 100 x 140 mm.

Following a wager between the French businessman C.T. Weymann (creator of imitation leather coachwork) and the American Moskovics (designer of the famous Stutz), a 46 h.p. Hispano-Suiza sports model (left) pitted its strength for 24 hours against a Stutz at Indianapolis in April 1928. The affair ended with a crushing victory for the Hispano, the Stutz having given up the race after 19 hours on the road.

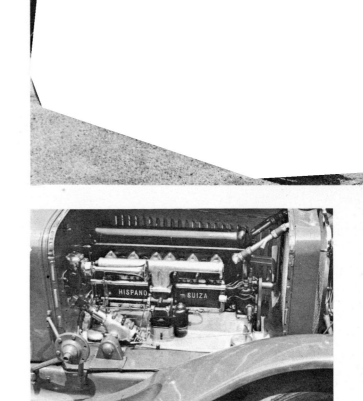

A Boulogne 45h.p. model appears on the right, its cleanly designed overhead-camshaft engine below.

Over the years, too, the Hispano became a symbol of all that was chic. It showed up in the literature of the period in books, as in Michael Arlen's *The Green Hat*, a bit of which I quote: "Open as a yacht, it wore a shining bonnet; and flying over the crest of the great bonnet, as though in proud flight over the scores of phantom horses, was that silver stork by which the gentle may be pleased to know that they have just escaped death beneath the wheels of a Hispano-Suiza car, as supplied to His Most Catholic Majesty." There was even one opus of the gilded life called *L'homme à l'Hispano* by Pierre Frondaie.

People wonder about the name Hispano-Suiza: "What's this Spanish-Swiss stuff got to do with a French car?" Mark Birkigt was a young Swiss who got some rich Spaniards to back him in 1904 and formed the *Société de Construction d'Automobiles Hispano-Suiza* in Barcelona. Even the very early cars to come from Birkigt's drawing board were full of new ideas that became commonplace years later. The T-head, the cylinder cast as a unit (*en bloc*), the shaft drive with torque taken up by the rear springs (Hotchkiss drive), and, on a racing Hispano of 1912, a piston-type pump supercharger, which not only pumped mixture into the cylinders, but also pulled the burnt gases out through an extra exhaust valve.

But it was the so-called Alfonso XIII model, developed from the successful racing cars of 1910, that first made the Hispano famous. This was officially known as the 15T, and if the term "sports car" had been known in 1912, that's what it would have been

called. It was a delightful little machine with a T-head, four-cylinder engine of 3,622 c.c., and an incredible bore-stroke ratio of 80×180 mm. It would do better than 70 m.p.h.—fast for 1912—and better than 90 when souped up and stripped down for racing. Furthermore, it made a distinctive and musical exhaust noise which captivated the motor sportsmen of the day, including the Bourbon on the throne of Spain whose name it acquired.

Most of these Alfonso models were, by the beginning of World War I, being made in a recently opened factory near Paris, but the Barcelona factory continued their production until 1920, although with a new four-cylinder, overhead-camshaft engine not unlike the aero-engine in concept.

In 1931, Hispano-Suiza took over the Ballot Company and brought out some very nice but unexciting six-cylinder, push-rod engined machines, hardly to be mentioned in the same breath with the fiery aristocrats of the Twenties.

However, there was to be one more fabulous Hispano, the V-12, which was launched in 1931, just in time for the Depression. This lordly *voiture de Grande Luxe* had a 9½-litre engine and developed 220 h.p. It was capable of about 105 m.p.h. and would go from 0 to 60 in 11½ seconds, not bad for a 5,000-pound carriage.

But somehow this king of cars never generated the excitement of the 37.2. The Hispano had been a car for the great wild days of the Twenties. The Thirties were a time for lesser machines.

MERCEDES BENZ

Above: 300 SL Mercedes-Benz. Right: The blown eight-cylinder models were produced by Mercedes from 1935 to 1939 and were sought after by sports car enthusiasts and lovers of luxury cars. This model, Type 500 K, dates from 1935. It develops 160 b.h.p. "with compressor" and has a 5-litre power unit.

Lusty-looking giants such as the SSK Mercedes-Benz of 1929 (following pages) were the beau-idéal of the wealthy young blades of the late Twenties. Their prodigious, 7-litre, super-charged engines delivered 225 h.p. with the "kompressor" engaged.

If Rolls-Royce, during the great years of the Grandes Marques, typified the British ideal in a road machine —silence, superlative craftsmanship, together with a certain lean and quiet understatement of quality— then' Mercedes-Benz was typically German. While also of superb construction, the Mercedes-Benz of those days was an altogether different sort of animal, especially in its sporting versions which are the ones most worth considering. They were flamboyant in look, Teutonically harsh in character.

The firms of Daimler, who were building the Mercedes, and Benz were married in 1926.

The Daimler Company, before joining Benz, was in its own right one of the great marques of all time. It had been so ever since Wilhelm Maybach (who was associated with old Herr Daimler) designed in 1900 the machine which instantly made every other car in the world impossibly old-fashioned.

This new car had a honeycomb radiator, gate-change gear-lever, and accurate control of engine speed by means of a throttle, made possible by mechanically opened inlet valves. (Until then the inlet valves in all cars opened by suction). Although made by Daimler in Cannstatt, this new *wunder-wagen* bore for the first time the name Mercedes, after the daughter of one Emil Jellinek.

Jellinek, Daimler's agent and Austro-Hungarian consul in Nice, rubbed shoulders with the fast-moving, gilded set on the Riviera in those free-spending Edwardian Days. The change in his fortunes came about when he astutely contracted to dispose of the entire factory production if Daimler would name the car after the apple of his eye. He had no trouble selling the new Mercedes to his rich friends who were enchanted by its silence and reliability as a touring machine and its near invulnerability as a racing car. For in 1901 a fast tourer was a sports car *and* a racing car (once you undid the back seats).

In 1903, there appeared the legendary "Sixty" Mercedes. A "Sixty" cost some £2,500 in 1903. But, consumed with heart-burning eagerness, many a gold-laden young buck paid several times this much to get one ahead of his friends. Herr Jellinek became much richer, and so proud of his cars, that he changed his name to Jellinek-Mercedes.

The "Sixty" had a giant four-cylinder engine of

9,236 c.c., and low-tension, make-and-break ignition. To make it easier to start, a ratchet-and-pinion device was fitted to raise the exhaust valves from their seats.

The "Sixty" was fast. In July, 1903, when three 90 h.p. cars ready for the Gordon-Bennett Race were destroyed in a fire that levelled the Cannstatt works, the factory borrowed three "Sixties" from private owners and, with one of the cars driven by Jenatzy, the red-bearded Stirling Moss of his day, won the race. He averaged 49.25 m.p.h. for 325 miles and at times reached 85 m.p.h.

Between 1903 and the end of World War I, Daimler built a spate of fine Mercedes cars for both touring and racing, but not until the Twenties did they build machines that delighted enthusiasts as much as the memorable "Sixty".

The first sporting Mercedes-Benz was the 33/180, or K, and it was certainly the least desirable. It appeared in 1926, the year the firm became Mercedes-Benz. Designed by Ferdinand Porsche, who had come to Mercedes from Austro-Daimler in 1923 and who was later to design the Auto-Union Grand Prix cars,

the Volkswagen, and the Tiger Tank, it was claimed to be the first "off-the-floor" car anybody could buy (if he had £2,500 to spare) that would do 100 m.p.h.

A friend of mine owned one and I was terrified every time I rode in it. It had the usual long loco-motive-boiler hood from which huge external exhaust pipes curled like nickel-plated pythons. Filling the cavernous space under the hood was a 6.2-litre, single overhead-camshaft engine complete "mit kompressor" which cut in when you were daft enough to press the accelerator well down.

I don't recollect even seeing anything like 100 m.p.h. on the speedometer of this high and unwieldy conveyance, but I do remember that at 40 or so it took the best part of a city block for its hopeless brakes to bring it to a halt.

It would seem unlikely that so cumbersome and dangerous a car as the K could be redesigned and made usable, but Porsche not only made it usable, he made it one of the great cars of all time. He lowered the chassis, bored out the engine slightly (to 6,789 c.c.), and installed power brakes (which still didn't stop too well).

127

This new model was called the 36/220, or S, and its 6.8-litre engine developed 120 h.p. at 3,000 r.p.m. without the supercharger and 180 h.p. when the supercharger was cut in.

This supercharger or "kompressor" was the unique feature of these cars. Gear-driven from the front of the crankshaft and running at three times engine speed, the standard-size blower (there were two larger sizes) blew air at eight-and-a-half pounds per square inch *into* the carburettors instead of sucking a gas-air mixture *from* the carburettor and *then* pumping it into the cylinders, as is usually the case. A clutch cut the blower in only when the accelerator was pushed down, so that most running was done with the "kompressor" out of action.

This six-cylinder engine also had a single overhead camshaft driven from a vertical shaft at the rear. Two valves per cylinder were operated by rockers while the cylinders, of cast iron, were of the wet liner type and sat in a bath of cooling water in the light alloy block. The crankcase and head were of aluminium, the only gasket being between the block and the head. Elsewhere, precisely ground and lapped surfaces were of such high accuracy as to preclude gaskets. The crankshaft rode on four main bearings and a pump delivered heated oil to the crankcase from an auxiliary tank.

In 1929 this engine was enlarged to 7 litres and put into a new model known as the 38/250, or SS. With a 7 to 1 compression ratio, it now delivered 170 h.p. unblown and 225 h.p. with the "kompressor" cut in.

The SSK was a variation of the SS, but with a shortened chassis (K for *kurz*).

The SSKL was a similar machine, but with a chassis drilled as full of holes as a Swiss cheese to lighten it (L for *leicht*). This type was used for racing and with the so-called "elephant" blower developed some 300 h.p. Private owners could buy an SSKL, but somehow (and this is still true of Mercedes-Benz today) they could never approach the results the factory got out of its cars. For example, in 1931 Rudolf Carraciola in an SSKL won the German Grand Prix against two Bugatti Type 51's driven by Varzi and Chiron.

This was the time of Mercedes' greatest racing successes, but the production sports cars of the mid-Thirties were the obese 500K and 540K (this time K stood for "kompressor"). Softly sprung, and woolly engined, albeit well-made and beautifully finished, these machines had lost the purposeful character and performance of their predecessors. Even today they are much in demand by collectors of "classic cars".

Nowadays, Mercedes-Benz, in addition to a line of excellent lesser cars, also manufactures the 300 series. The de luxe 300 Touring machine and the superb 300 SL sports car certainly qualify as Grandes Marques. If you own one, cherish it and treat it with kindness, for, doubtless, thirty years hence, it will be sought as eagerly as its ancestors are today.

The Mercedes-Benz 230 SL, latest in the line of famous Mercedes G.T. cars.

BUGATTI

At best, I've never been more than a *demi-Bugattiste*, a heretic, unfaithful to the cult of *Bugattisme*. Although I have owned and driven and even suitably revered the name of Bugatti, I have committed the unpardonable sin of flirting with other gods, of allowing myself to think that other cars sometimes, under special conditions and for particular purposes, may be almost equal to the Bugatti.

Your true-blue *Bugattiste*, under pain of having his Bugatti Owner's Club badge torn from his car, would admit no such heresy. He's almost right, for the Bugatti was as unique as its maker, Ettore Bugatti.

Bugatti sprang, in 1881, from a family of artistic Italians in Milan who hoped that young Ettore would follow the family traditions and go in for sculpture. Luckily for the world, he didn't. Instead, he became a master sculptor in metal for motor car chassis. Each part of every car Bugatti ever designed bears the stamp of his genius. It is crisp, functional, and beautiful for its own sake.

As I write this I am looking at some of those brilliantly clear photographs people used to make, early in this century. They are close-ups of the mechanism of a de Dietrich of about 1904. The clean, flat surfaces, the sharp edges are as pleasurable to look at and as efficient as those in the very last Bugattis. And Bugatti was a mere boy, not yet twenty-one, a minor whose father had to sign the contract when Ettore joined de Dietrich in 1902 as their designer.

Nor were the de Dietrich people fools, for Bugatti had already made a name for himself as an automotive genius who had designed and built race-winning machines since he was eighteen—and this without any formal engineering-school training.

The de Dietrich works were in Alsace, then a German province. In time, Bugatti left to work for other car builders—Mathis, Peugeot, Duetz—but when he set up his own factory in 1909 it was in Alsace, at Molsheim, near Strasbourg.

From 1909 until 1939, Bugatti turned out fewer than 10,000 cars, but they were of thirty-six different models. Of these many were racing machines, the most successful ones ever built. In 1925 and 1926 alone, Bugattis won over 1,000 races!

Bugatti never built an uninteresting or unexciting car, unless it was the relatively quiet Type 44, which is sometimes known as "the Molsheim Buick".

The Type 43 was the sporting version of the Grand Prix 35B, the car that had done most of the race winning. The 43 had a straight-eight, 2.3-litre engine and was supercharged by means of a Roots blower at eight pounds per square inch. It developed some 120 h.p. and a good 43 could exceed 110 m.p.h., a remarkable speed in 1927 when it first appeared. The three valves per cylinder were operated from fingers actuated by a single overhead camshaft. Expensive maintenance never bothered Bugatti. He assumed you were rich. Roller bearing con-rods and crankshafts—which meant disassembling the crankshaft in case of trouble—and non-detachable cylinder heads were normal in his designs. The Type 43 was typical. The chassis, too, is typically Bugatti, with deep side rails just below the dashboard area, but tapering to unbelievable delicacy at the front end. The springs were reversed quarter-elliptics in the rear and in front half-elliptic, but of such stiffness that one almost feels M. Bugatti might as well have left them off. (He did build a racing car without rear springs once). The front axle, common to almost all Bugattis, was nothing less than jewellery. Of polished steel and hollow, it had square apertures through which the springs were thrust. The flat-spoked wheels were of cast aluminium, the brake drums an integral part of them.

But what is it like to own and drive one of these high-strung animals—say, a Type 43?

In the first place you must be a very special kind of man, imbued with the fervour of *Bugattisme* to stand the machine's foibles. On a cold day, for example, it is nearly impossible to start. (Bugatti told complainers to keep their cars in heated garages). So you drain the oil and water, heat to taste, and re-feed to your engine. If it is going to start it will now burst into life at the first turn of the starter. But if you are a true believer, you'll hand crank first with the switch off to ease the pistons in their cold cylinders. You then idle at, say, 1,000 r.p.m. for ten minutes to warm things up. Idle much slower and you'll be taking out the sparking-plugs for cleaning.

But a Bugatti is worth the trouble. Once on the road, nothing except perhaps an Alfa Romeo of the Thirties can give such joy. The front wheels point exactly where your hands on the steering wheel tell them to. You corner like a god. The clutch feels light at first, but as you gain speed it needs a swift kick to allow you to flick the gear-lever from notch to

131

BUGATTI

Preceding pages: The Type 55 Bugatti. La Royale, the Type 41 Bugatti (right), often called the Golden Bug, was designed as a "voiture de grand luxe" for the use of kings and princes. Its chassis alone cost £7,000 in 1927, the year it first appeared. It had a fourteen-foot, two-inch wheel base and a Gargantuan 13-litre engine which developed no less than 300 b.h.p. It was capable of 125 m.p.h. and could be throttled back to 3 m.p.h. without changing gear. At 72 m.p.h. the engine only turned over at 1,000 r.p.m. The Royale was guaranteed and maintained free of charge for the life of its owner, each of whom Ettore Bugatti presented with a special white elephant radiator-cap ornament. On the running board sits the late Jean Bugatti, son of "Le Patron".

The famous driver Albert Divo was a champion who earned fame at the wheel of many different cars. Here he is seen (centre, right) in a 35B type 8 cylinder Bugatti, with supercharger. At the bottom of the page: the 57S, here shown in the Atalanta coupé version. The shorter, lower chassis houses the 170 b.h.p. engine. Dry sump lubrication: maximum speed 125 m.p.h. at 5,500 r.p.m. Page 136: Ettore Bugatti designed this Type 59, 3.3-litre car as a full Grand Prix racing machine. The model seen on these pages was converted for road use, and was capable of 175 m.p.h.

notch. (At low speeds, however, the multi-plate clutch —a tricky device on a "Bug"—doesn't quite release and you make embarrassing noises unless you just slam the lever through).

When a Bugatti needs work you'd best be an enthusiastic and knowing mechanic yourself, for there are not half-a-dozen men in the country who can be trusted to operate on it. To do a carbon and valve job means removing the cylinders—the head doesn't come off—and before you can do this on some models you have to remove the rear axle. On the Type 43 and some others, the roller bearings of the crankshaft are lubricated from jets set in the side of the crankcase which receive their oil through small-diameter copper pipes. A little lint in a pipe can mean trouble, of course. But *Bugattistes* never go near a dismantled engine with a rag. Camel's hair brushes only, *mon vieux!*

The Type 55 which came out in 1932 was one of the great sports cars of all time. It had a Type 51 Grand Prix engine (slightly de-tuned) in a Type 54 Grand Prix chassis, which had proved lethally dangerous as a racing car. This 2.3-litre engine had twin-overhead camshafts, eight cylinders, and a slightly larger supercharger than the Type 43. It blew at ten pounds.

The 55 was very much like the 43 on the road but rather faster and with much greater acceleration. It was capable of going from 0 to 60 in just over nine seconds and had a top speed of 120. It could do 100 m.p.h. in third!

In 1935, a new kind of Bugatti appeared, designed for use by people impatient with all the charming idiosyncrasies of the near-racing type of Bug. This new series was the Type 57, with a 3.3-litre, eight-cylinder, twin-overhead-camshaft engine. Although built in the usual Bugatti style, this "Normale" model somehow caused the cognoscenti to weep into their Pernod. "Bugatti is 'going Cadillac' like everyone else," they moaned.

But soon Bugatti brought out additional versions of his new machine, first a supercharged 57, the 57C, and then a much lower chassised, higher-compression type, the 57S (for sport), which in supercharged form was known as the 57SC. The weepers could dry their tears now, for these 57's proved themselves to be the greatest cars for road and sport that Bugatti had ever built. They compared in power and speed thus: The 57—130 h.p., 95 m.p.h.; the 57C—160 h.p., 105 m.p.h.; the 57S—190 h.p., 125 m.p.h., and the incomparable 57SC—220 h.p., 135 m.p.h.

Ettore Bugatti still had not been convinced of the benefits of independent front suspension. He compromised by splitting the ever-beautiful, polished-steel front axle in its middle and joining the halves with a knurled collar. This allowed an almost imperceptible amount of independent movement for each front wheel. (You can't blame him for not wanting to give up that wonderfully handsome axle). Further, he fitted De Ram shock absorbers, marvels of complexity which theoretically adjusted themselves to the exigencies of the road.

In 1936, a stock 57S driven by Robert Benoist crammed 135.4 miles into an hour on the Montlhéry autodrome in France, and in 1937 and 1939 57S Bugattis won first place at Le Mans.

The war ended the Type 57's. The Germans, the Canadians, the Americans all had their way with the Bugatti factory.

Ettore Bugatti died in 1947. He had during the war designed a 350 c.c., overhead-camshaft engine and a 1½-litre engine for a new small sports car.

A successor to the 57, the famous Type 64, was ready to be brought out, but it came to nothing.

At the Paris Car Show in 1951 a new Bugatti was exhibited, the Type 101, and although a few of these exist, no real production ever got started. In 1955 the people who now run Bugatti's factory brought out a 1½-litre, Grand Prix car with a transverse rear engine, which made a brief appearance in the ACF Grand Prix. It bore the red oval name plate, but is it a Bugatti? Is any car that Ettore himself didn't design a Bugatti?

A 37 Bugatti (p. 137 top) that has been restored completely in every detail. It is driven by a 1,496 c.c. 4-cylinder engine without supercharger. It was launched for the first time in 1927 and reached a speed of 106 m.p.h. It has the same typical design as the famous 2-litre, 8-cylinder models. One of the greatest "sports cars" of the early Thirties was the type 43A Bugatti (p. 137 bottom). It included the technical details of the famous Grand Prix models. Possessing a genuine 105 h.p. it could go faster than 100 m.p.h.

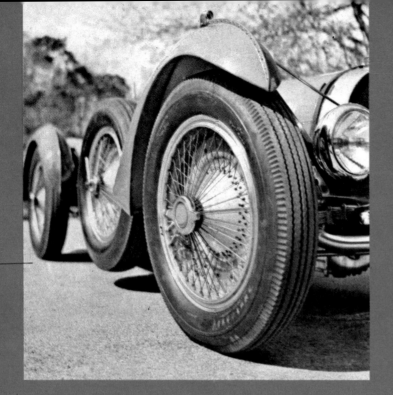

DUESENBERG

The J-type Duesenberg has an 8-cylinder, 6,880 c.c. engine developing 265 h.p. The 1934 coachwork by Franay includes a sliding roof. Following pages: "SJ" supercharged Duesenberg. This 1935 model was one of only two such short-chassised machines ever built. Its straight-eight, twin-overhead-cam-blown engine was said to develop 320 b.h.p. The short wheel base (142½ inch) roadster accelerated from zero to 100 m.p.h. in 17 seconds and did 104 m.p.h. in second gear.

A drawing in the advertisement pages of *Vanity Fair* in the early Thirties shows an imperious beldame talking to the third gardener. Behind them stretches a manicured landscape calculated to make the Hanging Gardens of Babylon look like the greenery adorning a traffic roundabout. A yachtsman, oozing billions aboard one of his J-class yachts, fills another page.

On each of the ads there is but one line of chaste lettering: "He (or She) drives a Duesenberg."

Duesenberg's advertising agency knew what it was doing, for it was emphatically a car only for the very rich. Duesenbergs, even in those days cost upward of $14,000 and I know of one with ultra-posh coachwork that cost nearly $25,000. Since Duesenberg confined himself to building the chassis, the coachwork was tailor-made for the client by the leading coachbuilders of the day.

The tycoons got their money's worth, too, for the Duesenberg (built in Indianapolis) gave them the comfort and size and prestige of a Rolls-Royce or Isotta-Fraschini, plus the tigerish power and speed of a Bugatti (although hardly a Bugatti's handling qualities). Furthermore, it was as beautifully constructed of the very finest materials as any car, any place, any time.

Imagine what a sensation the J Duesenberg must have caused when it was announced in 1928. Here

was a car of 265 h.p., with a top speed of 116 m.p.h. which would do 90 m.p.h. in *second* gear. This in a day when 100 h.p. and 90 m.p.h. in high was considered prodigious in the U.S.A.

The Duesenberg engine was a straight-eight of just under 7 litres. Its four valves per cylinder were operated by chain-driven, twin-overhead camshafts. It had aluminium pistons and connecting rods and a chrome-nickel-steel crankshaft with five main bearings no less than two and three-quarter inches in diameter. Although the crankshaft was carefully balanced at the factory, it had a unique vibration damper bolted on between No. 1 and No. 2 cylinders, consisting of two cartridges—one on each side of the crank cheek—94 per cent full of mercury. The mercury churning about inside the cartridges effectively absorbed any torsional vibration. This huge engine developed its peak horsepower at 4,200 r.p.m.—very high when you consider the weight and size of its reciprocating parts and its fairly long stroke of 4¾ inches. But Duesenberg engines were built to stay in one piece—as is proved by the number of them still running as sweetly as they did thirty years ago.

Three-speed gearboxes transmitted the drive from a two-plate clutch by way of a torque tube to the hypoid rear axle which had a duralumin housing. The semi-floating axles were an amazing $2^3/_{16}$ inches

in diameter, but were bored out to save weight. You find this concern for weight-saving in greater use of light alloys than was common in those days — but not in places where weight-saving meant sacrificing strength. The alloy-steel chassis frame, for example, had a depth of 8½ inches and had six cross-members. Like Bugatti, Duesenberg knew that a rigid chassis meant good roadholding.

Springing was by semi-elliptics all around. Braking was hydraulic.

The Duesenberg had a fascinating dashboard. In addition to the expected instruments, it boasted an altimeter-barometer, a tachometer, a stop-watch chronometer, and a brake-pressure gauge. It also had four warning lights which were wired to a sort of mechanical brain. One of these lights went on every 750 miles to remind the driver to change the oil, another glowed at 1,500-mile intervals to tell him the battery needed water. The other two were connected to an engine-driven chassis lubricator. If this was sending the right doses of oil to various destinations, like the clutch throwout bearing or the spring shackles, a red light signalled that all was well. If its reservoir was empty a green light glowered at you.

In 1932 an even more potent Duesenberg was produced: the SJ (S for supercharger). This one had a vertical centrifugal blower which operated at six times engine speed. At 4,000 r.p.m. it blew at five pounds, but revolved at 24,000 r.p.m. Centrifugal blowers, a peculiarly American type, don't do much at low revs, but even so the SJ engine was claimed to put out 320 h.p.; 104 m.p.h. in second gear, and over 130 m.p.h. in high. A 5,000-pound roadster on a short wheelbase (142½ inches) it could, they said, accelerate from 0 to 100 in seventeen seconds!

Only once did I see a Duesenberg in action on the road in its heyday. I was driving a 1,750 c.c. blown Alfa Romeo on Mr. Vanderbilt's Long Island Motor Parkway one day in 1933 and I was, I fondly imagined, acting quite the racing driver. I must have been doing about 75 (on one of the rare straight stretches) when, with a long trumpet blast, a black convertible sedan shot by me like a bolt of lightning. I tried to catch it, and even though I gained a bit on the twisty parts of that narrow road, I never even got close enough to find out if it was a J or an SJ.

The J and SJ Duesenbergs were by no means the first cars Fred Duesenberg and his brother, August, had built. Fred was the leader and, like Royce and Bugatti, he was a self-made engineer. Coming from Germany as a boy in 1885 he had, by 1903, already built a racing car. By the Twenties the Duesenberg was one of the more important racing machines in the world, winning the Indianapolis 500 in 1924,

DUESENBERG

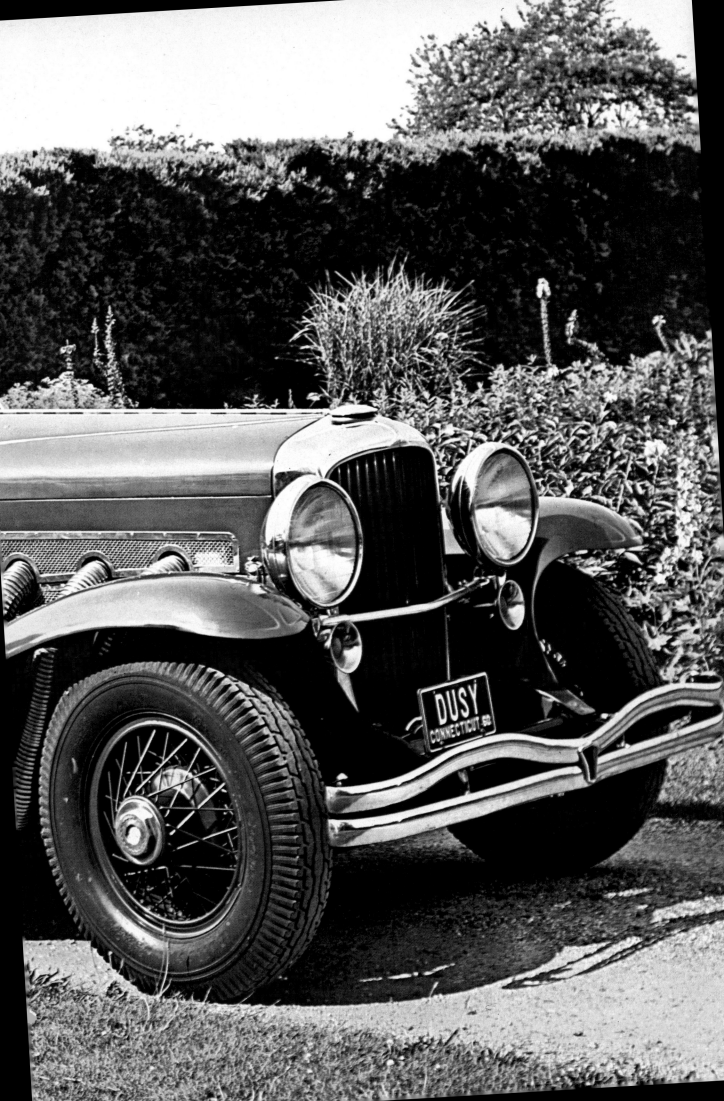

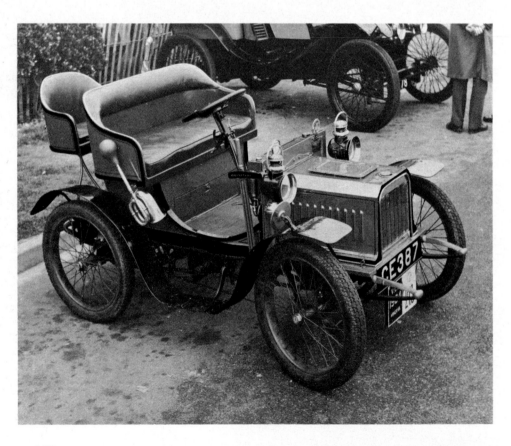

1925, and 1927 after having been (in 1921, driven by Jimmy Murphy) the only American car ever to win the French Grand Prix.

In 1920 the Duesenberg Model A, based on the racing cars, with a 90 h.p. engine, liberal use of aluminium and four-wheel hydraulic brakes (pioneered by Duesenberg) created a stir. Although not expensive ($6,500), considering its quality, it was not a financial success and in 1926 Auburn-Cord, under the control of E. L. Cord, a very shrewd stock-market operator, became Auburn-Cord-Duesenberg.

Now, for the time being at least there was plenty of money and the Duesenberg J was the result.

Fred Duesenberg died in 1932 after an accident in one of his cars, but Dusies were produced until 1937—amazing when you consider how few people would buy such a machine in the early Thirties. Of some 480 J's and SJ's manufactured, more than 200 still exist—a far greater proportion than that of any other great classic—Bentley, Bugatti, Alfa Romeo.

Perhaps they *were* built better than any other car ever made.

MINERVA

The firm of Minerva was created by a strong-willed, persistent and far-sighted industrialist, Sylvain de Jonc, and its history is a clear proof of the innate love of the Belgian people for high-quality mechanical achievements.

De Jonc first made bicycles in 1897, came to motor-cycles two years later and began making cars in 1904. At this period huge factories had been built at Berchem, near Antwerp.

The first light-car models were just as good from every point of view as the famous de Jonc motor-cycles, but the Belgian make became really famous in 1908, when the sleeve-valve motor, developed by Knight, was adopted. At a time when this type of

motor made a noise that could only be suppressed with difficulty, even on luxury models, Minerva was one of the firms that was able to commercialise silent, powerful cars.

The Minerva sleeve-valve model was very well built and soon became a favourite with clients from the leading smart set. The models were well proportioned and had nothing of the "monster" about them. Henry Ford I was a Minerva client, and the wonderfully silent engine attracted the attention of André Citroën when he came into the car business, taking over the old firm of Mors.

After the 1914-18 war Minerva was as well known as the makes of super-cars. The 30 h.p. 6-cylinder model naturally found favour with the best American clientèle. It was so successful that one American firm making luxury cars, Diana, literally copied the elegant shape of the radiator.

Minerva was also successful with its straight-eight models, still of the sleeve-valve type. The 32 h.p. sports car and the 40 h.p. model of the Thirties deserve a leading place among the great classic cars of the world. Special mention should be made of the "rapid 25 h.p.", which was excellent on the roads and in 1930 carried out a long-distance run from Ostend to Marseilles and back again; this remained famous, as did a test run of 6,368 miles in 142 hours.

After the death of the firm's director in 1928 the famous marque went through a difficult period when faced with strong foreign competition. It could not survive the second World War.

The 20 h.p. 6-cylinder Minerva (top left) built in Antwerp from the end of 1925, was one of the greatest of European cars. It was remarkably well built and possessed a Knight sleeve-valve engine equipped with Scintille ignition. The braking system included Dewandre-type servo-brakes. This "torpedo" dates from 1926. From 1905 onwards Minerva built an important range of models, from the light 5 h.p. 1-cylinder model shown left, to cars of 20 h.p. This small vehicle had a 635 c.c. engine.

ISOTTA-FRASCHINI

After Rolls-Royce and Hispano-Suiza, the double name of Isotta-Fraschini is probably the one which is most closely identified with the old-fashioned luxury of the great years of the Twenties and the very early Thirties.

Before it became a marque favoured by princes and maharajahs, the Isotta-Fraschini had enjoyed a very good reputation from the beginnings of motoring in Italy.

The two founders of the firm, Cesare Isotta and Vincenzo Fraschini, had originally been importers for Renault cars from France. But after they had made certain of co-operation from their respective brothers, Isotta and Fraschini embarked on building cars on their own in a new factory which they had set up in the Via Monterossa in Milan.

The outstanding event in the history of this famous firm was the arrival of a very promising technician, Giustino Caltaneo, who joined them within a few years. Originally, he had been merely a draughtsman, then he became engineer and later was chief of the technical department.

After having produced successful high-speed racing cars, which became famous in the hands of the well known driver Trucco, amongst others, Caltaneo was one of the very first to undertake the problem of front-wheel brakes. His original patent dates from 1910, and is therefore contemporary with the work of H. Perrot, in France.

The Isotta-Fraschini cars had front-wheel brakes from 1911 onwards.

After having taken an extremely important part in the building of aeroplane engines during the 1914-1918 War, the firm returned in 1920 to their traditional luxury car with a wonderful chassis equipped with a straight-eight, with a capacity of 6-litres.

The great period of the Isotta-Fraschini cars began then, and the magnificent Italian 8-cylinder model took its place among the fantastic fairy-tale cars of the age. The United States, and, in particular, the

Hollywood film-stars, took to them with enthusiasm. Rudolf Valentino possessed one along with his other cars.

After the model 8 came the 8A which was more powerful still, possessing a 110 h.p. motor and a cylinder capacity of 7.37 litres. These enormous cars could be seen in Paris, London and New York, equipped with splendid coachwork. Although the Isotta-Fraschini was heavy, it was capable of attaining speeds of 87 m.p.h.

During 1926, the firm was so successful that it produced more than 500 models.

But the prices of 1929 and the difficult years which followed hit Isotta-Fraschini hard. In 1931, an even more powerful model was brought out, but it could not prolong the survival of the big luxury car for very long and about 1935 the firm converted to successful buses and lorries.

In 1947, just after the second World War, Isotta-Fraschini attempted to go back to luxury car production, and brought out a revolutionary chassis with a V8, 125 h.p. motor at the rear. Unfortunately, only a few prototypes were built and tried out, and on September 24th 1949, the firm went into official liquidation.

No more was heard of the famous initials "I.F."; but today they are much sought after by vintage car enthusiasts.

This type 8A Isotta-Fraschini saloon (preceding pages) which spent more than thirty years in Britain, illustrates the peak of Italian classicism. This vast car had 8 cylinders in line, a capacity of over 7 litres and developed 120 h.p. For a long time it was the favourite car of princes and Hollywood stars. The big AN type Isotta-Fraschini "torpedo" (page 146) left the Milan factory in 1909. Its big 4-cylinder engine of 4,942 c.c. developed 30 h.p. It was one of the first cars of this marque to possess a cardan transmission. The Type 8 Isotta-Fraschini of 1920 (right) was the first real luxury car of the post-war period. It had an 8-cylinder engine of 5,901 c.c. developing 80 h.p. Its line is extremely pleasing and its front-wheel brakes were a remarkable novelty for 1920.

BENTLEY

Mention the words "Bentley" and "Le Mans" to an Englishman. A bugle shrills in his head, he straightens up a little, he stands alongside Nelson at Trafalgar.

For it was the thin green line of Bentleys at Le Mans that, in the Twenties, successfully upheld the motoring prestige of England against the onslaughts of the savage machines from the European continent and even from America (in the form of Stutzes and Chryslers).

During the Twenties, those years of the locust for other English racing machines, the Bentleys won at Le Mans four times running, as no cars did before and none have since.

Walter Owen Bentley, like many other great British engineers, first learned to revere fine mechanism and honest workmanship as an apprentice in the shops of the Great Northern Railway. But a few years before World War I he deserted locomotives and became a partner with his brother in a small company which had the British concession for the sale of a French car, the D.F.P. (Doriot, Flandrin et Parent). For a few years the Bentley brothers had a moderate success selling, and even racing, D.F.P.'s. The war put an end to D.F.P. sales, but not before Bentley had made a notable innovation in engine construction—the aluminium piston.

Intrigued by an aluminium souvenir paperweight in the form of a piston that a French foundry had sent out to its customers, Bentley got the idea of having aluminium pistons made up for his racing D.F.P., with exciting results. Until then pistons were made of cast iron or light steel and broke at high revolutions. The light aluminium pistons not only permitted higher engine speeds but higher compressions, due to better heat dispersal. And, of course, greater engine power resulted.

During the war, W. O. Bentley sweated over the design of rotary aero engines and, in fact, succeeded in coming up with what were considered to be the most successful rotaries used in British aeroplanes, the B.R. 1 and B.R. 2 (B.R. for Bentley Rotary).

By November, 1919, he had a chassis to show at the Motor Show at Olympia in London. It wasn't, however, until September, 1921, that the first 3-litre Bentley was delivered to a customer.

The 3-litre was just the car wealthy young Britons of those feverish post-war years were waiting for. It had, for its day, the speed and ferocity of a racing machine, but yet was docile enough to drive to a tea-dance in Mayfair. Almost instantly the name Bentley became synonymous with all that was smart and sporting in motor cars, and long before production ceased only ten years later, 1931, it easily ranked in prestige with Rolls-Royce.

During the six years or so that the 3-litre cars were made, various other models were included in the 1,600 or so machines that left the factory. (Some 500 still exist). Among these were the "Red Label", "Black Label" and "Green Label", short-chassis, 100 m.p.h. models and the standard, stodgier, "Blue Label" types.

In 1926, a 6½-litre Bentley appeared—the "Big Six"—with an engine whose six cylinders had the same dimensions as the 37.2 Hispano-Suiza (100×140 mm.). In this engine the camshaft, unlike that in the 3-litre, was driven by a fascinating system of connecting rods and eccentrics from the crankshaft.

Between these two variations of a 6½-litre car, an enlarged version of the 3-litre appeared in 1927: the beloved 4½-litre Bentley. Since its four-cylinder engine had cylinders of the same dimensions as the six, many parts were interchangeable with it. These 4½'s are today considered most desirable by the connoisseurs who are the members of the Bentley Drivers' Club in England. And who can blame them? For snugged down in the leather seats of an open Van den Plas four-seater, with its cut-away door for the driver's right arm, its outside brake lever, and its satisfyingly purposeful, if not easy, gear change, a lover of vintage cars is as close to heaven as he'll ever get.

In 1930, that formidable, almost unbelievable motor car, the 8-litre Bentley, arrived to stun motorphiles. This noble carriage was not designed as a sporting vehicle, but to transport nabobs in the height of luxury at speed.

In spite of their racing successes in the next five years, Bentley Motors went under in 1931. At first it was thought that Napier's would acquire the name. Indeed, W. O. Bentley even started designing what could have been one of the great cars of all time: a 6¼-litre, overhead-cam Napier-Bentley.

But it was not to be. At the last moment, in court, at the receiver's sale, Rolls-Royce snatched the prize.

In 1933 a new car, a warmed-up and lowered small Rolls appeared. It too was called a Bentley!

Preceding pages: The incomparable 8-litre Bentley of 1931. Designed not as a sports car, but to carry luxurious, closed coachwork, very few of them had the type of open body seen here. The single-overhead-camshaft engine developed 220 h.p. Ever since 1953 the "Continental" type Bently (above, right) has accustomed sports-car lovers to completely streamlined bodies. As usual the h.p. rating of the 6,230 c.c. engine is kept confidential. The "Blower" Bentley (right) had an intriguingly complex supercharger with carburettors mounted out in front, protected only by a screen of coarse chicken-wire (to keep rocks out). Only some fifty of these 4½-litre cars were blown. In this form, they developed 182 b.h.p. At Le Mans in 1930 Sir Henry Birkin took the lap record in a blown 4½ at 89.7 m.p.h.

150

ALFA ROMEO

Preceding pages: A 1934, 2½-litre supercharged Alfa Romeo. Above left: The exquisitely built engine of this car develops 140 h.p. Above right: A 1925 RLSS 22/90 which has a 3-litre, push-rod engine. Centre: A Giulietta Spider. Below: The highly streamlined coachwork by Pinin Farina on an Alfa Romeo Giulietta Chassis was inspired by the 1955 Superflow bodies carried out on the 6-cylinder experimental chassis. The general effect is harmonious and quite uncluttered. The traditional Alfa Romeo radiator shell was in fact reduced to a central grill motif, and this was one of the big successes of the Turin Show in 1961.

The Alfa Romeo of the Thirties was as great a car as the Bugatti—and vice versa.

These are the only two sports cars ever made about which there can be any argument as to superiority. No others were even in the same league.

A.L.F.A. (Anonima Lombarda Fabbrica Automobili) built French Darracqs as far back as 1909. Business was just so-so until a young engineer named Nicola Romeo took over at about the time of World War I, added his own name, and called the outfit Alfa Romeo.

Almost immediately after World War I, Alfa Romeo began to make its name known on the road circuits and race tracks of Europe with the famous P2 racing two-seaters. These had 2-litre, twin-overhead camshaft, eight-cylinder, supercharged engines and dry-sump lubrication. Driven by such crack drivers as Ascari, Campari, and Mazetti, they cleaned up in enough races to win the world's championship in 1925.

But Alfa Romeo had not yet learned the lesson that a great sports car should be a de-tuned racer rather than a hotted-up tourer. The sporting machine they offered in 1925 was the 3-litre RLSS developed from their 15-55 four-cylinder and 21-70 and 22-90 RL six-cylinder touring machines.

In 1927, however, Alfa Romeo started building cars which owed much to the designs of the successful P2 racing machines. The first of these had a 1½-litre, single-overhead-camshaft, six-cylinder engine. This freely revolving engine (about 4,500 r.p.m.) in a car weighing about a ton, developed 60 h.p. and prodded the thing along at about 75 m.p.h.

By 1929 these machines had developed into the most delightful of sporting conveyances: the six-cylinder Gran Sport 1750 c.c. supercharged twin-camshaft 17/95 model. I have owned several of these charming and exciting machines and I still think that they and their later and larger brothers, the eight-cylinder 2.3's, are the most exhilarating sports cars I have ever driven—and I include everything up to the latest Ferraris.

The engine of the 1750 Alfa is one of the most exquisitely finished mechanisms ever to be installed in a motor car. Even the Bugattis must take second place to it. Its twin-overhead camshafts are driven by a vertical shaft at the rear of the engine. The Roots supercharger (blowing eight pounds) is driven from the nose of the crankshaft. On the left of the blower is affixed a dual Memini carburettor, and from its right springs an amazing *tour de force* in light-alloy casting technique—the intake manifold. The wafer-thin cooling fins following its every convolution must be seen to be believed.

The 109-inch chassis is quite conventional, though made of the finest materials. The bodies were usually by Zagato; simple, graceful two-seaters with lean sweeping fenders and typically Italian, high-off-the-ground running boards. Within the tucked-in uncallipygian tail there is room for a top, a pair of batteries, a 30-gallon petrol tank and, surprisingly, some luggage.

When you climb behind the wheel, after having first tickled the carburettor to flood it, you wonder how anyone with a normal behind can sit next to you. The instruments are cunningly hidden under the cowl. To see them you must bob your head, thus blowing the horn on the steering-wheel centre with your chin.

Turn the key and press the starter button and the engine literally explodes into action. Select first gear and let in the clutch (which has an undeserved reputation for fierceness) and you're off with the oddly Alfa-ish whew-p, whew-p from the exhaust. The gears, the camshaft drive, the blower add to the music. As you go up through the gears you realise that this little baby can *go!* (0 to 60 in under ten seconds—105 m.p.h. in high—in the latest types of 1750 which put out 105 h.p.)

The steering is characteristically Alfa. You learn not to grip the wheel, but to let it oscillate through your fingers slightly as the front wheels hit irregularities in the road. Otherwise the car snakes.

You take corners at impossible speed—I firmly believe a 1750 will out-corner any car ever built—by just wishing the car around, helped by an almost imperceptible movement of your wrist.

The eight-cylinder, 2.3-litre Alfa which came out in 1931 (though the 1750 was made until 1934) was much the same, but more powerful (140 h.p.). Its blower, however, lay alongside the engine and was driven by a train of gears. Racing versions of the 2.3 and the later 2.9 ended Bugatti's mastery of road racing.

The 2.9 Alfa Romeos had basically the same eight-cylinder, twin-cam engines as the 2.3's, but by 1938 the 8C-2900-B, as it was known, had become a little decadent, with enveloping bodywork and independent front suspension. Although its 180-h.p. engine could propel it at 125 m.p.h., it wasn't nearly as much fun to drive as the Alfas of a decade earlier.

Right after the war Alfa Romeo brought out a 2½-litre machine at a fabulous price, but I think they'd just as soon forget about that one.

The nicest machines Alfa Romeo makes today are the Giulietta's, but I do miss that wonderful intake manifold of the 1750. Perhaps the new 1962 model will be worthy of the Alfa Romeo's of yesteryear.

DAIMLER

The history of the big British firm Daimler is the best way of illustrating the interest that the British have always had in car manufacture right from the beginning.

Originally, it was the work of a far-sighted man who was able to make a group of enterprising Englishmen share his enthusiasm for the car produced by Daimler from 1890 onwards.

After Frank Simms had established contact with the German firm, the Motor Syndicate, the first important organisation in Great Britain for Daimler products, was set up in 1893. In 1896 the first Daimler entirely built in Coventry came out of the factory which was directed by the engineer Critchley.

In the same year the "new" Daimlers took part in the Emancipation Rally (14/11/1896), and they also went on a rally from John O' Groats in Scotland to Land's End in Cornwall, which caused a considerable stir. Daimlers were so solid and well built that the sports-loving King Edward VII ordered his first one in 1900. For fifty years Daimlers were to keep the great privilege of being the official cars of the British Royal family, but after the year 1950 lost this

dignified status to the stately products of Rolls-Royce.

At a period when the elementary valve mechanism made it almost impossible to achieve the silent running suitable for a luxury car, the Daimler Motor Company very soon took an interest in the sleeve-valve motor conceived by C. Y. Knight. The English marque achieved a remarkable degree of perfection after 1905 through a long series of practical tests which culminated at the end of 1908 in the commercial production of the "Knight silent engine".

After that the Daimler became a classic car of the British aristocracy. The noticeably silent running of the sleeve valve engines with four and six cylinders was closely in harmony with the extremely austere opulence of the Daimler limousine and coupés. These handsome cars could be recognised by the moulding of their radiators, and comfort was obviously more important than elegance. During the first world war, the famous cars of the Military Headquarters were similar to this, with couchette seats and card-tables.

After making a considerable contribution to wartime aviation, Daimler returned to their traditional production of cars in 1919. In 1928 the 6-cylinder

models were replaced by the famous 12-cylinder ones known as the "double-six", which were as quiet as electric cars. These chassis were equipped with something that was very new at the time, the first hydraulic clutches built in conjunction with a Wilson preselector gearbox.

After 1933, however, valve motors had become very silent and Daimler gave up the Knight motor in their range of 6- to 8-cylinder cars and also in the Lanchesters, a make which they had taken over.

Between 1939 and 1945, Daimler again played an important part in the British war effort, although the factory was severely bombed in 1940. After 1945, Daimler produced some outstanding cars with magnificent coachwork, such as the limousines of Lady Docker, wife of the then Company Chairman.

Daimler made an effort to enter the light sports-car field, and had a certain amount of success, but the financial status of the old company was very precarious. At the present time their very interesting sports model as well as their luxury V-8 cars are produced under the management of Jaguar Cars Limited.

Saoutchik, who was used to building splendid coachwork for princes and heads of state, mounted this very representative saloon on the 8-cylinder 5,500 c.c. 1952 Daimler chassis. The designer succeeded in combining his typically "flamboyant" style, in which the curved lines were emphasised by wide chromium mouldings, with the demands of an "official" car.

Following pages: A 1934 C26 Voisin of the "Cimier" type. Its 6-cylinder engine developed 140 h.p. The wholly aluminium coachwork was designed by Gabriel Voisin.

THE ERA OF THE GREAT CLASSICS

By now jolting, unreliable cars had disappeared and had been replaced by successful models which were dependable, tested, and better to look at. Motor car history during the Thirties can be compared to the achievements of the Renaissance in the development of the arts and the enriching of our civilisation.

We come now to the age of the outsize, the gigantic, the multi-cylinder super-cars which led to a magnificent display of genius, refinement and luxury and caused engineers and coachbuilders to vie with each other to a fabulous extent.

Cars were built by the yard, with a minimum chassis measurement of nearly 10 feet, and the overall dimensions sometimes approached 20 feet.

The motors fitted to these chassis varied from 4,000 to 13,000 c.c., spread over 6, 8, 12 or 16 cylinders which, depending on the whims of various designers, were of the V-type, with single, twin or treble camshafts, and reinforced by one or two superchargers. The enamelled, cadmiated, engine-turned bodies were made of various materials, including cast steel, aluminium, magnesium and molybdenum. Coil and distributor ignition was used, or else single and twin magnetos. The motors were cooled by ventilated, pumped water, or, when air-cooled, a turbo-fan was added (Franklin Airman V-12). Lubrication was carried out by the splash, fully forced, or dry-sump methods, minimum capacity varying between 2 and 5½ gallons according to requirements. Petrol tanks holding 44 gallons made journeys of about 125-155 miles possible, depending on the driver's mood and stamina, the degree of damp or heat, the steepness of the roads, and the amount of traffic about.

Designers no longer jibbed at good finish, and in fact it became all-important.

Radiators, which publicised the makers' names, were gigantic, made of chromium-plated bronze and shining with flashy dimmers; some of them had an aggressive, pointed shape, with austere-looking stone-guards fixed in front. The radiator-caps were graced with delicate winged nymphs, either languishing or leaping into the air; other mascots included birds in flight, engraved signs of the zodiac, or designs that were cabalistic, baroque, rococo, modernistic or futurist in style. Beyond these artistic creations stretched the interminable bonnets, cheerfully attaining lengths of nearly seven feet and more. Shelter was provided for the passengers in an apologetic way, and the means of entry were unobtrusive, with windscreens no wider than loop-holes. They were rather like windcutters or

Marmon convertible of 1932 equipped with the famous 16-cylinder o.h.v. engine which developed 200 b.h.p. Made with light alloys, this engine created a sensation when it first appeared in 1930. Marmon also produced the same model in 12 cylinders. The 1926 20 h.p. Panhard et Levassor sports model (right) with works sports car body. Equipped with a sleeve-valve 4-cylinder engine, with a capacity of nearly 2 litres, it could get up to 124 m.p.h. and beat many records.

butterflies wings, and were sometimes double by the back seats; they could be retractable, inclinable and detachable, while the centre part could be opened by means of racks, screws, spindles and cranks.

The great art, in designing a beautiful car, was to provide a space of just over one foot between the steering-wheel and the seat; in models of this type, which were more than 15 feet long, the passenger was regarded as a bit of a nuisance.

Colours were bright or else discreet in an obvious kind of way: clinical white on jet-black, off-white on nigger-brown. Sometimes the colours clashed, but there was something splendid about the result, reminiscent of Titian or paintings of the Fauvist school.

Upholstery-work varied, for a vast range of hides and skins were used. Real leather, with its characteristic smell, was cut and sewn in symmetrical designs, and the seats were softly-padded, sewn with mother-of-pearl buttons, silk braids and gold binding. Rich printed velvets and silky broadcloths were used on groups of sofa-like seats or "directorial" armchairs. Doors were highlighted with lines of bright colours, coats of arms or monograms; they closed with the

comfortable click of safe-doors, by means of huge locks, and their vast hinges were equipped with lubricators. The windows were operated by rack and pinion gear, and slid up and down with a soft hissing sound on felt runners.

According to the tastes, requirements and ages of the clients the manufacturers would deliver cabriolets, *coupés de ville* or limousines. The chassis was built longer or shorter when circumstances required, but the motor remained the same.

The instrument panels were made of walnut, mahogany or rare, exotic wood, or else they were inspired by competition from aluminium and polished, rubbed and engine-turned to the nth degree. The panels alone could cost as much as a cheap mass-produced car, for as a rule they required extra materials amounting to 165 feet of wire and 2½ feet of tubing, while their total weight amounted to 176 pounds.

In return for this considerable drawback the car-owner was entitled to an anemometer, a record of the date of lubrication, a water-thermometer, an oil-thermometer, an oil manometer, an oil viscosity gauge,

161

Top left: A torpedo-type Renault sports car on a short chassis; 40 h.p., 6-cylinder model, with fittings by H. Chapron. Centre: This Horch limousine of 1936-7 was equipped with an 8-cylinder engine. The firm also produced a convertible model with a 12-cylinder V engine. Bottom left: Coach, mounted on a Peugeot chassis; side-valve, 4-cylinder engine of 1927, with modernised coachwork. Wrap-round wings dating from 1935. Above: A Maybach "Zeppelin"; convertible, on a 12-cylinder chassis, 180 h.p., 1937/1938.

a thermometer indicating the outside temperature, as well as an ammeter, a pressure-gauge for hydraulic brakes, a gauge showing the electrolyte level in the batteries, another showing its specific gravity, an upper cylinder lubrication gauge, a rev. counter, a speedometer, etc. etc... 41 instruments in all. In addition to these necessary details there were control levers, dimmers and various types of control. At this period people were incurably gadget-minded and were quite hypnotised by the proliferation of instruments on the cars designed by Voisin, Duesenberg, Air-Flow and Marmon.

As a rule each piece of coachwork was carried out by hand, based on a specially built model; the bodies were faced with a trellis of fine gold which stood out in relief. The bumpers were mounted on telescopic shock-absorbers with Tecalemit greasers (Hispano, Voisin, Isotta and Rolls).

Although the boot came into general use the removable trunk kept its own traditional shape. It was expensive, for it was made of wood covered with tooled leather, embellished with studs and artistically designed locks, while the whole thing was reinforced with double straps fastened in cunning knots (Bentley, Bugatti, Hispano, Voisin and Horch).

There was intense activity in the sporting world, and at the same time there were many *concours d'é- légance* which displayed the taste and genius of the coachbuilders. At Le Touquet and Deauville the 8- cylinder 15 h.p. Delage D8 155, with almond-green coachwork, ran off with all the *prix d'honneur*. The passenger was the archly expressive Miss Betty Spell, wearing a toast-brown suit, an off-white boa round her neck and a pirate-style beret. The judges applauded with delight—it was a magnificent spectacle.

The banker Guérin caused a sensation with his 12-cylinder 54 h.p. Hispano coupé with coachwork by Franay: the lower part of the body was black, the upper part champagne colour, while the polished wheel-discs shone like brilliant sunshine. The judges were so blinded and bedazzled by all this that they awarded it the Grand Prix d'Excellence at Cannes in 1934.

In 1939 the judges at Monte-Carlo were left breathless by the Delage D8 120S, with coachwork by Villars. The car measured over 15 feet, and the mudguards were accentuated by riveted ridges extended by ailerons beneath. The cabriolet was midnight blue, with blood-red leather upholstery, while the chromium-plated, single-turn exhausts, in the Mercedes

Right: This streamlined Delage "coach", with a straight-8 95 h.p. engine, is a D8-85 model of 1935. It was one of the first cars produced before the amalgamation with Delahaye. Below: Itala Gran Turismo torpedo, 1912; the 4-cylinder engine was of 5,401 c.c., developing 35 h.p.

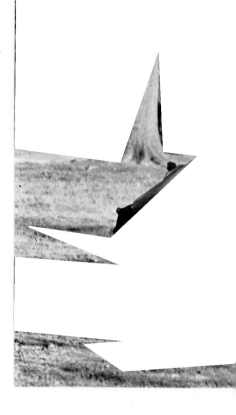

style, came down from the bonnet and emphasised the aggressive appearance of the car.

Gabriel Voisin's contribution to the history of motoring deserves to last for ever. When you encounter Voisin you enter an unusual world, and the orthodox-minded are not allowed in.

Only those with a good sense of humour and an intelligent, affectionate nature can appreciate cars which belonged to no one except their creator. And it's all wrong to use such a banal word as "car" to describe the mechanical devices created by the man who had three passions — aviation, automobiles and women.

"Voisin's aeroplane-cars were just Voisin creations". They were the embodiment of personal ideas, cluttered up, naive or revolutionary, they were neither bad nor exceptional cars, but cars with an individuality of their own, and even in their smallest details they were unlike any others.

The most remarkable achievement of this period was without question the Double-eight 16-cylinder Bucciali, designed by the Corsi Brothers, who had a passion for unusual and grandiose styles. They were ruined by their attempts to enter the car business, but some of their achievements were unique and some of their designs intensely original. These included the strange, vast, front-wheel drive vehicles, fitted with various kinds of engines, including a 30 h.p. "Continental", bore and stroke 85.7×114.2 mm. The wheels were made of moulded Alpax and had a strange outline, looking like sunflowers. This imposing creation took your breath away and transported you into a mysterious dream-world.

At the risk of being persecuted for life by distinguished and fanatical admirers of Rolls-Royce, I believe that the Hispano-Suiza was and still is the finest car ever made. The design and assembly of the engine shows the great attention paid to line and aesthetic effect, while the engine itself reveals a wonderful finish and a greater variety of metals than any used to date; cylinder-blocks with hardened sleeves, pistons made of ultra-light alloys, tubular connecting-rods, crankshaft with static and dynamic control, turned from the solid, sodium-cooled valves, powered clutch, brakes and steering, plus ride control; that sums up the characteristics of the 32 and 46 h.p. models, and the unrivalled, dignified 12-cylinder 54 h.p. model too.

These cars were eagerly seized upon by all the coachwork kings and received the blessing of the international aristocracy.

Passengers in the magnificent "Cicogne" were raised above the hurly-burly of the common crowd.

The same was true of the huge and powerful Horch-Maybachs, more in keeping with the fanatical German nationalists of the time than with the Latin character. At the opposite end of the scale the Alfa Romeos, real gems produced by the genius of Jano, had graceful, slender lines which contrasted strongly with the powerful heaviness of the Mercedes. The 8-cylinder 2ACT 6C and 8C 2905 with twin superchargers gave you a feeling of terrific intoxication on any kind of road. The mechanism was like pieces of jewellery, perforated as much as possible and encased in magnesium. Zagato, Castagna and Pinin Farina designed the most handsome models.

The engine of the 12½-litre "Royal Napoleon Coupé", its name indicating the zenith of attainment, weighed over 1,450 pounds. It was this car that took Ettore Bugatti right into the network of hilly roads on the Col de Saverne. Seated behind his chauffeur, the faithful Toussaint, with his bowler hat down over his eyes, he suddenly found himself thinking over the results of the year 1939 — he had sold 29 cars! About one hundredth of the demand existing in 1962. Not far from his factory, beyond the Rhine, the sky was clouding over: a terrible storm was on the way.

A great age in motoring would soon come to an end.

The millionth Buick (opposite) left the Flint factory in 1925. In accordance with the fashion of the moment it was a torpedo-style model of irreproachable design with many accessories popular at the time: running-board stops, detachable boot, protective covers on the spare wheels, divided windsoreens. The 1931/32 Chryslers (below) were distinguished by the very clean lines of the coachwork and by the windcutter "Duesenberg" shape of the radiator, a style which influenced fashions all over the world. This limousine has a floating 8-cylinder 105 h.p. engine.

MORE

AMERICANS

During the Twenties the appearance of the American motor car changed radically. Evolving from its early sit-up-and-beg look, its button upholstery open to the weather, the post World War I private vehicle provided protection as well as transport. Cross-winds were foiled by side screens, floors were sealed, wipers were driven by air or electricity.

By the end of the 1920's—at the beginning of the Second Depression—most cars were heavyweights, sun-visored, smooth-running and closed against the elements, incorporating many of the refinements and principles of comfort that we know today.

By 1932 the large, square elevation began to give way to wind-cheating stream-lining. With higher maximum speeds, wind pressure (over 12 pounds per square foot at 50 miles per hour) had become a factor that was worth considering. The sloping windscreen became a common feature, although the rear of the car still wore the tucked-in design of the horse-propelled coach or buggy.

Bonnets lengthened, allowing front wings and bumpers to cover up the complexities of the front suspension, giving a cleaner line to the foreward part of the vehicle. Still, tradition died hard and running boards, necessary in the days of high-floored interiors, had not yet been supplanted by smooth sides.

These were the general trends of American design during the first half of the fourth decade of this century. The great mass of production followed the slow progress to sleeker and more aerodynamic lines.

Yet there were a few individual manufacturers who tried—most of them unsuccessfully in the long run—to build distinctive luxury motor cars. For instance,

a really handsome Pierce Silver Arrow was made in 1933. It was at least five years ahead of its time in body design and performance, with a twelve cylinder, 175 b.h.p. unit, free wheeling, and power brakes. Its engineering and finish were greatly superior to most. It was bought by a few connoisseurs for $10,000—but failed to attract a large enough market to continue.

Another car of classic line and careful construction was the elegant sixteen-cylinder Marmon. A coupé with a motor made mostly of aluminium and which developed some 200 horse power was produced in 1931, a delight to the eye and a credit to the craftsmen that manufactured it. Unhappily the company of Nordyke and Marmon went out of business during the depression of the decade.

And so it was with many others. Great names that had been household words in the pioneer days of motoring vanished for ever. Names like Stutz, Peerless, Duesenberg, Franklin. This was the era in which only the strong survived.

But the decade was one of great technical progress. Cadillac brought out V-12 and V-16 models, independent suspension was introduced, automatic transmission and superchargers became popular, steering wheel gear changing was re-introduced and improved.

And towards the end of the period body design took on the look that survived into the Fifties. Radiator grilles and bonnet louvres became an integral part of the design, headlamps were swallowed by the front wings, bumpers curved into the body, and rear windows grew. The motor car of America had evolved from its close family ties with the horsed carriage and had begun a tradition of its own.

Preceding pages: The Mercer Raceabout, not well known in Europe, is a perfect example of the American pre-1914 War sports car. Its 5-litre T engine did not exceed 2,000 r.p.m., So that the driver did not get the feeling of travelling very fast. This could lead to trouble in an emergency, due to a somewhat inadequate braking system. On the other hand, the Raceabout had a flexibility which was comparable with the best European sports cars of the day. Opposite, at top: Sports coupé on 1928 Series L Lincoln chassis. The V-8 engine served as a model for Ford who brought out their famous V-8 in 1932. Centre: Chrysler Type 80 6-cylinder limousine of 1927. This was the first "Imperial", a rapid, powerful, silent sports car, with Lockheed Hydraulic Brakes.
Below: 12-cylinder luxury Packard Phaeton, 1933-4. These models illustrated the height of achievement in the classical style by this big American firm, which specialised in luxury cars.

LANCIA

It's a well-known fact that Fiat played an important part as a training-centre for technicians and engineers, and in this connection it's worthwhile remembering the origins of the Lancia.

The marque came into being when technician Vicenzo Lancia who, along with Felice Nazzaro, had been a top racing-driver at the Fiat works, decided to make cars himself, adopting his own personal ideas.

So Lancia and Co. was inaugurated in Turin in 1906, with the co-operation of his colleague and friend Claudio Fogolin. Although a fire destroyed the prototype, the first car was launched in 1908, a 4-cylinder 500 c.c. model developing 58 h.p. a high figure at that time. This first model, the "Type 51", was given the name of "Alpha", the first letter in the Greek alphabet, and succeeding letters were used for the whole range of Lancia cars up to 1931.

The personality and the creations of this firm have always astonished everyone. In the first place the V-formation engine — which can be seen again today in the little Appia — was very narrow, following a detailed study of 12- and 8-cylinder models undertaken in 1919.

Although this monobloc V-12 had been popular earlier it was not included in the range of models manufactured and was abandoned in favour of the 8-cylinder model of the same type known as the "Tri Kappa".

The "Lambda" — first produced in 1922 — was

amazingly successful; this V-4 cylinder model had a monocoque body, together with independent front suspension, and looked responsive. Tests in the Alps proved it had incredibly good road-holding power, and from a technical point of view it anticipated the developments of the Twenties. For years all the factory-produced cars were modelled on it and it wasn't abandoned until 1931, when Lancia built an extremely attractive 8-cylinder model known as "Dilambda".

After the crisis of the Thirties Lancia still kept their originality, producing the series named Augusta, Astura, Arteria, Aprilia and Ardea, all stamped with the personality of Lancia himself.

I remember very clearly an aristocratic Astura of 1935 with a very British look about it, and an indefinable Maybach touch in the design of the radiator shell. The creator of the model was Pinin Farina. It was a splendid tourer with a knife-edged line which is still a favourite with Rolls and Bentley. If you covered up the bonnets you could still mistake one for the other.

The Astura chassis attracted many coachbuilders, especially Pinin Farina, Bertone and Zagatto. Then there was the amazing streamlined coupé mounted on an Aprilia chassis, directly inspired by the Auto-Union V-12's, also streamlined, with a style that can be seen in the Abarth 1000 which set up records at Monza. The curved windscreen was fixed at an angle of 45 degrees, the wheels were entirely streamlined

This Lancia Flaminia Gran Turismo 2.800 develops 165 h.p. and is equipped with a light aluminium body designed by Zagato. It can reach a speed of 125 m.p.h. Right: Torpedo on Lancia Trikappa chassis, V-8 engine of 4,594 c.c., 98 h.p. Its speed was about 70-80 m.p.h.

with adjustable wheel-discs, and had a row of shutters for keeping the brakes well-cooled. The body enclosed the entire car and was gracefully downswept at the back; the roof was built in the tear-drop line and came down over two windows at the back, one of which was triangular and formed the culminating point. This little *chef d'œuvre*, which gave the impression of arrested movement, was also created by that master, Pinin Farina.

Then there were the Bertone creations, still using the Aprilia chassis. These were sumptuous limousines of 1937 with mudguards following unbroken curved lines, their central pieces constructed in three sections. Finally came his series of slender cabriolets on the Astura chassis. Their classic style was really beautiful and the cars were set off by colour combinations of a typically Latin type.

Lancia's achievements on the race-track are well known, and after the war the firm brought out some superb creations; the least of these were the unforgettable V-6 3,180 c.c. and the 300 c.c. sports model which earned fame so brilliantly in the hands of Fangio, Taruffi and Castellotti in the Pan-american Race of 1953.

Their powerful radiator-shell, with its row of air-inlets, gave the body an aggressive and undeniably fine appearance.

It's also worth remembering the V-6's, the 2-litre 300 c.c. and the 2-litre 800 c.c., supercharged, from the Le Mans 24 Hours in 1953, with suspension controlled by rows of pulleys and cables housed beneath the roof. This ingenious system was invented to compensate for variations in the loading of the rear tank and adjust the suspension.

And finally, nearer to our own times, came the amazing creation of the engineer Jano (who had already produced the unforgettable P3's with their roaring engines), the staggering Lancia D50.

This V-8 is definitely the finest in existence, with its V-opening of 90 degrees, its four overhead-camshafts, final chain-drive, detachable cylinder-heads without gaskets, complete with a de Dion back axle with unitary clutch, differential, and gearbox. Its ratio of 280 h.p. at 8,000 r.p.m. didn't do justice to this short-bodied fireball, and the lateral tanks, which were streamlined into the axis of the wheels, gave it a wonderful balance of line.

The new range of 2-litre cars with 4 or 8-cylinders, and the latest model, the 1500, with a V-formation opening to 60, 90 or 120 degrees, carries on the continuity and is a perfect example of the Lancia style.

The firm's generous *école* has brought results: the Aurelia and Flaminia models have followed the famous B20 and B22 and have shown quality while keeping up a tradition which has defied time itself.

Lancia only needed to adopt the front-wheel drive, and now they have done so. The Flavia shows how far this firm has kept its originality and made progress at the same time.

FIAT

The very name of Fiat stands for Turin and a whole national heritage, while the vast Fiat combine is an international centre of the automobile industry. It came into being in 1899, thanks to the enthusiasm and eclecticism of the two powerful Agnelli-Biscaretti families of Ruffia and Bricherasio. The letters F.I.A.T. stand for the "Fabrica Italiana Automobili Torino". Production commenced with a starting capital of 800,000 lire held by a parent company, the "Société de Construction et de Commerce des Automobiles".

This business, which has produced more than 3,500,000 vehicles and countless thousands of motors, lorries, aeroplanes, tractors and washing-machines, has been something of a miracle; the secret lay in its rapid growth which was due to the reputation it earned for conscientious car construction. The name of Fiat was well thought of soon after production began, because of its careful work and its continuous success on the racetrack. I have had personal experience of the high-

Left: Torpedo on 1921 519-type Fiat chassis; 6-cylinder engine of 4,766 c.c. capacity, developing 77 h.p. This roadster was built for eight consecutive years. Shown above is the most famous Fiat of all, which earned immortal fame by winning the Grand Prix of the A.C.F. at Dieppe in 1907, with an average speed of 70 m.p.h. It had a vast 4-cylinder engine with bore and stroke of 180 x 160 mm. and a capacity of 16,320 c.c., developing 135 h.p. at 1,600 r.p.m.

quality workmanship behind the models that brought the firm success.

It was the vast Fiat F2, formerly owned by the famous Felice Nazzaro, an 18-litre car with chain-drive and wooden wheels that taught me about Fiat workmanship. I rescued it from a swamp in the suburbs of Paris, where it had been lying half-submerged for 27 years.

The sliding leather-faced cone clutch was in a hermetically-sealed bell weighing a fabulous amount. Since I couldn't take it to pieces without the risk of smashing the bolts I decided to try it out without touching it. It worked just as well as when it was first made, although it had been subjected to damp and corrosive action for 30 years. That will give you some idea of how Fiats were built and finished in 1907.

And the whole car was built the same way. The huge 4-cylinder engine with bore and stroke of 200×190 mm. was uncommonly well-finished. The piston weighed nearly 11 pounds, while the big end (weight 13 pounds) was marked with the cylinder number and the Fiat initials, along with all the rocker-arms (which measured 8.6 inches,) the push-rods (2 feet 3½ inches), the rocker-arm stirrups, in fact all the related parts.

This car cost me nearly 2000 hours of enthusiastic work. The whole car was sanded and scraped, then the brass was cleaned, cadmiated and chromium-plated, while the cylinders were coated with mountains of crushed graphite. We kept the body proportions well balanced and the colours in harmony with each other.

The huge, thick wooden wheels were scraped down and left to dry on the furniture in my bedroom, which drove my wife to fury and despair, while I sawed up the pipes from my stove to make them fit

the end of the exhaust. We must have looked as though we were getting ready for a Grand Prix in the year 1900. We felt as though we were with the car just before the A.C.F. Grand Prix, the Coupe de l'Empereur in the Taunus mountains or the Targa Florio in Sicily, all races which the Fiat won easily.

One fine day in spring when a gang of breathless workmen were pulling on the engine with a rope, it sprang cheerfully to life. Six months of work were rewarded by a shower of glass and soot. It was a wonderful, shattering moment; no enthusiast could ever forget it. I confess I never felt comfortable when I sat in this monumental car, for the seats were 4½ feet high. It was very powerful, for it had a 160 h.p. engine with 1,600 r.p.m. and a lot of power in reserve, which made it difficult to drive. The clutch and the brakes needed superhuman strength to operate them. This massive thoroughbred ruined all my clothes, for a natural spray of oil was emitted by the back bearings and ventilated by the motor fan. You had to steer the enormous machine through a cloud of oil – the steering was amazingly easy – and work out the speed, which was distorted by the slow movement of the gigantic rockers. At two revolutions per second the valve control gear registered a speed of 62 miles per hour, whereas I felt I was going at a modest 37. Braking was chancy, and it was better not to leave it too late. I take my hat off to Felice Nazzaro, the ace of aces, who was able to keep up an average of 83 m.p.h. over a distance of 435 miles.

Fiat is also a rich centre of technicians and makes a great contribution to the progress of Italian industry as a whole. It is a well planned industrial combine, along with its steel-works, the Ferrieri Piemontesi, where there are 650,000 tons of metal being processed in plant built over an area of 1,500 acres.

★ ★ ★

GRANDS PRIX

Grand Prix racing is the highest type of motor racing, the kind of racing that involves a very special breed of men driving very specialised cars. The Grand Prix driver is totally dedicated to winning. The Grand Prix engine is a brute of great power, yet so delicate and highly stressed as to be ever on the verge of mechanical disaster, and so faddy as to choke on anything but exotic chemical mixtures.

Nonetheless, some people think Grand Prix racing is pointless. And this worries other people and prods them into making excuses for it. "The Grand Prix car of today is the touring car of tomorrow," they say. "Racing improves the breed." Or, "The racing circuit is the laboratory where new ideas are tried and proved." All of which is at least partly true.

For me, however, no excuses are needed. The excitements, the terrors, the noises, the colours of Grand Prix racing are wonderful in themselves, and the opportunity to appraise and appreciate fine driving and brilliant pit work is an added pleasure.

Once, in the Thirties, I took a train to a Grand Prix in France. I found myself crowded into a compartment with five excited young Frenchmen very hotly discussing the race. Although I had little French and they had no English, I was almost instantly embroiled. We made our points by pointing at pictures of drivers and cars and scribbling figures in the margins of *l'Auto*, the pre-war sporting daily.

Nothing in the world has ever stirred my blood so much as the shriek and bellow of Grand Prix cars practising on the course as I approached it on foot for the first time that day. As I got closer, the delicious castor smell of burnt racing-oil perfumed the air. And then when I saw the great vans which had brought the racing machines from across half a continent, vans bearing the prancing horse of Ferrari, the star of Mercedes-Benz, and the red oval of Ettore Bugatti, I almost expired with excitement.

Lounging with seeming unconcern around the vans and in the pits were the white-overalled drivers, absently watching the harried mechanics and fretful pit crews labouring over the cars. And all around were girls, gorgeous girls, hanging on the drivers, sitting on the pit counters, or frowning over still-blank lap charts and unstarted watches. You can see their daughters at today's races.

Preceding pages: This Grand Prix Delage was a master-piece of racing-car design in 1927. Its wonderfully complex, 1,500 c.c. supercharged engine had eight small cylinders and ran on ball and roller bearings. Delages ran four times in G.P. races and won every time. Ray Harroun's Marmon (above) won the first Indianapolis 500 in 1911. Below: The Italian champion, Felice Nazzaro, photographed at the wheel of his 6-cylinder 2,000 c.c. Fiat, with which he won the Grand Prix of the A.C.F. at Strasbourg in 1922, with an average speed of 78 m.p.h.

Then, almost suddenly, all the platforms and the fences were black with people. The cars stood in their places on the grid. The music from the loud-speakers stopped (you hadn't noticed it until then), and the crowd hushed. Only photographers scuttled in and out, rapidly operating the magazines of their Gaumont Spidos. As the loudspeakers gave the countdown (did they know this word then?), one and then another engine roared into life, some cranked by means of hand-held electric starters powered from storage batteries in little carts.

Ten seconds to go—and the air was vibrating with the shriek and clash of engines being blipped by their drivers. As the starter raised his flag, the engine noise rose to an unbearably shrill screaming and the cars on the grid shivered violently in a haze of oil smoke.

The flag whipped down. Like a single entity, twenty cars sprang forward in a horror of sound.

Grand Prix racing is different at Indianapolis, Indiana. The track there is a two-and-half-mile oblong with rounded ends, upon which cars of nearly identical specifications tear around and around for five hundred miles every Memorial Day (30th May). And they buzz around fast, too. Indianapolis race cars are as rapid as any machines running anywhere.

Indianapolis is unique, yet it is not too far away to have had European racers in its field from time to time. When Europe's spectators and drivers went off to war in 1914, the chief protagonists, Peugeot and Mercedes, continued to race against each other in the United States for two years. Ralph de Palma, driving his 4½-litre (ex-1914 Grand Prix) Mercedes; Dario Resta, a Peugeot. The results were inconclusive, the Mercedes winning at Indianapolis in 1915, the Peugeot in 1916. Indianapolis was not the only place where they raced each other. Among other contest was the famous one on the Chicago board track in June, 1916, when the Peugeot and the Mercedes sped, wheel to wheel, for three hundred miles. Four miles from the finish, the Mercedes had to go into its pit with sparking-plug trouble and Resta's Peugeot won at 98.6 m.p.h.

In 1917 the United States entered the war and racing stopped. But from the aerial dogfights over the Western Front came new ideas in engine design, new techniques in construction, new processes in metallurgy. Most aircraft engines were sixes, V-8's or V-12's, but Ettore Bugatti, the innovator, made an eight-in-line, and even a double-eight. Although little used in the air, it became the basis for successful racing-car engines for many years to come. Bugatti's plant in Alsace was occupied by the Germans, but Ettore's prototypes and blueprints were in safe keeping. That the eight-in-line idea was very much in everyone's mind by 1918, and on both sides of the Atlantic too, is proved by the fact that the Bugatti aircraft engine was being built by the Duesenberg brothers.

So, when Indianapolis had its first post-war Decoration Day race in 1919, what should appear but a Ballot straight-eight and a Duesenberg straight-eight. Neither of them won; a 1914 Peugeot driven by Howdy Wilcox was first.

During the years 1919-21, the Ballot proved to be a quite successful racing car—and the 3-litre Duesenberg was a sensation. Brash young Jimmy Murphy, in a road-racing modification of an Indianapolis Duesenberg, went over to Le Mans in 1921 and leading a strong Duesenberg team, won the A.C.F. Grand Prix, something no American had done before and none has done since. Everything American was still exciting and admirable in those post-war days, and the French were captivated by the typically American Murphy and his *formidable* Duesenberg.

The slickly turned out Duesenberg team may have

surprised the Europeans used to the rough bodywork of the usual Grand Prix machine of those days, but the superb finish and the sophisticated design of these 3-litre, single-overhead-camshaft engines and chassis astounded them, especially the beautifully executed four-wheel hydraulic brakes. The brake shoes were of spring steel, the hydraulic pistons on each wheel were machined out of blocks of marine bronze. The master cylinder was hinged to the chassis and moved as the brake pedal was depressed; the piston stood still. Oddly, the brake fluid was water with a little glycerine added to prevent freezing. It ran through a hollow front axle and kingpins to the front brakes.

Although the eight-cylinder engine put out only 115 b.h.p., it was sufficient to push the 1,750-pound car along over the rough and rocky course at a winning average of 78.1 m.p.h. Towards the end, it even ran with a pierced and empty radiator. Further, it set a highly commendable lap record of 83.2 m.p.h., which would not be beaten until 1929!

Now started a new era. The next eighteen years—until World War II—are considered by many to be the great period of Grand Prix racing. In the beginning, Fiat, Ballot, Sunbeam, Bugatti, Delage, Alfa Romeo, and even the American Miller, all fought for supremacy. But after 1923 a pattern emerged that lasted until the Second World War.

In 1924-25 the Alfa Romeo P2's carried all before them. Then the Bugattis had it all their own way, thanks partly to sheer weight of numbers. Alfa Romeo again became the king of the racing circuits from 1931-34, to be displaced during 1935-39 by the unbeatable Germans, Mercedes-Benz and Auto-Union. These great cars won most of the races during these five years, but other contenders arose to challenge them and win important Grands Prix too—the outsider Maserati, and in the 1,500 c.c. formula class, the English E.R.A., and Delage.

The "1500" was a fascinating, brilliantly conceived

Straight-eight Ballot (page 180) came out in 1919 and was designed by Ernest Henry, who had earlier designed the twin-cam Peugeot. The Ballot engine was inspired by Bugatti's World War I aero engine. These 5-litre cars were capable of almost 120 m.p.h. Above: Rolland-Pilain racing car, 1923 A.C.F. Grand Prix type (run at Tours). Engine with 8 cylinders in line, overhead camshaft, 4 carburettors, capacity of 2,000 c.c. Right: Voisin Supersport streamlined Torpedo, 18/23 h.p., 1922 Grand Prix de Tourisme type. These cars covered themselves with glory at Strasbourg and won the race at an average speed of more than 66 m.p.h. (4-cylinder engine with bore and stroke of 95 x 140 mm. without sleeve-valves).

Detroit Special American racing car of 1927 (left) built with parts from the front-wheel drive Miller racing car (the champion Tommy Milton is at the wheel). Right: The only American car to win a European Grand Prix was a straight-eight Duesenberg driven by Jimmy Murphy in 1921. Here is Bob Burman at the wheel. One of the great drivers of all time, Frank Lockhart, sits (centre, right) in the Miller Special. The fabulous 1,500 c.c. twin-over-head-cam, "91" Miller engine, supercharged by a centrifugal blower, which powered it, could produce 154 b.h.p. at 7,000 r.p.m. At Muroc Dry Lake, in a car powered by the "91", Lockhart once reached 171.02 m.p.h. He was later killed trying to beat the world's land-speed record.

machine. Designed by Albert Lory to run under the 1926-1927 international formula which limited Grand Prix engines to 1,500 c.c., it was ostensibly a two-seater (although the riding mechanic was by then a thing of the past). It was very low for its time. The absence of a passenger made it possible to seat the driver with his behind almost scraping the road, and the short drive shaft beside his left elbow. The chassis was normal for its day, with half-elliptic springing and four-wheel brakes (servo-operated off the gearbox à la Hispano-Suiza). To keep the radiator low, it was placed in front of the front axle, with its bottom edge below the line of the axle.

But it is the Delage's incredibly complex, expensive engine that continues to astound us as it astounded people in its day. This supercharged engine had eight small cylinders, twin-overhead camshafts, and it ran on no less than sixty ball and roller bearings! The twin camshafts had nine roller bearings apiece; the magnificent, forged, one-piece crankshaft ran on nine main bearings—rollers, too. So were the bearings for the eight con-rods.

It was the incredibly complex train of gears at the front of the engine that really made it such a *tour de force*. Over twenty gears—all on roller bearings—drove the camshafts, the magneto, the water pump, and two oil pumps. This engine could put out 170 b.h.p. at 8,000 r.p.m. The Delages ran four times in Grand Prix races and won every time. They also captured second and third place in two of the contests.

The Delage factory stopped racing in 1927, but ten years later Richard Seaman, the famous British driver, bought one of the old cars, and with the use of more modern fuel in a somewhat modified engine,

was able to raise its horse-power to 195! He then went out and carried away the honours in 1,500 c.c. class racing.

The Type 35 Bugatti, however, was perhaps the most successful racing car of all time. Ettore Bugatti certainly had been involved with racing cars for many years and with considerable success, but it was not until he evolved the Type 35 and its variations that he hit the jackpot. In 1925 and 1926, Bugattis were victorious 1,045 times. Obviously, these wins were not all in important races, for many amateurs owned Type 35's. They were not only factory racing cars, but catalogued models as well.

The chassis of the Type 35, which contributed so much to its unequalled controllability and road holding, was typically Bugatti. It had the extreme variations in depth of side members tapering from six-and-three-quarters inches at the dash to a mere three-quarters of an inch at the front goosenecks, and tapering rearwards to the reversed quarter-elliptic springs aft. In front, the Type 35's had, naturally, Bugatti's hollow, polished front axle.

The Type 35's of 1925, running under the 2-litre formula, had unblown, straight-eight engines. Bugatti inveighed against superchargers, claiming that they unsportingly increased engine capacity. A vertical shaft at the front of the engine drove a single-overhead camshaft which operated three valves per cylinder. The crankshaft was the usual piece of built-up Bugatti jewellery, running in five bearings. The inner ones were roller bearings, the end ones ball bearings; the con-rods ran on roller bearings. The mechanical racket from these bearings has led many a *Bugattiste* to think his engine was about to give up the ghost. Lubrication employed the usual Bugatti system of jets squirting oil at the revolving machinery. The blocks were cast in two four-cylinder sections, but the head was in one piece. The crankcase had tubes running through it from front to rear

INDIANAPOLIS MOTOR SPEEDWAY
15TH ANNUAL 500 MILE RACE 1927.
Frank Lockhart Miller Special.

that were supposed to cool the oil. I doubt whether this goal was ever realised.

These lovely, precisely built engines were easily a match for more powerful machinery due to their remarkable torque at low revs and their sturdy reliability. (Although they didn't develop much over 100 b.h.p. at 5,200 r.p.m., they have been revved to 7,000 without disintegrating). It was on these Type 35's that Bugatti's characteristic cast-aluminium spoked wheels, with their integrally cast-in brake drums, first appeared.

In 1926 the Grand Prix formula was reduced to 1.5 litres, and Bugatti had no choice but to supercharge his new smaller engines by mounting a Roots blower, driven by gears from the nose of the crankshaft. He called this variation of the Type 35 the

Type 39. At the same time he built for non-formula use (*formule libre*) his famous blown 2.3-litre Type 35B and in 1927 he added a 2-litre with supercharger—the 35C.

Around 1927, except for the reliable Delage, the beautiful horseshoe radiator of a Bugatti was almost always first across the finishing line, but a new Grand Prix formula that year (with no engine-size restrictions) and a new contender were to bring Bugatti's supremacy to an end.

Alfa Romeo was to be the new king. Alfa had been successful in Grand Prix racing in 1923 and 1924 with their P2's, but after a five-year lapse they returned in 1931 with new machines to glorify the name of Il Duce. Politics was getting mixed up with sport. Their first new car was the Type 8C—the

183

A P3 (below), still with cart-springs, is compared with a 1924, 2-litre P2
Alfa. Bottom of page: "Monoposto" P3 Alfa Romeo. This late example, with
Gianfranco Comotti in the cockpit, has been converted from elliptic-spring
suspension in the front to independent suspension on the Dubonnet system.
Opposite: 1933/4 Maserati Grand Prix car, with 8 cylinders in line, 2,500 c.c.
capacity, supercharged, which belonged formerly to the champion Etancelin.

"Monza"—with a 2.3-litre, straight-eight engine, supercharged from a blower mounted at its side and driven by gears situated between separately cast, four-cylinder blocks. The same gears also operated the twin-overhead camshafts and the oil and water pumps. Unlike the Bugatti and the Delage, the Alfa used no roller bearings. The Monzas developed some 160 b.h.p. at 5,200 r.p.m., and later Vittorio Jano, their designer, raised it to about 190 b.h.p. It had a conventional chassis with huge brakes, and a two-seater body (required under the formula rules), even though a mechanic was not carried.

Meanwhile, Bugatti had introduced its new development, the Type 51, with twin-overhead camshafts. The 51's and the new Maseratis prevented the Monzas, even when driven by aces like the great Nuvolari, from being decisively successful.

Alfa next experimented in some of their racers with two super-tuned, 1,750 c.c. six-cylinder, blown sports-car units side by side, with separate drive shafts, clutches, and gearboxes. The result was not too successful, but the next machine they produced —the Type B-2600, or the P3—was the most successful they ever raced. This was the "Monoposto". It had a single central seat, as two seats were no longer required under the rules. However, the twin-engined experiment had perhaps given Signor Jano the idea; the P3 had twin drive shafts in the form

of a V, with the apex just behind the gearbox. The engine was similar to that in the Monza, except that the block was now of electron with steel liners, and two small superchargers were fitted on its left flank. It developed 180 b.h.p. at 5,400 r.p.m. Between 1932 and 1935, the P3's, in the hands of such top drivers as Achille Varzi, Tazio Nuvolari, and Guy Moll, won over forty important races. In 1932 alone, P3's won the Italian, A.C.F., German, and Monza Grands Prix.

To challenge Alfa supremacy, Bugatti built that greatest of racing classics, the 3.3-litre Type 59 which developed 240 b.h.p. Alfa Romeo increased its engine size to 2.9 litres and managed to maintain its superiority, but there were two aerodynamically-shaped storm clouds on the horizon—Mercedes-Benz and Auto-Union.

A new formula for the years 1934-1937 started the Germans building. The *Association Internationale des Automobiles Clubs Reconnus* (A.I.A.C.R.), which controlled car racing, decided that racing cars were getting too fast and proposed a new rule, hoping to slow things down. (They kept doing this and cars just kept on getting faster). This new formula required chiefly that a racing car weigh no more than 750 kilograms (1,650 pounds) without fuel, oil, water, and tyres.

Hitler loved cars, and wanted to show the world

Above: The triumphant arrival of the German driver Von Brauchitsch on a 12-cylinder, 3-litre supercharged Mercedes-Benz at the 1938 Tripoli Grand Prix. Left: German Auto-Unions first appeared in 1934. By 1937 when the models above and left were seen their 5.9-litre engines were developing over 600 b.h.p. Earlier models had fabric bodies, but these later ones were panelled in aluminium. Page 187, top: Tazio Nuvolari in a twelve-cylinder Alfa Romeo at Roosevelt Raceway in 1937. Right: The Alfa Romeo "Alfette" first appeared in 1938, then reappeared immediately after the war. These type 158-9's had 1½-litre, eight-cylinder engines and two-stage supercharger. Toward the end of their career, their engines developed no less than 310 b.h.p.

that the *Herrenvolk* could build better racing cars and drive them faster than anyone on earth—faster especially than those "*verdammte Italiener*"—and he offered a prize of 500,000 Reichsmarks for the most successful German car. When the Mercedes-Benz's and the Auto-Unions appeared on the starting grids in 1934, the nightmares of Alfa Romeo, Bugatti, and Maserati became realities.

That first Mercedes-Benz of 1934—the W25—had a 3.3-litre, straight-eight, twin-overhead-camshaft,

blown engine that developed 350 b.h.p., in a light chassis with independent suspension all around, and enveloped in a light, aerodynamic body. It instantly made every other racing car look ancient.

The Auto-Union (built by a combine that manufactured the Horch, Audi, Wanderer, and D.K.W. passenger cars) was designed by Dr. Ferdinand Porsche, and was known as the P-Wagen. It had a light tubular chassis—in early models the cooling water ran through the tubes—and also independent

suspension by means of torsion bars in front and a transverse leaf aft. Porsche put his engine in the rear. This fantastic, 4.9-litre V-16 had a single camshaft between the cylinder banks which operated all 32 valves and produced 380 b.h.p. at 6,000 r.p.m.

At first, the Mercedes and Auto-Union suffered teething troubles. Alfa Romeo, for example, took the first three places in the A.C.F. Grand Prix at Montlhéry in 1934. But after that the Germans were invincible. Until the war, Grand Prix races were little more than contests between Auto-Union and Mercedes, between great drivers like Caracciola, von Brauchitsch and Fagioli for Mercedes, and Rosemeyer and Stuck for Auto-Union.

But the manufacturers didn't leave things there. Mercedes enlarged the engine of the W25 to 3.7 litres. With 400 b.h.p. it was clocked in speed trials at 197 m.p.h. for the flying kilometre! By 1937, with a further enlarged engine, it was developing 500 b.h.p. Under a revised 750 kg formula, a new model

the W125 using a 5.6-litre engine, developed 646 b.h.p. It did 193 m.p.h. in road-racing trim! The W125 chassis was, however, a considerable improvement over the W25, which had been tricky to handle. It was tubular, with torsion bars and a de Dion axle astern, and a new, lower, smoother body.

The Auto-Union, too, became more powerful year by year. By 1936 its engine's size had increased to 5.9 litres and was developing over 600 b.h.p. Its chassis was no longer used as plumbing (leaks had shown themselves), and it now had torsion bars at the rear, too. But despite experiments with its suspension and weight distribution, the P-Wagen was decidedly tricky to drive—even compared to the Mercedes-Benz, which the great British driver, Richard Seaman, likened to driving a family saloon at 100 m.p.h. on ice. Only one driver, Bernd Rosemeyer, ever succeeded in really mastering the peccadillos of the tail-heavy Auto-Union. Even Achille Varzi and Tazio Nuvolari disliked driving the P-Wagens.

Although Mussolini had not the millions to pour into racing that Hitler had, Alfa Romeo feverishly tried to improve their G.P. machines. In 1935 they increased their engine size to 3.2 litres and installed Dubonnet front suspension; in 1936 a 4-litre V-12 of

400 b.h.p. was tried. It was hopeless. The Italians, with their outclassed machines (including some very potent V-8, 4.6-litre Maseratis), didn't stand a chance.

In 1936, at Roosevelt Raceway on Long Island, over a figure-of-eight-shaped pseudo-road circuit, the Alfas and a 4.7-litre Bugatti showed what European racers could do against American cars. If I remember rightly, the best an American car could do was take thirteenth place. In 1937, the race was run again, but this time the Mercedes and Auto-Union teams arrived, too. They also overwhelmed the Americans, stupefying drivers and spectators alike with the earthshaking crash and scream of their exhausts, and their unbelievable speed.

Nuvolari whips along in the 1939 Auto-Union (upper left). This twelve-cylinder model (earlier machines were equipped with sixteen) had its fuel tanks moved to the bulges on the sides of the car from their previous position behind the driver. A Teutonic reunion (lower left): Mercedes-Benz Grand Prix cars of 1937, 1939 and 1955 line up to be photographed. Note the removable steering wheel held over the head of the driver in centre. Top right: A famous partnership of the years 1948/51: Etancelin and his 4,500 c.c. Talbot. Above: Alberto Ascari — another great Italian driver — sits the D50 Grand Prix Lancia at Monaco in 1955. This Lancia has a 2½-litre, V-8 engine with four overhead camshafts and a tubular space-frame chassis.

Above: Wolfgang Von Trips does a bit of grass cutting in a 1960 Formula I Ferrari. Upper left: The V-6 engine of the Ferrari "Dino" Formula I. At Spa, Tony Brooks drove this Vanwall (opposite page), winner of three Grands Prix in 1957, six in 1958. Its 2½-litre engine produced 270 b.h.p. on Avgas in 1958. In 1957, when the use of racing dope was allowed, it gave 290 b.h.p. The 1965 all-British B.R.M. (upper right) had an 8-cylinder, 1½ litre engine mounted in its tail. It is similar in name only to the original 16-cylinder car of 1947, the design of wich was too far ahead of its time to be a success. Jim Clark in a Lotus-Ford in which he won at Indianapolis in 1965.

When a new formula was decreed in 1938, limiting engines to 3 litres, supercharged (4½ litres unsupercharged), Mercedes had ready a fabulous new creation with a V-12, twin-supercharged, 2.9-litre engine, producing 483 b.h.p. at 7,800 r.p.m.—at about two-and-a-half miles per gallon. This engine was set diagonally, permitting the drive shaft to pass next to the driver's central seat. These cars now had de Dion rear suspension, too. Amazingly, although they had but half the engine capacity of the earlier machines, they were capable of 190 m.p.h.

Auto-Union met the 3-litre rule by chopping its V-16 down to a V-12, now with three camshafts. They were having trouble with too much weight aft, so they removed the fuel tank that sat between the driver and the rear-mounted engine, slid the driver back, and put fuel tanks on the sides. Alfa Romeo had no fewer than three new supercharged designs under the new 1938, 3-litre formula—a straight-eight, a V-12, and even a V-16. Maserati tried a blown straight-eight. But their situation remained almost hopeless.

With no chance of beating the Germans in formula Grand Prix racing, Alfa brought out the famous Type 158, 1½-litre car. Now they could at least beat the English, who had been doing quite well with their 1,500 c.c. E.R.A.'s. This Type 158, which was to be so successful after the war, had a straight-eight, supercharged, twin-overhead-camshaft engine developing 205 b.h.p. at 7,000 r.p.m. Maserati, too,

built 1,500 c.c. machines, but it was no use. The Germans brought out a 1,500 c.c. job, too—a Mercedes V-8 that developed 260 b.h.p. and surprised the Italians by beating them at Tripoli in 1939. Since the 1938 formula permitted the racing of 4½-litre unblown cars, two French machines appeared, the 4½-litre Delahaye and the Talbot. The advantage such cars had lay in their low fuel consumption, thereby saving pit stops. Taking advantage of this—and by dint of clever driving—the famous French ace, René Dreyfus, defeated Rudolf Caracciola and Herman Lang in their Mercedes-Benz's in the Pau G.P. in 1938.

In 1939, Grand Prix racing stopped. When it began again after the war, Bugatti was gone, and a new organisation, the *Fédération Internationale Automobile* (F.I.A.), was regulating Grand Prix racing. Only Italy had first-class racing machines ready to go: their 1½-litre, blown, Type 158 Alfa Romeos and the Maseratis. Also suited for modern racing, but to a lesser degree, were France's 4½-litre Talbots, and England's 1½-litre E.R.A.'s. The new F.I.A. formula for the period from 1947 to 1953 specified 1½-litre blown cars and 4½-litre unblown machines.

For the first few years nothing could touch the Alfa Romeo "Alfettes" which, through continued development and the use of two-stage supercharging, now developed 310 b.h.p. Nor were the new 4 CLT/48 Maseratis, now made by a new firm to whom the Maserati brothers had sold their name, able to do much against the Alfas, although they,

too, used two-stage blowers on their four-cylinder engines.

But a new star was rising which in years to come would completely dominate G.P. racing. This constellation was called Ferrari.

Before the war, Enzo Ferrari had operated the *Scuderia Ferrari* which, until 1938, had been entirely concerned with running Alfa Romeo's racing department. But now he decided to build his own machines. Up to 1960, Ferrari, with his knack for quickly designing and building new machinery to meet every changing quirk of Grand Prix racing, had produced over thirty-seven types of Grand Prix machines. I have not the space here to deal with them all, so the highlights will have to suffice.

The first G.P. Ferraris were the Type 125's, which appeared in the Italian Grand Prix in 1949. These tiny, tubular-chassised, 1½-litre machines designed by Gioachino Colombo already had the over-square V-12 engines which have since been so characteristic of Ferraris. Supercharged, these engines developed 225 b.h.p. at 7,500 r.p.m., but were no match for the Alfas that year. In 1949, Alfa Romeo did no racing and Ferrari's 1½-litre machines had things their own way. However, in 1950, Alfa entered a new version of the Type 158. This was the 159, which developed 350 b.h.p. at 8,500 r.p.m.

But Ferrari dropped his 1½-litre blown machines. Having noted the advantage the 4½-litre French Talbots had in not having to stop for refuelling during a race, he made a quick about-turn and decided to build unblown 4½-litre machines to counter the

nearly invincible Alfas. These 4½-litre, 330 b.h.p. V-12's (later increased to 380 b.h.p.) were the work of a new designer, Aurelio Lampredi, who also designed a new tubular-framed chassis with de Dion rear suspension for his new engine. This big new Ferrari was still unable in 1950 to vanquish the 1½-litre Alfas and their formidable combination of drivers, Fangio and Farina. But the next year it did better, winning the British and German Grands Prix, although Alfa was now squeezing 385 b.h.p. from the 1½-litre engine—at a petrol consumption rate of one-and-a-half miles a gallon!

After 1951, Ferrari reigned supreme for several years, for at the very height of their success, Alfa Romeo gave up Grand Prix racing.

In addition to the Grand Prix formula, the F.I.A. had for some years sanctioned another racing category known as Formula II, for 500 c.c. supercharged cars or 2-litre unblown machines. With Ferrari practically unopposed in Formula I, Formula II, by decision of the F.I.A., became the Grand Prix formula for 1952 and 1953. Ferrari had somehow known this was coming and had ready a Formula II four-cylinder, 2-litre unblown engine, plus a 2½-litre version for the new 1954 formula. In 1952 and 1953, the Formula II 2-litres won outright and Alberto Ascari took the world's championship both years.

Things changed in 1954 as real Grand Prix racing came back, although hardly with the wondrous sound and fury of pre-1939. All of the machines which appeared on the grids of the *Grandes Epreuves* that year were 2½-litre, unblown cars. No one took advantage of the other approved engine size—750 c.c. blown. Maserati developed its old Formula II, six-cylinder machine into the potent 250 F, now with a space frame using a grid of small-diameter tubing.

Mercedes-Benz came back. Although the Germans had been personae non gratae in Grands Prix for a few years after the war, they could have entered G.P. racing for several years prior to 1954. Now they entered the lists with the new Type W196, 2½-litre racing machines. As usual, the Germans were ahead of the game in design. Their straight-eight, 275 b.h.p. engines (a far cry from their 600 b.h.p. engines of the Thirties) had twin-overhead camshafts driven by a train of gears from the centre of the crankshaft; the cylinders were separated into two blocks of four (à la Monza Alfa Romeo of twenty years earlier). Further, they used fuel injection and desmodromic valve gear, in which the valves are positively closed as well as opened by the camshaft. This engine was mounted at an angle in a beautifully made space frame, which had independent suspension fore and aft. All four brakes were inboard to reduce unsprung weight.

Surprisingly, Lancia, which had never raced in *Grandes Epreuves*, announced that it was going racing, too. Their engines were V-8's with four overhead camshafts developing some 275 b.h.p. They used the fashionable space frame, too; their gear

ɔ the road's edge as to cut the tops off weeds with ɪeir hubcaps.

If I was ignorant about sports cars before 1930, ɦe great mass of Americans was, too, and it was to ɑke some fifteen years before the words "sports car" ɔecame coinage in the United States.

It had not always been so. In the early days of motoring, one of the surest ways of advertising the virtues of a make of car was to have it win races. At first, manufacturers raced their normal production models against each other, but as competition became keener, the cars they brought to the starting line became less and less like the machines they were offering to the public. These specialised versions were lighter. Through careful tuning and higher compression their engines were more powerful. Above all, their bodywork was leaner, starker, and rakishly charming.

Before long these machines, which helped sell the stodgier, seven-passenger tourers and landaulets of a manufacturer's line, became out-and-out racing cars. However, there were sporty types, impressed by their wins on the track and road circuits, who would have none of the landaulets. They wanted the race cars to drive on the road. Often they were able to buy last year's racing car, attach mudguards and acetylene lamps, paint the whole thing red, install a muffer, and out-roar, out-speed, and out-do with the girls every other young blade in the township.

In Europe, at first, as in the United States, sports cars were merely road-equipped racing machines or, as was common, especially with big Mercedes, they were family limousines with their monumental bodywork stripped off in summer and replaced by a pair of bucket seats, or one of those charming two-seater bodies of woven wicker that looked for all the world

as if it had been stolen out of somebody's summerhouse.

It was easy to convert a chain-drive machine like a Mercedes to sporting use since it was fairly easy to raise the rear-end ratio for high speed by merely changing the size of the sprocket. But not only Mercedes' were turned to sporting purposes. In Germany, Benz and Horch were also so used by the sabrescarred sons of the aristocracy. And in France, Belgium, and England, many a big-chested Panhard, Metallurgique, or Napier found new speed as it was stripped of heavy carriagework and let loose with only a pair of flimsy racing seats as its burden.

But it was from the trials for which Prince Henry of Prussia offered a trophy in the years from 1908 to 1911 that there emerged a type of machine which was the direct ancestor of the sports car of today. From 1908 to 1911, the Prince offered a trophy for a motoring "Tour" that was not a race nor, in our sense, a rally, although part of it at least consisted of a speed trial. The winner was chosen by means of

Top of page 198: Mercedes-Benz hardtop-roadster, type 300 SL, with an official rating of 240 h.p. Above: A sleek, Italianate 250-G T Ferrari. Below: The E-type, 265 b.h.p. XK-engined Jaguar, available with roadster body (shown here) or with Grand Touring coupé body. Because of an immensely strong integral body-chassis construction, the open model, capable of over 150 m.p.h., is no weaker structurally than its coupé-bodied sister.

a complex formula that pleased no one. And each year all the losers swore that they'd never have anything to do with such a ridiculous event again. What irked the losers mostly was that instead of a "Tour", the "Prince Henry" became a pretty rough race, in spite of the fact that the cars were required to be touring machines, complete with mudguards, lights, and enough room for four passengers.

The participants didn't know it but they were engaging, for what was probably the first time, in sports-car racing.

At least two of the machines arising from these "Tours", the Austro-Daimler and the Vauxhall, were direct links with the sports cars of our time. They were neither stodgy touring cars nor were they racing cars. They were, perhaps, the first genuine sports cars.

The "Prince Henry" Austro-Daimler, built in Vienna and designed by Ferdinand Porsche, won the speed trials in 1910—which, by the way, was the most important of the tours; in 1911 they degenerated into a mere procession—and also won the entire event by being placed second and third with duplicates of the winning machine.

These 27/80 Austro-Daimlers had four-cylinder 5.7 litre engines with huge valves inclined at forty-five degrees in hemispherical combustion chambers.

Above: Austro-Daimler AD6 torpedo sports model, 6-cylinder, 3-litre capacity, 1926 (Austria), designed by Ferdinand Porsche. On the right, an Ultra-Sporting Briton: the low-chassis "100 m.p.h" Invicta, capable of some 95 m.p.h. This car had a six-cylinder, pushrod, twin-carburettor truck engine and a disconcerting habit of spinning like a top. Aside from this annoying peculiarity, the Invicta was a most pleasant vehicle to drive, and won the Monte Carlo Rally.

The car's valves, in cages, were operated by a single overhead camshaft driven by a vertical shaft from the crankshaft. Its twin magnetos were driven from the lower end of the shaft. This engine has never ceased to amaze me, for it is almost identical in design to that in the 1907 Welch I drive, even to the archaic, total-loss oiling system. However, with its light steel pistons, oversize valves, and better carburetion, the Austro-Daimler developed some 95 b.h.p., nearly twice that of the Welch, although their cubic capacity was almost identical.

The chassis of the Austro-Daimler was quite ordinary, the rear wheels chain-driven. It was very high-geared and the gearbox had close ratios, another sports car virtue that still has not been learned by some manufacturers in our time. Top speed was over 80 m.p.h.

The "Prince Henry" Vauxhall was a rather different beast. It had a far simpler engine, a 3-litre L-head of notably unexciting specifications, but with the ability to turn up 2,500 r.p.m., which was a high speed in 1910. It developed 52 b.h.p., the later 4-litre versions 75. Although these were capable of only 75 m.p.h. (really nothing to be sneezed at in 1914), it was the manner of their progression that gave them their charm and made their fame. With a very low unsprung-to-sprung weight ratio—the "unsprung weight" is that not borne by the springs, such as wheels, brake drums, differential—it had a lightness and delicacy of handling such as we cannot know in the heavier cars of today. During the visit of a British team at an Anglo-American Rally, I watched Laurence Pomeroy, a famous motoring journalist and a first-class driver, take his Edwardian Vauxhall around the track at Thompson, Connecticut. Not only were its lap times quite as fast as cars fifteen years its

One of the more popular British sports cars is the Austin Healey 3,000 (below). Built by BMC, the huge English manufacturing combine, the Healey has a 3-litre, six-cylinder, push-rod engine and gives remarkably good performance. Its top speed is over 110 m.p.h. and it can reach 60 m.p.h. from rest in just under ten seconds. It has disc brakes forward and drum brakes on its non-independently sprung rear axle. The Porsche Type 356B-1600 coupé (bottom) is but one model of the various Porsches which were originally based on Volkswagen. They range from "cooking" versions like this, to the extremely potent road-racing types. Although its opposed-four engine is only 1,582 c.c. and has a compression ratio of 7.5:1, it develops 70 b.h.p. and is capable of very nearly 100 m.p.h.

Above: The Triumph TR 4 hard-top coupé, 4-cylinder engine, 100 h.p. Below: The MGB has a 1.8-litre power unit, dual carburation and develops 95 b.h.p.

Above: An American Stutz car, 8 cylinders in line, overhead camshaft-driven. This car took part in Le Mans, 1928 (it was placed second, beating the world record for road-speed, 5-litre category). Opposite page, upper left: The engineer-designer racing driver Jean-Albert Grégoire after completing the Le Mans 24-hour Race in 1927, in which he drove his Tracta Gephi car with frontwheel drive. The "Competition" Delahaye (upper right) won the "Fastest Road Car" race at Brooklands in England in 1939. This 1936 model had a 3½-litre engine adapted from that used in Delahaye trucks. It could better 110 m.p.h. A Lagonda similar to this 1937 Lagonda "Rapide" (bottom of page) won at Le Mans in 1935. The "Rapide" used the same Meadows commercial engine which had earlier powered the Invicta.

junior, but its road holding and the precision of its steering were easily their equal, too.

But the "Prince Henry" Vauxhall's claim to greatness lies in the fact that it was the direct ancestor of the 30/98 Vauxhall, with the Bentley one of the more notable English sports cars of the Twenties.

Obviously there were machines besides the Austro-Daimler and the Vauxhall emerging as true sports cars: Bugatti, Hispano-Suiza, Mercedes, Aston Martin. Their names would grow greater after the war. Sadly, the names of the great American sporting machines—Mercer, Stutz, Simplex—were doomed to wither away, almost to be forgotten until their resurrection by the antique-car enthusiasts of our time.

The dozen or so years between the end of the Great War and the onset of the cold chill of the Depression were, at least to those who love the spidery starkness and near brutality of the vintage sports car, the great days of sporting machinery. Each country's sports cars bore the stamp of its national characteristics, its geography, its economics.

England, in contrast to the countries of continental Europe, had not only a wealthy upper class, but also a large, educated middle class with a sporting tradition. Therefore, in addition to the expensive, hand-fitted, large and powerful machines such as the Bentley, Britain produced a host of small, comparatively

cheap sports cars for the growing middle-income enthusiast. Also, since few English sports cars were built for export they were well-suited to the English road, which was billiard-table smooth, incredibly twisty and narrow, and seldom climbed mountains. Typical pre-World War II English sporting machines were the Invicta, Riley, H.R.G., Lagonda, Vauxhall, Sunbeam, Frazer-Nash, A.C., Alvis and, of course, the M.G. Although I am sorely tempted, I can deal with but a few of these here.

Of all these cars, I believe I know best the Invicta, specifically the "100 m.p.h.", 4½-litre, low-chassis model. I owned one for seven mostly happy years, starting in 1943. The car I had was built in 1934 and was one of the last of its type—chassis No. S-155. It had a six-cylinder push-rod engine, with twin S.U. carburettors, developing some 115 b.h.p. at 4,000 r.p.m. Approaching 4,000, these engines begin to feel pretty rough, and I still recollect with horror the time I found No. 3 main bearing lying in the crankcase when I undid it for cleaning. But otherwise the Invicta was a charmer. It was fast (about 95 m.p.h.— 0 to 60 in 14½ seconds), wonderful looking, with its plated outside exhaust pipes, and honestly and ruggedly built. Although its steering was impeccable, its strong, elliptically sprung chassis had a built-in vice. Because too much of its weight was in front and of its ultra-low underslung frame, it had the maddening habit of swapping ends. For very little cause it would spin around and I'd find myself facing the way I had come. In spite of these peccadilloes, Donald Healey won the 1931 Monte Carlo Rally outright on a similar car, and in 1933 an Invicta driven by A. C. Lace on the Ards Circuit in Ireland put in a faster lap than Sir Henry Birkin's 4½-litre Bentley. If the Invicta, which cost some £1,500, could have weathered the Depression, its faults could have been designed out and Buick would have had to call one of its models by another name.

If any car was built with one end in view—to give its driver all the wild excitement of driving a spirited motor-cycle—it was the untamed and highly original chain-drive Frazer-Nash. From 1924 on, many models were brought out the "Colmore", "Boulogne", "Exeter", "T.T. Replica" and more—and they were fitted with almost every type of sports engine that came into their maker's ken. It's difficult to find two Frazer-Nashes that are alike. The manufacturers would bolt together almost any combination you wanted. But no matter what the model, all Frazer-Nashes had a delightful and archaic system of chains

to drive the back wheels—not unlike that in the James Steam Carriage of 1833. From a head-snapping clutch, power was transmitted through bevel gears and then by a rattling rat's-nest of chains and sprockets to the rear axle. (Sprockets could be quickly changed so that you could have any gear ratios you fancied). Sliding dog clutches locked the desired sprocket to a cross-shaft and made lightning gear changes simple. The solid rear axle, without differential, made corners feel funny, the hard quarter-elliptic springs discouraged lady passengers, and the quick-as-a-wish steering required the driver to watch where he was going every minute, but driven with verve and zeal no sports car was ever more fun.

In 1935 the factory, to the dismay of dedicated "chain-gangsters", dropped the wonderfully stark models, although they'd still make you one to order until 1938 or so, and brought out a British version of the German B.M.W. A pity, that!

For the impecunious young sports-car Englishmen of the Thirties, there was a fair number of low-priced, low-powered, albeit pleasingly sporting little machines from which he could choose. The Singer, the M.G. "Midget", the Austin "Nippy" were typical.

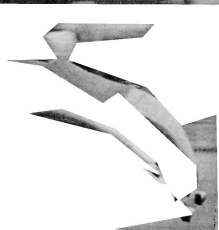

Cecil Kimber, in 1923, modified a Morris Cowley and called it an M.G. (for Morris Garages). It was so successful in rallies and hill climbs that the Morris organisation went into the production of M.G. sports cars similar to the 1927-28 model shown above. In 1929 the first M.G. "Midget" appeared (left). A later version of this — the TC (above, right) — took America by storm in 1946. The TC had a four-cylinder, 1,250 c.c. engine, which gave 55 b.h.p. and approached 80 m.p.h. Its precise steering and good road holding were a revelation to American drivers. Centre right; M.G. TD, launched in 1951, with an engine capacity of 1,250 c.c., the first M.G. to have independent front wheels. Below, right: M.G. TF, launched in October 1953. Engine capacity 1,250 c.c., later 1,500 c.c.

Of these the M.G. Midget soon became the most popular and had more to do with spreading the cult of the sports car than any other machine ever built. Although the Midget did not appear on the scene until 1929, the M.G. (for Morris Garages) had been around since 1923 when Cecil Kimber modified a Morris Cowley for competing in trials and rallies. Until 1929, the M.G.'s had been quite successful, medium-sized sporting machines of about 2 litres. But the first Midget had an engine of only 847 c.c., which put out some 20 b.h.p. This engine and the chassis, were based on those in the popular Morris "Minor", but with modified manifolding for better breathing. An overhead camshaft operated the valves and was itself driven from the crankshaft by a vertically mounted generator, which odd arrangement persisted for years in spite of the trouble people sometimes had with oil from the valve gear dripping into the generator.

This tiny M.G. was immediately joyfully hailed by the young sports motorists as the ideal machine for trials, club racing, and fun on the road. For in spite of its measly 20 horse-power it was a lively little devil. With its light wood and fabric bodywork it weighed only a bit over a thousand pounds. They loved its jaunty look, too, for it was low-built, with cutaway sides and a saucy, pointed tail.

It wasn't long before people were hotting up these little machines and racing them in spite of their having fabric universal couplings and fuel tanks over the driver's knees. The factory wasn't far behind them and produced a super-sports version known as the "Montlhéry" Midget. These had their engines reduced in size to fit into the 750 c.c. racing class. With improved chassis, bigger engine bearings, downdraught carburettors and such, they developed over 30 b.h.p. while a few with 9 to 1 compression put out 45 b.h.p., and in supercharged form no less than

60 b.h.p. at 6,300 r.p.m. This car covered itself with glory at Montlhéry.

It was far back in 1932 that the typical M.G. Midget, with its long sweeping wings and the slab fuel-tank, first appeared. This was the J2, and it was from these J2's that all the subsequent M.G.'s that have appeared down the years were developed: the P Types, the TA's and finally, after World War II, the TC's which made the U.S.A. sports car conscious.

The Briton enjoyed his sports car. He entered rallies (the rally of those days was still a form of motor sport instead of a numbers game for electronic engineers) and he entered trials. These trials, which still are a part of the sports motoring scene in England although nowadays the cars entered in them have evolved into weirdly specialised mechanisms, consisted of a number of slimy, muddy, ditches set at a steep angle. With their flair for understatement, the British called these rock-strewn mud holes "trials hills". The idea was to rush along with hundreds of other mud-plastered entrants from one of these obstacles to the other and climb each one non-stop against the clock, often at night and in the rain. If you got stuck in a morass, you not only lost points, but suffered the indignity of being dragged to the top by a traction engine.

Until the war, the English sporting driver's mecca was Brooklands. This motor-racing track, irregular in shape, several miles around, and complete with steep bankings, was built as early as 1907. Here, the Briton could not only watch Grand Prix types competing at week ends, but also join in sports-car racing. One of the favourite events sent masses of sports cars of every complexion charging off in a one-hour "blind" to see who could go farthest in that time.

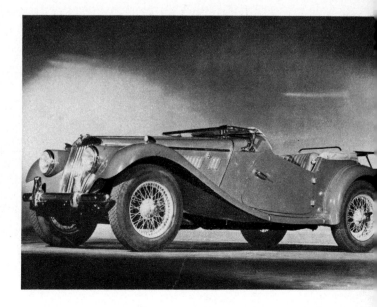

Luckily, this 1923 U.S.-built Kissel (right) couldn't go very fast, its two-wheel brakes being what they were. In spite of its rakishly sporting look, it was breathing hard at 70 m.p.h. for its six-cylinder engine developed only 65 b.h.p. The chain-driven Frazer-Nash of 1935 (below) has a 2-litre, twin-overhead-camshaft Blackburn engine and does 85 m.p.h. This car looks as if it has a rear seat, but that after-compartment is largely taken up by chains and sprockets. Bottom: This 3-litre Sunbeam of 1926 had the first twin-overhead-camshaft engine to be offered to the public in a non-racing machine. It had the high compression ratio of 6:1 and produced 90 b.h.p. — good for its day. It was capable also of almost 90 m.p.h. Note that its front mudguards fitted the wheels very closely and steered with them. Bottom right: The Sunbeam's engine. Page 209: The 6-cylinder de Vasselle Hotchkiss, which won the Monte-Carlo Rally in 1935.

Moreover, for a small fee it was possible on quiet weekdays to take your sports car out on the track and have a wonderful time going as fast as you liked.

Alas, Brooklands is no more. During the recent war, the track was requisitioned and after the war its board of directors sold it to make way for industrial sites.

France during the inter-war years was the only other car-building European country where enough middle-class young men existed to support the manufacture of sports cars other than Bugattis, Hispano-Suizas, Delages, and Delahayes. The Salmson, Lombard, Sénéchal, Amilcar, and Chenard among others, were all comparatively low-powered, medium-priced cars with a character that was almost uniformly Gallic.

As much in the French idiom as any of them, and the most famous as well, was the Amilcar. That Amilcar I used to gape at was, most likely, the 1923 Grand Sport. These early "Amils" had such incredibly narrow bodies that the seats were staggered to give the passenger a little elbow room. These 1923 cars were known as the Type C.G.S. and had four-cylinder, L-head engines developing 40 b.h.p. The light and fragile-looking chassis sat on half-elliptic springs in front and quarter elliptics aft, and even then had four-wheel brakes, although about as big as ice-hockey pucks. These Amilcars looked as if they might turn over while standing still. A view under the hoods at their puny, crudely finished engines was a dismal prospect.

But looks were deceiving. The Amilcar was an amazingly potent little creature. It won hill climbs right and left. One of them won the twenty-four-hour Bol d'Or; another came in fourteenth at Le Mans in 1924, qualifying for the Rudge-Whitworth Cup. As for lasting power, you still see them around.

An entirely different kind of Amilcar with a six-cylinder, supercharged, twin-overhead-camshaft engine appeared in 1926—the G6. This expensive and desirable road version of an Amilcar racer was guaranteed to do better than 100 m.p.h., but unfortunately only a few were ever built.

I cannot resist mentioning one other French sports car, the Delahaye. Although most Delahayes were lush and flamboyant machines for the rapid transport of French millionaires and their curvaceous mannequins who posed beside the cars in *Concours d'Elégance*, Delahaye in 1936 produced as lean and purposeful a sports car as anyone could desire.

This "Competition" model had a push-rod, 3½-litre, three-carburettor engine which was said to be a hotted-up version of the engine used in Delahaye trucks. Although it was no beauty to look at, it was a tough and durable power plant. In sports form it produced a very creditable 160 b.h.p. at 4,200 r.p.m. and pushed the light two-seater along at better than 110 m.p.h., enough to win the "Fastest Road Car" race at Brooklands in 1939. This much-talked-of competition was organised by a group of Englishmen, each of whom was confident that he had the speediest machine on the road. Even though it caught fire just before the start, the Delahaye, driven by Arthur Dobson, got out in front and was never overtaken by the other racers—including two Alfa Romeos (a 2.6 and a 2.9), a Talbot-Lago, and a very potent Delage.

Germany, after World War I, did not have the economic climate to support the sale of quantities of sports cars to middle-class young men; there were too few of them. Although the Germans were quite successful between the wars in international sports-car competition, the cars were mostly Mercedes-Benz's entered by the factory.

Domestic sports-car events after Hitler's rise were

A 1939 "Competition" Delage like the one above, left, won the Tourist Trophy in 1938. It had a six-cylinder, 3-litre engine. Lushly curvaceous is the 3-litre, 1946 Delage (left). The body is by Figoni and Falaschi. A German "Sportwagen", the Type 328 B.M.W. of 1937 (below), had a tubular chassis, rack-and-pinion steering and independent front suspension. Figoni and Falaschi built the opulent body (top of page 211) for the twelve-cylinder, 1939 Delahaye. Centre: A 1936 A.C.F. Grand Prix Delahaye sports car, 6-cylinder engine, 3,447 c.c. Maximum speed 115 m.p.h. Bottom of page 211: A throwback to the vintage years, the British H.R.G. was made until 1955. It had stiff, underslung, half-elliptic springs aft and quarter-elliptics forward. Available with either 1,100 or 1,500 c.c., four-cylinder, single-overhead-camshaft engines, it could approach 90 m.p.h. with impeccable road-holding. The engines were bought from Singer and modified.

quasi-military affairs, the be-swastikaed cars driven by S.S. types through rivers and over rocky fields. A Jeep would have licked them.

The only notable pre-war sports car besides the Mercedes-Benz was the Type 328 B.M.W. made by the Bayerische Motorische Werke, which also makes the B.M.W. motor-cycle and which, during the war, made the engines for the deadly Focke-Wulf 190 aeroplane.

The 328 B.M.W., which superseded an earlier push-rod engined sports car, the Type 55, was in 1937 far more like the sports cars of today than its contemporaries. Light (1,800 pounds), tubular chassised, independently sprung in front, with rack-and-pinion steering and hydraulic brakes, it had an astounding performance for a comparatively low-priced moderately powered machine. It had an 80 b.h.p., 2-litre engine with three carburettors. In fact, the current English Bristol engine is a modernised version of the same power plant, using the same complex push-rod system to operate its overhead valves in hemispherical combustion chambers.

The 328 was capable of almost 100 m.p.h. and a racing version whose engine developed 135 b.h.p. won the shortened, wartime *Mille Miglia* at an average of over 103 m.p.h.

Italy is the birthplace of the violent automobile. Ferrari, Alfa Romeo, Maserati, Lancia, call Italy their home. Ettore Bugatti was born in Italy. Only there is motor racing a national sport as important as cricket in England or baseball in the United States. Ninety-nine out of a hundred youthful Italian males have no hope of ever acquiring enough lire to buy a Ferrari. But let some rich young Signore dive out of an Appenine hairpin corner in a Ferrari and scream through the narrow, cobble-stoned street of a

mountain village and every boy flattened in a doorway to give the screeching *macchina* room feels that *he* is mashing the throttle to the floor, that *his* hands are on the steering wheel to guide the car around the next impossible hairpin.

The handling qualities of Italian sports cars owe much to Italy's terrain and the temperament of her drivers. Her cars must have magnificent steering and brakes and unburstable engines to cope with steep Alpine roads, dead-straight, engine-killing autostrade and, above all, zealous, lead-footed drivers, each of whom thinks himself a Tazio Nuvolari.

After Alfa Romeo and Ferrari, Lancia and Maserati are the great names among Italian sports cars. Between the wars the Maserati brothers built Grand Prix machines, upon rare occasions fitting mudguards and lights to one of them for a sports-car race. Such

In road races of the early Fifties, the Cadillac-engined English Allard (left) set the pace. Farina's taut and functional body styling for Fiat-powered Cisitalias of the late Forties (top of page 212) started a fashion that still persists. Their Fiat engines were usually 1,100 c.c., push-rod, four-cylinder types, which developed about 60 b.h.p. The cars had tubular chassis and could do better than 90 m.p.h. The RS-60 Porsche sports racer (centre) has its overhead-camshaft engine mounted forward of the rear axle; its 135 b.h.p. produces almost 150 m.p.h. A similar "Spyder" won the 1,500 c.c. class at Le Mans in 1957. The Maserati 3,500 GT (below) has a six-cylinder, twin-overhead-cam engine, approaches 130 m.p.h.

Maserati sports car as existed were models like these, de-tuned by their owners for road use. It was not until after World War II that sports Maseratis were offered for sale by the new owners of the Maserati name. The cars the Maserati brothers were to build, post-war, would be known by a new name—Osca.

Lancia, however, was a big name even before the Great War, although the cars of that period made little pretence of being sporting machines. In 1922, Lancia brought out the Lambda, a touring car of unusual design, but the idea that it might be considered a sports car never entered the makers' heads. Over the years, however, as drivers experienced the Lancia's superb road holding and steering, enabling it

often to do better time over twisting, difficult roads than many breathless and screaming sports cars, it endeared itself more and more.

The early Lancia Lambdas were long, flat, plank-like touring cars of an early type of integral construction. The four-cylinder, 2-litre engine was the first of the narrow "V's" which have since become a Lancia trade-mark. A single overhead camshaft operated the valves. The carburettor was mounted, of all places, at the rear of the engine and fed the cylinders by way of a passage running through the centre of the head. Early models had three-speed gearboxes, later ones four-speed. But even the latest Lambdas were hard put to better 80 m.p.h.

In 1951 this Type C, XK-120 Jaguar (left) won the 24-hour Race at Le Mans. A speed of 140 m.p.h. is claimed for the Type 507 B.M.W. sports coupé (lower left). Its 3.2-litre, V-8 engine, which develops 178 b.h.p., is made almost entirely of aluminium. Just before World War II the A.C. Ace (below) appeared in this country, and a few were exported to the United States. Pleasant sports tourers with no pretensions to high performance, their six-cylinder engines were designed in the 1920's. They had aluminium blocks with wet liners and a single-overhead camshaft; 80 b.h.p. was developed. The Aceca coupé (bottom) is descended from these machines. It handles beautifully, and its Bristol engine is capable of 105 m.p.h.

It was the Lambda's unique front suspension that gave it such lovely road manners. Its springs were long coils inside big vertical tubes which served as kingpins. These tubes also contained the hydraulic shock absorbers, and the whole front end was knitted together by a formidable bridgework of tubing and braces, part of which continued rearwards to form a cradle for the engine. The vertical tubes containing the springs ended in little round plates in the front mudguards, and the same kind of people who talked about sealed engines in Rolls-Royces warned that these plates must not be removed lest a spring fly up and drill through your forehead. Never saw it happen to even one mechanic, I'm sorry to say.

After six years of war, the factories of Europe that had been building sports cars were either masses of bombed wreckage or had turned their machines over to the making of the stupid hardware of modern war. It appeared that it might be years before anybody would build sports cars again.

It was astounding, naturally, to see the sports-car builders begin almost immediately to make mouth-watering machines for motor sport. But what was even more astounding was the way Americans suddenly, violently, fell in love with the sports car.

It was, of course, the M.G. TC that started it. Dainty as a button, lively, its handling was a revelation to Americans resigned to the slow and mushy steering of the barge-like cars they were used to. For the Detroit machines of the late Thirties and Forties were far more clumsy than American cars of today.

Those few of us who had been long involved with machines like Bugattis and Alfas were just a little annoyed at this sudden invasion of our domain by parvenus in checked caps, and by the salesmen with recently learned British accents who graced the sports-car showrooms springing up everywhere from Passwater, Texas, to Peculiar, Missouri. But there was no denying that the rush was on. At first the new boys bought mostly British cars, for they were more easily available. But in the Fifties, as the factories of the continent swung into production, the now sophisticated American sports-car buyer began lusting after Mercedes-Benz's and Porsches, Cisitalias, Alfa Romeos and Lancias, and even Maseratis.

For the American sports-car enthusiast learned fast. He joined sports-car clubs and avidly read not only the British motor magazines, but the new and excellent American magazines like *Road and Track* and, latterly, *Car and Driver*.

Today, wonder of wonders, there is even a great American-built sports car, the Corvette, made by, of all people, General Motors. (Unfortunately, the beautiful, though high-priced Cunningham is no longer in production).

But most surprising of all is the way Americans have embraced all types of motoring sport. Before the war sports-car racing was indulged in by a small group of very "in" types who called themselves the Automobile Racing Club of America. They raced a weird agglomeration of everything from G. P. Bugattis to a Ford-engined Amilcar, wherever they could —even, in 1940, through the roads and around the exhibition halls and pavilions of the dormant New York World's Fair grounds.

By European standards such sporting events were as nothing. The Europeans had for years engaged in sports-car racing of such magnitude as to be beyond the imagination of Americans.

Take the Italian *Mille Miglia*, for example. The *Mille Miglia* was not, in its heyday, a mere race. It was a form of national hysteria. The 1,000-mille course itself, a gigantic figure-of-eight starting in Brescia in the North, with its waist at Bologna and its southern loop touching Rome, was a piece of grandiose insanity. It climbed the often fog-shrouded Futa and Raticosa passes, it ran over long and straight stretches burning in the coastal sun, and twisted through cobbled mountain villages. And everywhere were people, millions of hoarsely screaming, wildly keyed-up Italians, gesticulating at the drivers, pointing out the next turn (often wrongly, if he were, say, a German) and encouraging their favourites.

The first race was in 1927. Minoia, driving an O.M., won at under 50 m.p.h., taking over twenty-one hours to run the course. By 1933 the great Tazio Nuvolari had cut the time to sixteen hours. In 1955 Stirling Moss in a Mercedes-Benz did it in slightly over ten hours—at an average of 97.9 m.p.h. Along the straights he got up as high as 170 m.p.h.

Each year the race got wilder—as well as faster. At the beginning only catalogued machines might

A 166 M Ferrari: Built in 1949, its 2-litre, V-12 engine gave 125 m.p.h.

n-overhead-cam Maserati engine.

Sports-racing Maserati dashboard.

Famous "Birdcage" Maserati.

Lotus sports-racing car.

Drivers sprint towards cars in Le Mans start at Sebring.

Lister-Jaguar at speed.

Aston Martin — Salvadori up.

The late Alfonso de Portago at Sebring.

Sports-racing Ferrari in practice.

217

enter, but towards the end so-called "prototypes"—mainly disguised Grand Prix machines — left the starting ramp at Brescia at one-minute intervals to force their way through the hundreds of sports and Gran Turismo machines in many different handicap classes, which were already screeching south, often in rain and darkness.

It was amazing that only a few spectators and drivers were killed each year, but in 1957 a spectacular Spaniard, Alfonso, the Marquis de Portago, new to the race, blew a tyre after being warned that he needed it changed and charged into a crowd of spectators, killing fourteen of them including six children. Since then by government decree the *Mille Miglia* has been toned down to a quite boring event, more like a rally than a race.

Such racing is, course, impractical in the States, although before the war I tried to interest the authorities in running a race over the perfect road circuit that exists in New York's Central Park.

No sooner had a few sports cars been unloaded in the States (and sometimes dropped on the dock by Anglophobe longshoremen) than their happy owners slapped numbers on them and went racing. In the East, Watkins Glen and Bridgehampton welcomed the newly revived sport to their streets and country lanes. Towns in California followed suit. But as cars got faster and the richer boys started bringing in Ferraris and Cadillac-engined Allards, the races were moved to airports and to closed circuits, at least one of which — the twelve-hour race at Sebring, Florida —has achieved international recognition.

Although there is still, happily, much racing around the country in smaller machines like Alfa Romeos, Triumphs, and Austin-Healeys, modified to meet the requirements of the sports-car clubs, much sports-car racing is now in the hands of tough professionals, and even the sports-car magazines are prone to sneer at what they call the "gymkhana, chequered-cap school of motoring enthusiasts".

The sports-car owner can still—if he has a built-in electronic brain—get some fun out of another form of motoring competition, the rally. The American type of rally originally was patterned on the famous European rallies like the Alpine Trial and that great-grandfather of all rallies, the *Rallye Monte Carlo*.

Each winter when the gales roar across the Polish plain, when Scotland and the Scandinavian peninsula lie coated in ice, and the wolves howl among the Balkan snows, cars from all these uncomfortable places converge on sunny Monte Carlo.

The "Monte" started in 1911 when twenty-two cars entered. Today, as many as three hundred start from Warsaw, Lisbon, Glasgow, Palermo and many other large European cities. No matter where a rally car starts, it will traverse almost 2,000 miles of European road in January, go through controls and time checks, and cross the glacial passes of the Alps. Cars lose points if they are too late or too early at controls, which requires much painful navigation and mathematical calculation, or if they arrive at Monte Carlo battered and patched up. The more smashed bumpers, the more lost points. And it's mighty easy to smash things up on icy Alpine hairpins at night when the specified average time between controls is about 10 m.p.h. faster than any sane driver would attempt on midsummer's eve. Surprisingly, so many cars arrive in Monte Carlo without loss of marks that it has been necessary to hold eliminating trials. Before the war one of the trials was the notorious

David Brown's Aston Martin DBR1/300 (bottom, left) was one of the most successful British sports cars that ever engaged in international competition. In 1959 it won the Tourist Trophy, Le Mans, and the 1,000-kilometre at the Nürburgring, thereby gaining the world's sports-car championship, never before won by a British machine. Shown here is Roy Salvadori driving at Le Mans, where, with Carroll Shelby, he won at 112.5 m.p.h. Traditionally, British sports cars have been four-square devices, complete with in-built headwinds. But the English, as evidenced by the Lotus Elan above, have begun to outdo the Italians with a number of their latest sports cars. The Lotus, built with a stressed fibreglass body, is powered by a 1,558 c.c. unit with two Weber carburettors, developing 105 b.h.p. net at 5,500 r.p.m. It has all-round independent suspension and a separate steel chassis. Launched in 1963, this car has improved in its design and performance considerably over the last years.

"Wiggle-woggle"—a complex series of figures-of-eight done against the clock. One year an enterprising Roumanian entrant in some fiendish manner attached his brakes to his steering, so that applying the anchors automatically threw him into a calculated skid, sending him around the wiggles and woggles faster than anyone else.

The rules are different from year to year and nowadays the organisers are like as not to send the tired contestants out for a gay road race at night over a mountain circuit, have them engage in a speed hill-climb, or even race around the Grand Prix course at Monaco in their efforts to find the ultimate winners. There is one over-all winner and various class winners, depending on engine size.

Before the war, Athens was a favourite starting point for the more dauntless types. But even they would arrive (if they arrived at all) shaken by their adventures. One cold year, Athenian competitors reported that many high-banked Balkan rivers were difficult to cross because the enterprising natives had removed the plank bridges for firewood. A competitor named Ostaczinski, a member of a Polish team from the Balkans, once swore to me that the only way they could hold off a pack of ravening wolves that pursued them was by throwing empty slivovitz bottles at them.

But the contestants' tall tales and adventures are not always funny. There are many tragic stories and examples of heroism.

In 1932, for example, a Mrs. Vaughan, a surgeon and an inveterate rally competitor, in company with a young lady medical student, was within a few hours of the finishing line in a Triumph when they came upon the grisly wreckage of several cars. They got out of their car and, in imminent danger of having following competitors smash into them, set four broken legs before going on to win the *Coupe des Dames.*

When they arrive in Monte Carlo, the crews, having lived together in their cars for several sleepless nights and hungry days, are barely on speaking terms. Until recently, after some hours of sleep, sunshine, and good food, they would polish their cars for the *Concours d'Elégance* and the *Concours de Confort.*

And it is in these contests that the big Rolls-Royces and Bentleys did best. Here they could show off their specially fitted coachwork complete with built-in toilets, hot and cold running water, tape recorders, trick road lights on stalks (for poking under fog banks), and electric wipers for the headlights. It's a wonder they ever reached Monte Carlo at all under

219

The term "sports car" is used quite loosely. To some people a sports car is a near-racing machine, to some it is a car used mostly for the fun of driving. But even sedate-looking closed machines like the Lancia Flaminia (left centre) can have the attributes of the genuine sports car. This car's 2½-litre, V-6 engine develops 131 h.p. It can be handled with such verve and enterprise and can put up such high averages that it surely merits its description as a sports car. Upper left: An English Morgan, stripped for racing, on the course at Marlboro, Maryland. It has a TR-3, four-cylinder engine developing 100 b.h.p. Above: A British-built, Bristol-powered A.C., also at Marlboro. This car is capable of 110 m.p.h. Page 220, bottom left: Italian 1,200 c.c. Fiat Spyder Roadster. Bottom right: English Sunbeam Alpine II. Its 85 b.h.p. engine is capable of 100 m.p.h. Left: On the starting line at Danville, Virginia; Alfa Romeo Giulietta Spyder in the foreground.

the weight of this fascinating junk, in addition to the usual stuff Monte Carlo rallyists carry: shovels clipped to the wings, unditching apparatus, spare snow tyres, bottles of gas for filling tyres, plus a dashboard and cockpit-ful of instruments for navigating and calculating the course.

When it comes to calculating instruments, the American rallyist need take second place to no one. If you've ever wondered what it might be like to get inside an electronic brain, just sit down next to the driver of an American rally car. For the American rally depends more on calculating microseconds and hundredths of a mile than it does on brilliant and dangerous driving over impossible roads, which American cops tend to discourage.

Most rallyists, therefore, rally just for the fun of the game—and a chance at the little silver trophy awarded to a winner. This makes no fortunes, but your rallying regular is an intense and dedicated man. Why? I think, mostly, it works something like this. Suppose that after much high-pressure salesmanship you have finally convinced your wife that a sports car is necessary to your common happiness. You at last own that brazen-voiced little machine of your dreams. Now you see yourself, helmeted and goggled, as the scourge of the racing circuits. Your wife has other views.

"You mad?" she says. "You with four kids and hardly any insurance. Anyhow, you might break our darling new car. If you're going anywhere in it I'm riding with you."

So you enter a rally. It's fairly safe, you've heard it's fun, and you can take your wife along. And even if you're racing, you have a nice big racing number on the side of your car.

When you get to the place where the rally starts, you find lots of people just like you and your wife, but you also find quite a few serious looking, two-man teams who seem to be electronic wizards, fooling with enough stop watches, calculating machines, surveyor's odometers, and other navigational gadgetry to take them into orbit around Jupiter instead of just a pleasant two-day jaunt in the Catskill Mountains. But like them you set your only watch to the time signals some important-looking officials are bringing in on a portable short-wave radio, while other unsmiling officials test your car for mechanical fitness.

At last it's your turn to leave the starting line. Your wife is rustling a sheaf of instructions and fiddling with a stop watch.

A man says, "Go!" Your wife presses the button on the watch and starts reading the instructions:

First Leg: Average speed 39.8 m.p.h.
1. Turn right at airport gate
2. Turn left at Clarke's Store
3. Turn right at Essex Road
4. Bear right at red barn to Rte. 9

Second Leg: Average speed 31.6 m.p.h.
1. Turn right at Wharton's Antique Shop
2. Bear left at Sea Horse Cafe

. . . and so on for page after page.

You get lost in exactly 12 minutes 10.2 seconds by your stop watch.

The only time I ever tried this I not only got lost, I immediately got mixed up on the average-time business, to the annoyance of the grimly serious timing-officials who hid behind privies and haystacks, their hands full of clip-boards and stop watches.

When the day's rallying was over, I joined the contestants in the hotel where they stayed overnight before starting off again in the morning. Here they had a whale of a time arguing calculating machines, tenths of seconds, and lost points.

I started to talk to a white-moustached gentleman at the bar who was wearing a brass-buttoned blazer on which was sewn various sports-car club insignia. I said something about Bugattis. He moved away.

I never did see the end of that rally, but I read that an engineer and a tax estimator won the 523-mile run by being only 74 seconds off schedule.

That's what you need to win. Numbers in your head—sawdust too, maybe.

European manufactures have always taken rallying seriously. When one of their cars wins such an event, its success is loudly trumpeted in advertising. Even if a car doesn't get anywhere near first place, it may be publicised as being "... first in the class for 150 c.c. cars driven by left-handed lady pinochle players". Most publicized of all international events is the "Rallye de Monte Carlo". Above: an M.G. 1100 scuds through the foothills of the Alps. American rallyists tend to stuff their cars with displays of glittering instruments (centre). This Saab boasts four expensive stop watches, three Curta calculators, and a smart little gadget that counts wheel revolutions. Patriarch of all such games is the "Rallye de Monte Carlo". Below: Louis Chiron flags off a Monte Carlo Rally car on the mountain circuit.

LINKS WITH
THE PAST

Every time my venerable fifty-four-year-old touring car and I pull into Mr. Wilcox's garage, which has stood opposite the village green since well before my car was built (it was H. A. Wilcox's Bicycle and Automobile Repair Station in those days), we go through the same experience. As I descend from the driver's seat so that Mr. Wilcox can lift the cushion to fill the fuel tank, the town loafers—who hang around the service station now that the general store is no more—give up leaning on the side of the garage building and with elaborate casualness stroll over for the fiftieth time to make a careful examination of the old machine. A few cars stop on U.S. 1, and their drivers join in the rapping of mudguards and the fingering of brass. By now a small crowd has gathered, and when Mr. Wilcox lifts the hood to add some oil, three heads join his under the hood in a careful survey of the engine.

"Ay-yuh," they say, "they don't make 'em like *that* no more."

"Please don't touch the brass," I say (finger-marks leave brownish green spots on the painfully polished brasswork).

"Solid brass," they say admiringly.

"Look at all that bronze in the engine."

"You can't get leather like that any more." (They don't know it was re-upholstered just a year ago).

The newest, bedizened, 485-horse-power Detroit Wunderbird can drive up to the pumps, but none of the crowd bemused by the ancient car will grant it even a glance.

People seem to be infatuated with old cars. Some of us are even so crazy about them that we own them and drive them. Is it because they are working relics of an imaginary, happier past? Is it because people are enchanted by their simple, well-made mechanisms and delightfully archaic look? Are some of the people who own them merely rich snobs?

People succumb to antique motor cars for all of these reasons and many others, too. There are now over 20,000 members of antique car clubs in the United States, though this lusting for elderly vehicles is not only an American disease. The virus exists all over the world. British Clubs like the Veteran Car Club of Great Britain and the Vintage Sports Car Club are older than their American counterparts. There are antique car clubs in every corner of the Commonwealth. Le Teuf-Teuf is a French Club, the Allgemeiner Schnauferl-Club, German. There is even a Classic Car Club of Japan!

Although most of the members of these clubs own at least one ancient motorised chariot, and a few of the richer ones own many more (I know one man who owns over two hundred), a few do not. This group may only want to receive the excellent magazines some clubs publish, or they may be interested in one of the more exotic offshoots of the hobby. Some collect brass headlights and bulb horns or old catalogues and instruction books, which they pursue with all the zeal of an archaeologist hunting the Dead Sea Scrolls.

The excitement of the chase—the tracking down and dragging home of a hoary and derelict machine—is one of the great, nerve-wracking pleasures of the game. Before I found my own grey-beard of a car, I went out on safari with the man I mentioned, the one who owns the two-hundred-odd ancient vehicles. He doesn't like publicity, so we'll call him Spencer.

Spencer, a millionaire, arrived at my place to pick me up wearing a tattered pair of overalls.

"No sense in letting the characters who might be willing to sell an old car think I'm rich," he explained. We climbed into a decrepit truck to which was hitched a trailer built for hauling cars.

"Once you buy an old car," Spencer said, "it's a good idea to drag it right home. Some of the types who've hung on to old wrecks for years are odd fish who change their minds. That's why it's a good idea to pay cash and get a receipt. If you give them a cheque, they sometimes refuse to cash it and the deal is off." Spencer had a definite series of stops in mind for this day's hunt, places where he had spotted old cars whose owners had refused to sell. "A man might throw you off his farm when you try to buy his old Ford in May, but be happy to sell it to you in December. You've got to keep coming back." He told me about one old man and his Ford.

One day Spencer, who seems to have an extra eye in the side of his head which sees old cars in the dim darkness of archaic garages, spotted an ancient Ford in a garage as he drove past. He stopped and approached the elderly gentleman who appeared to be running the establishment.

"That's a nice Model T Ford you have in there. May I look at it, sir?" (Spencer is very polite, especially where old cars are concerned).

"You may, son, you may." Spencer examined the car and, trying to hide his excitement, asked if he might buy the machine.

"That car serves a very special purpose, son. You see, it sets over a hole in the floor and if we moved the car, how'd we keep people from falling in?"

"Perhaps I could pay for filling in the hole, and then you'd sell me the car."

"Better look at the hole first, son." Spencer looked and changed his mind. It was a gigantic old greasing pit and the cost of filling it would have bought not

Preceding pages: Huge antique car meet at Hershey, Pennsylvania. The 1907 Welch which appears on the title page is seen (top left) as it looked when it was first discovered. Right: The dismantled engine of the Welch sits on the floor of Ralph Buckley's Antique Auto Shop during restoration. Mr. and Mrs. Warren S. Weiant (top right) sit in their 1899 Locomobile Steamer which was the official American entry in the 1959 Brighton Run in England. Note the mirror covering part of Weiant's left leg. This mirror was not for viewing the road, but for taking a look at the water gauge on the side of the car. The famous Twin-Six Packard (above) first came out in 1915. This car with its twelve-cylinder, 6½-litre engine was as flexible and smooth-running as a modern machine. Its only disadvantage was its two-wheel brakes.

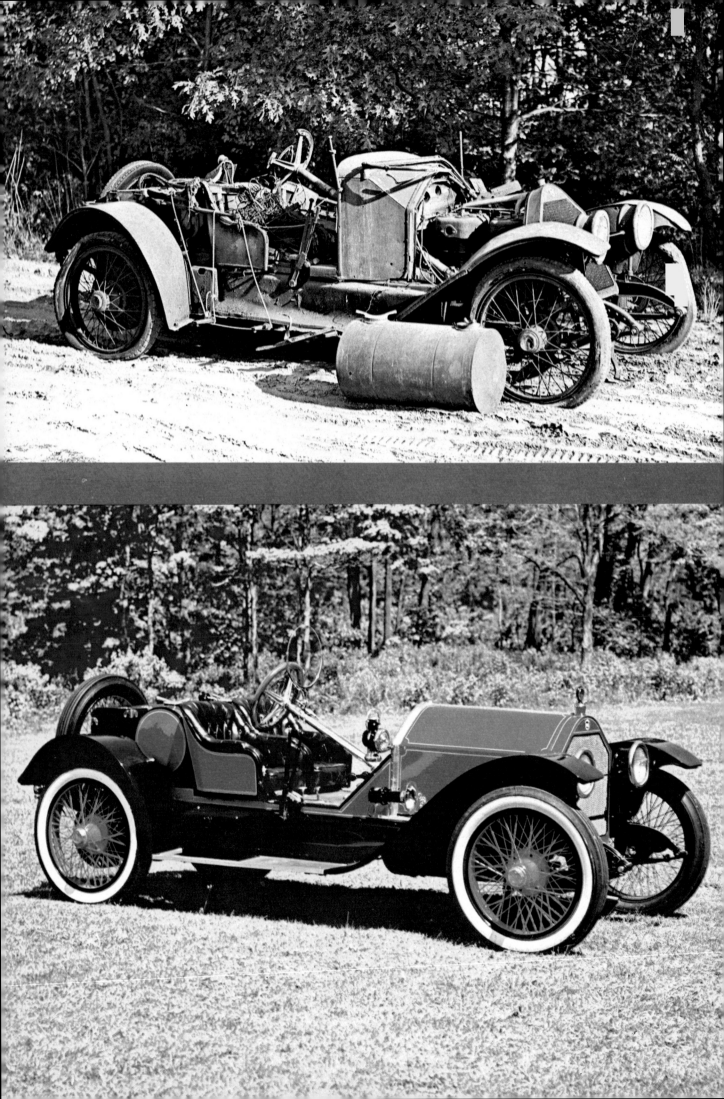

one, but three flivvers. Looking around the old garage, Spencer noticed a very rare type of Model T cylinder block, serving as a step between the front part of the garage and a room on a higher level in the rear. He tried again.

"Would you care to sell me that cylinder block, sir?"

"And what would I use for a step?" Spencer offered to have a carpenter come and build a proper step.

"Used to this block, son."

"But it's all shiny and slippery," Spencer pointed out. "You might break your neck, sir."

"That's right, son. I dern near did the other day."

"Tell you what I'll do," offered Spencer. "I'll trade you another block exactly the same size with the top all roughed up to take off the slipperiness, if you let me have this old one."

"It's a deal, son."

Spencer rushed back to his garage, but in all that welter of ancient car parts, he could find no spare Ford block. The only one in the place was operating under the hood of a nicely restored car. Spencer did the only thing any antique-car man could do. He ripped apart the more modern engine to trade its block for an older one. After all, he might have use for it some day.

We stopped at a junk yard.

"There's a wonderful 1913 Isotta-Fraschini in here that I've been trying to buy for a long time," explained Spencer.

He pointed out a rusty little mess, half-sunken into the ground, with the lower halves of its wooden-spoked wheels rotted away. The part of its wooden body that still remained was weathered to a silvery greyness, and pathetic little tatters of once-red leather upholstery stirred in the breeze. The steering wheel was gone, the hood had vanished, and the engine, exposed to years of snow and sun, was a small pile of corroded aluminium, blackened brass, and rusty iron.

"Very nice," I muttered politely.

The junkman bustled over. "Hello, Mr. Spencer. Looking over my little beauty again?"

Spencer nodded and a murmured conversation started. I moved out of earshot so as not to hinder any delicate negotiations to come. But there were no nego-

tiations, and Spencer and I got back into the truck.

"I've been offering that guy a lot more than that little car is worth, just because it will fit into a spot in my collection. It would cost thousands to restore, but he's just sentimental and won't sell. He knew that car when they were both young and to him it's still new and whole and shiny. In the meantime, he just lets it rot away so that in a few years it will unfortunately be beyond restoration."

Not all antique cars are found in such deplorable condition, Spencer explained. Sometimes cars are found in almost the same condition as they were when new. These are often the well-cared-for but never-used pets of wealthy families, who keep them warm and dry and full of oil in memory of dear old grandpa.

With thousands of collectors avidly hunting down early cars, it is becoming harder, although not entirely impossible, to find pre-World War I machines. Many people are settling for cars of the Twenties and even the Thirties. Certainly, many cars of this period were important classics; however, some of the vehicles on which much labour and money is being lavished actually are no more than mass-produced iron.

Many people have an exaggerated idea of what an antique car is worth. Hearing that a collector has paid $7,000 for, say, a gem of a 1911 Lozier, they will demand thousands for the ruin of Uncle George's 1911 Metz that he left to rot in the barn in 1912. They don't realize that perhaps nine-tenths of the Lozier's value lies in its wonderful restoration. Further, the Lozier was a high-quality car to begin with. The Metz, as Uncle George would have sadly told you, was a dog when it was new. Fifty dollars might be too much to pay for it.

An antique bought from another collector who has already gone through the pangs of restoration may be a heart-breaking disappointment, since often some so-called "restorations" by ham-handed collector-mechanics can practically ruin a car.

Some people are not satisfied with bringing a car back to its original condition; they try to improve it. They chrome-plate parts which were originally nickel-plated. They install the latest plastic upholstery upon the seats of an elderly landaulet. They paint the undersides of mudguards white. They fake the ages of cars by building early-style bodies on later chassis, etc. These are minor crimes. But they also replace tired parts, like gearboxes and differentials, with recent types from junk yards, and hide modern self-starters under the floorboards. To a meticulous restorer, these crudities are reprehensible.

Miraculous metamorphosis: This unrestored 1916 Stutz Bearcat looked a little rough before a year of labour by Kenneth Rohl and William Hoffman. Note the anachronistic cowl which had to be stripped off. Rohl and Hoffman, who are not professionals, did all the restoration except the painting and upholstering.

Amateur restorers are sometimes indifferent mechanics who can ruin irreplaceable parts beyond repair. You'll note I said "sometimes". Many a book-keeper or dentist who rushes toward his disassembled darling in the garage every night for five years does as painstaking and correct a restoration job as anyone could hope for.

If a man has the time and the ability *and* the burning desire, home restoration is the cheapest way. Professional restoration can be costly. The greatest expense, by far, is for labour, at, say, $4.00 an hour. Since it can take as many as 2,000 man-hours to bring a car back to life, commercial restorations are out of the question for many people.

Purists use as much as possible of the original car in their restorations, even tracking down things like the original sparking-plugs for their engines. The advertising columns of the antique-car-club magazines are filled with piteous pleas from such seekers after parts for their cars. It is possible, however, to buy new sparking-plugs and archaic sizes of tyres for most old machines. New parts for the really ancient vehicles are non-existent, and it is necessary either to fabricate them or to cannibalise a non-restorable car of the same type. Collectors purchase so-called "parts-cars" for this purpose.

After Spencer—his trailer still empty—had let me off at my house, I began to think about an old car a friend of mine had mentioned to me. He said it was a Welch of about 1905, that it lay in a carriage house on an estate that was about to be sold, and that he thought it could be bought.

I began reading everything I could on Welch's, which wasn't much, but I discovered that the Welch had been a high-quality car with one of the first overhead-camshaft, hemispherical-combustion-chambered engines and a fascinating multiple-clutch transmission. This was enough. By the time the caretaker of the estate let me in to look at the car, I was near feverish with desire.

The Welch was a shocking sight. It was vast, its rear disappearing into the gloom of the coach house it shared with some ancient carriages. It stood there like a weird prehistoric monster under its huge, rafter-scraping top. Its colours were indistinguishable; paintwork, woodwork, leather, brass were all the colour of thirty-one years of dust. But one look under its hood at that crazy engine and I had to have it. I haggled not. I bought it.

When a friend of mine came up with his trailer to disentomb it and haul it home for me, we found that the carriage-house door in front of the car had not been opened for thirty-one years either. A crowbar helped that. The tyres, which had been held off the floor, looked fine—round and plump; the Welch had slept on jacks. But when we tried to pump them up, the air just wheezed dismally out of unseen lesions; the tyres had petrified to wood-like hardness. Later

Vintage Sports Car Club in England races elderly sports cars. A 1,750 c.c. Alfa Romeo of the Thirties (above left) leads an Hispano-Suiza of the Twenties. Dave Garroway (above) interviews Robert S. Kiborne III near T.J. Lester's 1913 Lozier at the start of the 1957 Anglo-American Vintage Car Rally.

they had to be sawed and chiselled off the rims. Surprisingly, they supported the Welch as we towed it, creaking, out of its resting place and aboard the trailer. The brass acetylene headlamps, though dented, were complete, but one of the sidelamps was missing. We questioned the caretaker—he knew nothing about it. My friend nudged me and rubbed thumb against forefinger. I pulled out a ten dollar bill, and miraculously the sidelamp materialised. (A sidelamp like that is worth fifty dollars.)

When we finally got the Welch into my garage (the tyres were like broken-up papier-mâché from bouncing on the trailer) and had a good chance to examine it closely and soberly, I was overcome with remorse and foreboding at the enormity of the crime I had committed against the economic fortunes of my wife and kids, at the impossibility of ever making a car out of that horrifying mass of junk.

The Welch was a horror. It resembled pictures of 1907 Welch's but slightly. (We quickly discovered it was an '07, not an '05). It had been "modernised" in the style of 1915. Its one-man top was a gruesome anachronism, as was its windscreen. Some unfeeling wretch had added front doors and 1915-style mudguards. Its *derrière* had a rounded, decidedly un-1907-ish vulgarity.

"Isn't she beautiful?" I asked my wife.

"Very," she answered.

I set to. I threw away the top, ripped off that stupid windscreen and those front doors. I started to investigate the car's insides, unscrewed things, lost nuts in the distant fastnesses of its mysterious gearbox, barked my knuckles, covered myself in half-century-old grease. I gave up.

Luckily, a friend of mine was willing to take it into his Antique Auto Shop in Pleasantville, New Jersey, and restore it for me. He and his helpers took the Welch to bits; if anything was unscrewable from any other part it was unscrewed. Then they started to build a new Welch from the old parts. First they sandblasted the chassis frame to remove the paint and rubbish of half a century. Then they erected upon it the engine, the transmission, the front and rear axles. If any part was worn or broken it was rebuilt as new.

When it came time to replace the bodywork, pictures of old Welch's were studied and measured and replicas of the original mudguards were fabricated. That odd, rounded rear of the body was found to be but superimposed tinwork and was peeled off to reveal the original coachwork beneath.

231

Above is a partial view of the collection of vehicles and chassis owned by Messieurs Pichon Père et Fils at Cières, France. All the cars, even the oldest ones, are in perfect working condition. Below is an extremely rare car: the famous Panhard et Levassor model of 1894, used for a long time by Emil Levassor himself and known as "Number 5"; Phénix 2-cylinder engine with hot-tube ignition. Above right: M. William Vaux and his "detachable" 1905 Daimler. Lower right: In front of the Rochetaillée-sur-Saône Museum: a 1911 Léon Bollée, a 1908/1910 Panhard Levassor and, in the background, a 1923 Renault 6-cylinder 40 h.p., torpedo type sports car.

A year went by. One day my friend phoned me to come and get my car. I had, of course, been down to Pleasantville a few times in the interim. The first time I couldn't even find the car, it was in so many small bits and so dispersed about the shop. The second time I had seen the engine, all polished brass and shining steel, being set into the frame. This time I couldn't quite believe my eyes, for as I rounded the corner and drove up to the shop, there, shining in sparkling paint, its brasswork shimmering in the sunlight, was a brand new 1907 Welch.

But what do you do with an ancient car once you've found it and brought it back to life? You can drive it, of course, as I do my other car. But there are some disadvantages to such use, due mostly to people in modern machines. Their drivers gape at you instead of at the road, and it's horrifying to watch the number of near accidents you cause by being a visual attraction.

Most ancient cars are used largely in connection with the events organised by the antique car clubs: meets, parades, and rallies.

Don't for a moment imagine that an antique-car meet is approached in any attitude of levity. To the participant in a big meet, such as the giant conclave of old cars held in Hershey, Pennsylvania, each autumn, it is a deadly serious and heart-burning business. For weeks before a meet he tries to divine the attitudes and foibles of the judges who will be examining the cars grouped in the same class as his (there are some nineteen different classes separating the steamers from the petrol-driven cars, the 1905 cars from the classics, etc.). Will the judges be impressed with a periwinkle-blue cylinder block? Should he paint the wheels or leave them natural?

But mostly, he—and his wife—and his children—clean the car. Cleaning the car doesn't mean just cleaning the car—not to the trophy-hungry antique-car club member. After he gets it much cleaner and shinier than you would dream possible, he *really* starts cleaning. He attacks crevices with tooth-brushes, even pipe cleaners, and not just on the body-work, either. He delves into the dark recesses of the engine, he waxes and polishes the drive shaft. The sacred brasswork is a career in itself, requiring hour after hour of dedicated rubbing with the owner's

"Commemoration Run" from London to Brighton each November attracts hundreds of pre-1905 vehicles and millions of spectators. Left: A group of competitors leaves Hyde Park. An iron-tyred 1895 Panhard Levassor (above) leads the procession through London streets. On the right, a competitor stops en route to adjust his 1902 Panhard Levassor. Top of page: The start of a handicap race for vintage sports and racing cars at Silverstone.

Left: Light two-seater Type 13 Darracq, 1913. 4-cylinder engine, 13 h.p., maximum speed: 40 m.p.h. Below: 1916 Pierce-Arrow Model 66 Raceabout during the first Anglo-American Vintage Car Rally in England in 1955. Right: A 1908 Hutton. Entered in the 1957 Anglo-American Vintage Car Rally, the Hutton had been built by Napier for the Isle of Man Tourist Trophy Race.

favourite brass polish, selected from among the many kinds whose merits have been seriously discussed between his fellow brass polishers.

The richer antiquers avoid this labour. They have squads—nay battalions—of flunkies to prepare their machines for meets. I know of one such gentleman, a far-western oil tycoon, who boasts even a "Chief Curator" for his vast collection of beautifully restored cars. (This is *not* the man who has so many antiques he piles them on end to save room).

It's delightful to drive towards a meet in your nicely tuned and polished antique car, waving happily to other antiques on their way to the meet, but you and the other people on the road are taking the grave risk of not winning a trophy that day. The smart and experienced cup hunter brings his machine, swathed in protective coverings, aboard a specially built trailer. Not for him an engine spotted with oil from actually being run, or a chassis defiled with the dust of the road.

At the meet the cars of each class are lined up in groups to await the judgment. Sometimes it takes hours of waiting for the judges to get to your car, but this period is one of the pleasanter aspects of the day. You talk to the people around you, discussing cars and other meets where the unspeakable judges had not the perception to give your beloved machine even an honourable mention.

Suddenly, the moment of truth. The judges, grim-faced, clip-boards in hand, surround your car. Each carries a marking chart for your car which rigidly allots (or subtracts) points for condition of brass, of upholstery, of paintwork, cleanliness of engine, etc. They even ask you to start the engine, noting how readily it commences, how it sounds (after this the trailer-the-car-to-the-meet boys feverishly polish away any specks of oil that may have sullied their lavender engine blocks).

There are even contests for people who dress up in costumes that they fondly imagine are of the same

236

period as their cars. This dressing up in funny clothes and false moustaches is dying out somewhat in the more sophisticated eastern meets, but in the Far West it is still de rigueur for women to wear plumed hats and lace dresses, while the men appear in top hats (to which are affixed goggles), string ties, violently checked tail coats, and spats. If you showed up at a British meet looking like that, they'd chuck you into the Thames.

The big British meet is the Commemoration Run from London to Brighton each November. This event celebrates the Emancipation Run of 1896 which marked the end of the notorious Red Flag Law. Limited to "veteran" cars,—under the rules of the Veteran Car Club of Great Britain, only machines built in 1904 or earlier are "veterans"—hundreds of such early cars leave Hyde Park, usually on a miserable, rainy morning, bound for Brighton on the south coast. More spectators show up along the way to cheer on the snuffling cars than at any motoring

event—over 3,000,000 in 1960 — and there is no nonsense with trailers. You get your car to Brighton under its own power or you don't get a plaque.

Another thriving British organisation, The Vintage Sports Car Club, looks back to the great past of sports and racing machines. They concern themselves with such sports cars as existed before 1931. But they don't just polish them and look at them; they race them and engage in tough climbing contests.

In 1954, Cecil Clutton, the president of this vigorous outfit, organised a contest between the Veteran Motor Car Club of America and his Vintage Sports Car Club; the Anglo-American Vintage Car Rally. Early American sporting vehicles sailed for England to engage in a contest with ten pre-1931 British sports cars. After eight days of rallying, hill climbing, and bending races (a race in and out of artificial obstacles), the British won. Two years later the Americans had their revenge in a return contest in the States.

MASS
PRODUCTION

FRANCE

It is hardly necessary in the opening paragraphs of a chapter on mass production to dwell at length on the importance of the part played by the motor car in the everyday life of industrialised nations.

This can be judged from the 111 million private cars which consume petrol on all five continents: more than 73 million in America, 29.3 million in Western Europe, 2 million in Africa, 2.4 million in Asia, 2.9 million in the Pacific and 1.4 million in the countries of the Soviet block. During the last two years, world production has fluctuated between 13 and 15 million cars per year, half of which are manufactured by American factories.

Other factors, both technical and economic, have also favoured the motor car industry: thanks to mass production, conveyor belts and automation (transfer-machines in particular), the motor industry produces high quality products at relatively low prices. The man in the street tends to forget that a motor car is a very complex thing, with more than 20,000 parts in a single car!

Mass production has brought this achievement within reach of the average man to such an extent that by 1st January 1964 there were in France 7.5 million cars on the road (i.e. one car for every 6.4 inhabitants), as against 1.8 million in 1938. If one takes into account a virtual standstill in production for a period of more than seven war years, this achievement is fairly impressive.

In 1938, 16 manufacturers – Berliet, Chenard, Citröen, Delahaye, Hotchkiss, Licorne, Ford, Panhard, Peugeot, Renault, Rosengart, Simca, Salmson, Talbot, Voisin and Bugatti – produced a total of 183,000 cars.

In 1950, twelve years later, ten of these makes were still being manufactured. Berliet, Chenard, Licorne, Rosengart, Voisin and Bugatti had disappeared. The year's output exceeded 250,000 units.

In 1964, fourteen years later, 4 large and one small manufacturer – Renault, Citroën, Peugeot, Simca and Panhard – were still in the running, and one new small factory had sprung up: Facel. Nevertheless, total production was six times greater than in 1950, for in 1963 it totalled 1,520,000 units. The tendency to merge is particularly noticeable, since the four large manufacturers account for 98% of the total production.

A survey of the trend towards mergers shows that in the last ten years Simca has acquired Ford S.A.F. and Talbot, while Panhard has seen its fate linked with that of Citroën. New mergers are always possible, and agreements with friendly foreign firms multiply: Régie Nationale (i.e. Renault) has crossed the Atlantic to reach an agreement with American Motors, approached Italy for talks with Alfa Romeo, and co-operated with Man in Germany in the field of heavy commercial vehicles. These agreements are, however, fairly limited, both on the technical and the commercial level. Simca now comes under the Chrysler Corporation (which holds 63% of the capital), but their policy is still one of French design, employing French labour and using French materials.

Through this industrial concentration, the present production of the French industry has expanded beyond the wildest dreams of any manufacturer in 1938:

700 2 CV Citroëns per day. This car was built by Pierre Boulanger to the formula of "four wheels under an umbrella enabling a countryman to carry a basket of eggs without breaking one of them". 158,000 2 CV Citroëns originally launched in 1947 were manufactured in 1963.

1,000 Renault R4's per day. (The millionth R4 rolled off the line on February 1, 1966.) This model was first introduced in October 1961 to replace the then popular 4 CV of which more than a million were built in 15 years. With the 4 CV came the firm's first attempts in the field of front-wheel drive.

Preceding pages: Fiat luxury saloon, 2,300 c.c. type, engine with 6 cylinders in line, speed 93 m.p.h. Its "trapeze" style coachwork, allowing wide visibility, is characteristic of the world-wide tendency which originated in Italy and inspired cars like the BMC range and the Peugeot 404. Above: Citroën DS 19 designed by Henry Chaperon. Right: Peugeot 404 with bodywork by Pinin Farina of Turin. There is a coupé of the same model and both are equipped with a fuel injection system.

Besides these two utility models, French industry provides the motorist with four popular, mass-produced cars which belong essentially to the economy class of under 6 h.p. totalling 3.6 million units in France alone – or almost half the cars on French roads.

The Dauphine, introduced in 1956, is well known not only in France but also throughout the world, and more than 2 million units have been manufactured. Gordini-Dauphines, the 'upgraded' model, come off the production line at the rate of 500 a day.

The Renault R8, the current 5 h.p. model, came out in August 1962, with which the firm hoped to retain customers interested in a more modern design.

The R16, introduced in 1965 and made at the new Renault factory in France, is a four-cylinder 1470 c.c. model of completely fresh design.

The Citroën Ami 6 was launced in 1961. This 3 h.p. model is still faithful to front-wheel drive, and differs from the 2 h.p. model in that it has distinctive bodywork, that it is extremely comfortable and that its performance is good. Over 500 cars of this model are produced daily – the production rate has increased since the new factory in Rennes opened in 1964.

The Simca 1,000 was also introduced in 1961. Seven hundred cars come off the production line daily. Just like the R8, the Simca 1,000 is a good

Opposite left: The Renault Caravelle has 2 + 2 seats, with a hard-top sliding roof; engine with 5 bearings, 950 c.c. capacity, 4 cylinders; disc brakes on all four wheels.
Opposite below: Simca 1000 coupé, designed by G. Bertone and mass-produced in collaboration with this designer; capable of 84 m.p.h.
Above: Panhard 24 CT. When this new model made its debut in 1963 it created quite a stir. However, the motor is the same as the one used in Panhard's P.L. 17, Tigre 848 3 c.c. which develops 60 h.p. at 5,750 r.p.m. Its top speed is 95 m.p.h.
Right: Facel 3; equipped with the Volvo sport 1.8-litre engine which develops 108 h.p. at 6.000 r.p.m. All four wheels have servo-assisted disc brakes. Its top speed is 113 m.p.h.

example of the present functional trend in popular cars. In line with this trend is the transverse-engined Peugeot 204, that manufacturer's smallest vehicle since the last war.

In the range of medium-sized cars, French factories daily produce 500 Simca 1300's, (a model first seen in 1963 and which now houses an engine developed from the Aronde unit), and 250 Peugeot 403's.

At a higher price level, one finds the more powerful French makes, namely:

The Peugeot 404, this firm's bread-and-butter line, the Sochaux battle horse since 1960, manufactured at a rate of 800 units a day. Peugeot, as is well known, is the oldest of the four largest French firms; it is also the most provincial and is still a family firm. Nevertheless, its products are world famous for their quality.

The Simca 1500 is the sister of the 1300 but with an engine permitting much higher speeds.

Mass production of this smart model started in October 1963.

Years ahead of its time, the car from the second largest firm in the French motor industry, considered the most individual, Citroën favourably impressed world technicians with the DS 19, a model which is brimful of original features. The ID and the DS are successors to the famous front-wheel drive 11 h.p. car, which, after 23 years of its production (1934-1957), held the world record for one-model longevity. The latest version of the DS 21, the Pallas, was introduced in 1965, and in addition to general refinements of construction and trim, has quartz-iodine lamps as standard, and incorporates a system of self-levelling headlights.

As one can see, the 1960's started in France with the birth of a wide range of new popular models, with a capacity varying between 600 c.c. and 956 c.c. The Renault R8 is a good example of the

French motor industry today with its choice of engine power. Its 956 c.c. capacity is exactly within the tax limit for the 5 h.p.: it shows how much influence taxation can exercise on the construction and development of a car. In France taxation is the real chief engineer of the motor industry.

At the other end of the scale, the range of two-litre cars is noticeably reduced: only one model (DS - ID), as against three in 1956. The Vedette and the Frégate have disappeared, and a replacement does not seem called for. There is nothing comparable, then, with the Fiat 2,300, the Mercedes 220, or the 2.4 Jaguar. Customers must needs turn to foreign makes, and this in a country where famous names are evidence of the quality which French technicians can attain in this field.

Left: René Bonnet Djet 1100 c.c. Top speed of 110 m.p.h., rear-engined, discs on all four wheels. A more powerful version is also made.
Right: Alpine coupé G.T.4., a Tour de France G.T. model derived from the Renault R.8 and Caravelle. The engine comes in either 956 or 998 or 1,108 c.c.s and develops 55 to 80 h.p., depending on the model. Maximum speed about 115 m.p.h. Disc brakes on all 4 wheels.
Below: The celebrated 15 CV Citroën, planned in 1934 as a 4-cylinder pushrod-operated overhead-valve engine, bore and stroke 72 x 80 mm., 1,200 c.c., was for over twenty years the toughest of the great European cars. Opposite: A Daimler Majestic saloon, 8-cylinder V-type engine, 4,500 c.c. capacity, capable of 121 m.p.h.

GREAT BRITAIN

Immediately after the last war British Car manufacturers began production of civilian vehicles with the same – or only slightly modified – designs as they used in the Thirties. For years they ran happily along on technical knowledge gained a couple of decades previously, feeding their products to the eagerly waiting and patient British public, who had been deprived of new transport for some eight years.

The situation lasted until the late Fifties. Then with a thud, the bottom began to drop out of the market. European cars were flooding into Britain. Even with import and purchase tax they sold well.

Some hard thinking was done in high automotive circles. Finishes began to improve, new designs appeared, imaginative plans were laid.

By 1960, the world began to remember that "Buy British" was an invitation to purchase quality (if not service) and exports climbed.

British manufacturers realised that their fortunes stood or fell by the designs — and the finish — of the products. The planners shifted into top gear again, with the result that for a second time in two years British cars — of the popular and the connoisseur type — are leading in worldwide appeal.

B.M.C.

Under the blanket heading of B.M.C. are the marques Austin, Austin Healey, M.G., Morris, Riley, Wolseley. In the makers' lists are seventy-four different variants on offer.

The Austin Healey Sprite, a comparatively recent small sports car costing under £650 has been redesigned and has acquired an almost identical twin in the M.G. Midget. The Austin Healey 3000 sports car has lately been given an increase in power by the addition of another carburettor and other refinements.

Most popular of all in the B.M.C. range – and fast becoming a mark of the discerning "man about town" are the fantastic little Austin and Morris Minis. With their revolutionary "sideways" power units and amazingly roomy interiors, plus front wheel drive, high cruising speed and liquid suspension, this diminutive pair have scooped the market in city-drivers.

For the sportsman, the driver who likes to astonish his fellow roadsters, there are the Austin and Morris Cooper, the latter of which won the Monte Carlo Rally in 1964. Now with the 1100 variants and the more recent 1800's, all based on the Mini formula, BMC's range is the largest in the country.

FORD

To fill the gap between its small car, Anglia, and its heavier models, the Zephyrs, Ford introduced the Classic in 1961. It had a power unit of 1,340 c.c. and developed 54 b.h.p. Its equipment included two pairs of headlights in the modern style, and its rear window raked back much like that of the Anglia. Soon after it was launched Ford put out the exotic Capri model, a two/four seater with identical machinery to that of the Classic.

In 1962 Ford took the plunge with a completely new pair of Zephyrs in four- and six-cylinder models, plus a Zodiac which as usual is a six-cylinder Zephyr with trimmings. The same year the Cortina appeared, and the following year saw the launching of the Corsair. Now with the 1498 c.c. Cortina GT winning many international rallies, the Lotus Cortina and the Anglo-American Ford GT gaining laurels on the circuit, Ford has truly entered the sporting world.

VAUXHALL

This thriving subsidiary of the American organisation, General Motors, was not long ago in some trouble over the design of its car, the Victor. Its American influenced design was not fully appreciated in Britain, and sales sagged. Now it has been completely redesigned in the contemporary European manner, and is a sleek and beautiful car. The wheelbase, length and track are bigger than the previous model, and the bodywork has a smooth line that was noticeably absent in its predecessor. In addition to the standard version, Vauxhall have the VX/490 which sports two carburettors and front-wheel discs.

The big-built over 2½-litre Cresta has been re-designed and bears the unmistakable family stamp of General Motors. It is a smooth, 6-cylinder saloon made for speed and comfort. In the small car range the Viva, produced in 1963, sells like hot cakes.

ROOTES

The Rootes Group produces the Hillman in its various forms, the Singer Gazelle and Vogue, the Sunbeam and Humber.

The Sunbeam Alpine, dart-shaped and rapid, has for some years been enhancing its excellent reputation. The small Hillman Imp and Singer Chamois have been added to the group's range, and the Sunbeam Tiger with its V8 4.2-litre engine takes them into the 'big-banger' field.

TRIUMPH

With the same chassis as its forebears the Triumph TR4 and now the TR4A were built with new and sporting bodylines. At under £1,000 the TR4A now provides buyers with a 2,138 c.c. power unit and potential speeds of over 110 m.p.h. The scaled-down version, the 1147 c.c. Spitfire has proved a best-seller, and the new Triumph 2000 and 1300 are fast carving a place for themselves in the world's markets.

The now well-tried Herald range – the 1200 and 12/50, and the six cylinder Vitesse, with their all-round independent suspension and sectionalised bodies, continue to be popular on the family front.

JAGUAR

Since the war Jaguars have adopted the philosophy of making elegance and performance doubly attrac-

Page 246, top: Vauxhall VX 490 model, 1508 c.c. capacity, 88 h.p. Centre: A British Ford Cortina. Bottom: The British Motor Corporation's M.G. 1100. Its transverse engine and unique hydrolastic suspension make this model one of the most advanced in the automotive world. Right: Austin-Mini-Cooper saloon, front wheel drive, luxury finish. Sideways mounted engine of 990 c.c. capacity, maximum speed about 87 m.p.h.

tive by not charging the earth for their products. From the 2.4-litre Mk 2 at just under fourteen hundred pounds to the "E" at nearly two thousand, the company has given value – much more than normal value – for money. And it has paid them handsomely.

The Jaguar E-type, now with a 4.2 litre unit, develops a potent 265 b.h.p. at 5,400 r.p.m., a long way from the old XK 120, its great-grandfather.

The Mark 10, which now also houses the 4.2 unit, gives 255 b.h.p. at 5,400 r.p.m. – and yet is completely docile in town traffic.

ASTON MARTIN

"For the fortunate few", as one motoring magazine puts it, the Aston Martin range is small and exclusive. That is, it excludes anyone with less than £4,998 to spend on private transport! Crowning effort of the David Brown organisation is the Aston Martin DB6 convertible. With a top speed in the Grand Prix class — its maximum under test in Britain was over 150 m.p.h. — this car can accelerate from rest to 70 m.p.h. in less than 10 seconds.

The DB6, successor to the DB5, was introduced in October 1965 and is a true four-seater. With its 3,995 c.c. Vantage engine developing a shattering 325 b.h.p. at 5,500 r.p.m., this is a car for the expert and the connoisseur.

LOTUS

Engineer Colin Chapman, head of the Lotus Company, is the only major racing man in Britain to give serious thought to selling modified versions of his essentially track-event vehicles to the ordinary public.

The Elan is a tuned down, plushed up version of what was once a race-bred competition car. Its four-cylinder twin overhead camshaft Lotus unit of 1,558 c.c. capacity develops 105 b.h.p. at 5,500 r.p.m., all of which brands it a car for the enthusiast rather than a shopping vehicle for the family. On the circuit the car has won many international events. For the impecunious, there is the Lotus 7 and Super 7. These like the Elan, can be bought in component form to avoid tax, at £499 and £585 respectively. The Super 7 normally houses a 1,498 c.c. Cortina engine, much modified by Cosworth and extremely vivid in performance. The four cylinder unit delivers 95 b.h.p. at 6,000 revs with twin Webers, and has a maximum speed of a shade over 100 m.p.h.

This, of course, is by no means a comprehensive survey of the British motor industry. We have not, for instance, touched on Rolls-Royce, who go their regal way in company with Bentley, selling their magnificent products for modest ransoms, clothing their noble frames in bodies by the aristocracy of coachbuilders, Young, Mulliner, and Park Ward. We have not spoken of Rover, the established but far-sighted company whose policy of developing the turbine engine may well prove to be the pioneering of a future means of propulsion on the highway.

Then there are the smaller companies, Turner, T.V.R., Warwick, Gordon-Keeble, and the Fairthorpe organisation owned by Air Vice Marshal (Pathfinder) Bennett. All these have their eye firmly on the future of the industry.

Opposite page: Rolls-Royce Phantom V: limousine with large wheelbase, 8-cylinder engine of V-type with capacity of 6,230 c.c. Above: S2 type Bentley. Same engine as the Rolls-Royce; streamlined, low-slung coachwork, speed 112 m.p.h.

Below: Jaguar Mk X. Same 3,800 c.c. 240 h.p. engine as the Jaguar E-type sports model; speed about 118-124 m.p.h.

WESTERN
GERMANY

Above: Mercedes Benz 200 SE type saloon. 6-cylinder 2,193 c.c. engine, 134 h.p., fuel injection. Below: Volkswagen luxury "coach", 1,192 c.c. capacity engine, equipped with soft convertible roof; one of 5 million Volkswagens built since 1945.

We have here the second largest manufacturer in the world after the United States: 2.4 million private cars came off the production line in Germany in 1963, and this figure increased to 2.5 million in 1964, in spite of the disappearance of the Borgward group. In the matter of cars, the "German miracle" is most apparent: this miracle is largely due to the giant, that is to Volkswagen. In this firm, the term mass production is particularly valid: 4,500 cars a day, including 1,000 "VW 1500's" (this model first appeared in 1961 and does not seem to have been as fabulously successful as the famous "1200").

Volkswagens came out of the factory (or what was left of it) at a rate of 1,785 cars in 1945. In 1961, for the first time, Volkswagen exceeded the "million within the year". And since 1945 the bodywork has hardly changed!

This vast production, hinged until now on one single model, has made it possible for the German motorist to benefit from a particularly favourable price policy. Today Volkswagen is the *bête noire* of all European manufacturers of popular cars. It is their most dangerous competitor, both in its huge production and in the quality of its after-sales service.

Opel, on the other hand, was a General Motors bridge-head in Germany. It manufactured 555,000 private cars in 1963, the main part of the production being based on the famous Rekord model, which was available in several versions. In the autumn of 1962 appeared a new model at a rate of 1,000 cars a day.

This new model, bearing an old name, the Kadett, increases the ranks of 1,000 c.c. cars in Europe.

Another American bridge-head in Germany was that of Ford, who strengthened their position among the large firms and sent 167,000 Taunus 17 H's on the roads of Germany and the world during 1963. The TS version, with a hotted up engine, is for motorists who want performance.

In September 1962 Ford Germany launched the much-heralded Taunus 12M (code-name "Cardinal") a neat little car with front-wheel drive and a V4, 60°, 1,183 c.c. power unit.

Mercedes-Benz, most famous of all German makes, has just celebrated its 80th birthday. Its luxurious limousines bring the motorist quality, comfort, and high technical achievement. A car like the 300 limousine contains a perfect combination of the most advanced refinements: pneumatic suspension, disc brakes, direct injection and power-steering. And the 600 which came out in 1963 is rightly considered a rival to the Rolls Royce.

Auto-Union, which became a subsidiary of Mercedes-Benz in 1960, holds a dangerous trump card with its D.K.W. "F.12", now also available as a luxury model, the "F.102", of 1,175 c.c. The Roadster 1,000 Sp is also in this range, and is famous for the remarkable efficiency of its two-stroke engines.

Besides its 700 c.c. "Luxus" model, B.M.W. now has a 1,500 with a 4-cylinder engine inclined at 30° developing 90 h.p. Even before it was marketed, this sports saloon designed by Michelotti and equipped with disc brakes, attracted 25,000 orders from B.M.W. fans who had not even had the opportunity to try it out! It is also available as an "1800" and as an "1800 TI" version, developing 102 and 124 h.p. respectively.

N.S.U. continues to produce its Prinz 4 (598 c.c.) and has brought out several versions of the Prinz 1000. Latest of the line is the Wankel Spider, with the advanced rotary engine.

Porsche continues with its six-cylinder 911 two-seater coupe, and has introduced the 912, a 1.6 litre four-cylinder car with the same bodyshell.

Opposite page, top: Cologne Ford, Taunus type 17 M. Centre, left: NSU Prinz IV. Centre, right: Porsche 901 coupé. Below: B.M.W. "700" coupé. This page, top: Auto-Union, 1000 SP coupé. Centre: Opel, Rekord. Below: VW, Karmann-Ghia 1500 coupé.

ITALY

The Italian motor car industry, which is concentrated in the two strongholds of the north, Milan and Turin, has made continuous progress at an astonishing rate during the last few years. Before the last war it was severely limited, for the production of private cars was less than 60,000 per year, but now the industry is in full expansion, developing at a rate unequalled by any other European country: 100,000 cars in 1950, 320,000 in 1957, 1,100,000 in 1963.

For a long time Italy was a very poor country, but it is now undergoing great economic expansion. It is one of the few countries in a position to export labour and therefore has no problem in recruiting enough workmen for its own needs. Nor has the home market nearly reached saturation point. Italy is in fact the last motorised of the Common Market countries, with only one vehicle for every 17 inhabitants. Of course the proportion is much higher in Northern Italy, for in Calabria there is only one car for every 80 inhabitants.

Newcomers to Italy are always astonished by the Italian passion for cars, a passion which was anticipated by the scientific genius of Leonardo da Vinci several centuries before it could be turned into reality. It is in evidence at all times and in all places. Most Italians drive about in a little Fiat, but the famous names ring in their ears daily: Alfa-Romeo, Ferrari, Maserati, Pinin Farina, Mille Miglia, Targa Florio, Monza, etc.

In the field of mass-produced cars there is only one name: *FIAT*. In this connection Italy has the most concentrated motor car industry in the world. In 1963 Fiat built 900,000 private cars, which represents 81% of total production. The vast Turin company offers the consumer an extremely wide range: twenty models with engine capacities varying between 500 and 2,300 c.c. Output of the popular 600 (its capacity has been increased to 750 c.c.) reached 340,000 in 1963 and has far exceeded a million since it was first produced. The 500 is particularly suitable for use in town, while its younger sister the Giardiniera is an all-purpose vehicle which has aroused keen interest. The remarkable career of the Millecento continues—it is still produced at the rate of 180,000 a year, while that of the 1300-1500 models has a brilliant future: outstanding performances (the engineer Lampredi, who came from Ferrari, has equipped them with 72 and 80 h.p. units), disc brakes and compact dimensions. Finally, the 1800 and 2300 models offer the more demanding motorists the easy handling of the 6-cylinder type.

ALFA-ROMEO produce about 55,000 cars per year; the Giulietta, in its various versions, the quite recent Giulia, and a 6-cylinder 2600 which marks the return to the great Alfas of the past.

LANCIA continues to produce its three basic models Fulvia, Flavia and Flaminia, and the total production of the range reaches nearly 40,000 cars.

CISITALIA is offering an 850 saloon model, developed from the Fiat 600 D, with an increased engine capacity of 847 c.c. It has disc brakes.

ABARTH are noteworthy for their astonishing commercial success, perhaps the most outstanding of the last few years. Their model factory offers a range of unrivalled sports car types, with engine capacities of 700 to 1,300 c.c. The success of the little Scorpion reflects the determined and selective character of their director, Carlos Abarth, a former speed-cop with a passion for car racing.

MASERATI are known for their luxury Gran Turismo models. The 3500 with Lucas fuel-injection, now develops 235 h.p. The factory continues to make the astonishing 5-litre model, the highest cylinder capacity of any car produced in Italy.

FERRARI. The lord of Maranello, the Commendatore Enzo Ferrari remains the leading figure on the production and technical side. His thoroughbred cars are the products of continuous and unequalled success on the race-track.

Finally, to conclude this rapid description of Italian mass-production, on both small and large-scale lines, it should be noted that overseas manufacturers are beginning to establish themselves in Italy: Alfa-Romeo are assembling Ondines and Renault R4's, Innocenti are assembling Morris 1100's and there is now an "Italian Panhard" factory in northern Italy.

But Italy is also the country of coachwork, and what a rich field that is.

The strong influence exercised by the Italian master coachwork designers on today's style is well known. The greatest manufacturers in every country turn to the designers of Milan and Turin when they make

Left-hand page: Fiat 600 a small 4-seater equipped with a 767 c.c. engine in the rear. Above: Alfa Romeo Giulia Spyder with its elegant coachwork designed by Pinin Farina. It is equipped with a 1,570 c.c. engine which develops 106 h.p. It has a 5 forward speed gear box and can reach 105 m.p.h. Below: Fiat 2300 S coupé, built to a Ghia design.

255

Above: Lancia Flaminia GT coupé, coachwork by Pinin Farina. Below: Alfa Romeo coach, 2,600 c.c. 6-cylinder engine.

plans, and are ready to put the finishing touches to prototypes of future mass-production models.

During the last few years the Italian coachwork designers have been turning more and more towards mass-production of special coachwork for manufacturers who in this way can include these models in their regular production programme.

PININ FARINA is the leading coachwork designer. The daily output of his workshops is forty car bodies per day: Giulia Spyder, Ferrari 250 Gran Turismo, Flaminia coupé. His drawing-offices brought to life the Fiat 1200 and 1500 saloons, the Peugeot 403 and 404, the whole BMC range from the Austin A40 (it is in fact rather difficult to tell the difference at any distance between a Peugeot 404 and an Austin A60!) and the Lancia Flaminia.

Under the leadership of the engineer Luigi Segne, the firm of *GHIA* are equally prosperous. They are well-known through their long-standing collaboration with Chrysler, and for their daring futurist-style prototypes, such as Gilda, Dart and Selene.

The Fiat 2300S Coupé bears Ghia's signature, which is already familiar abroad, thanks to the coupés and saloons produced by Volkswagen Karmann-Ghia.

TOURING manufacture the Giulietta Sprint for Alfa Romeo, the Lancia Flaminia coupé and saloon, a Maserati 3500 Gran Turismo coupé, and carry out certain special types of coachwork.

BERTONE work mainly for Alfa Romeo. This coachbuilder designed the Giulietta Sprint coupé, and has built more than 200,000 of them since 1955. Lancia entrusted him with the manufacture, at the rate of 4 to 6 a day, of the Flaminia limousine, which was

designed originally by Pinin Farina. Bertone is also responsible for the coachwork of the NSU Prinz sports model, and the Simca 1000 coupé.

VIOTTI, ALLEMANO, VIGNALE and *ZAGATO* are active on a secondary level but are still responsible for some outstanding creations. Lastly *GIOVANNI MICHELOTTI* is noteworthy among the stylists: prototypes for Standard, Triumph, BMW, Osca and other firms came from his workshops. Michelotti also collaborates with Vignale and Allemano.

Above: Maserati coupé, 3,500 c.c. GT with fuel injection, coachwork by Touring. Below: Ferrari 4,000 c.c. Super-America model; 2+2 seater with streamlined coachwork by Pinin Farina.

257

EASTERN EUROPE

The U.S.S.R. is not usually open-handed with information about its production (especially as far as marques and types are concerned), and as a result it is difficult to get a clear picture of car output in this country. It is certain, however, that motor-car manufacture has remained very backward. Cars are considered as luxuries and there are only 700,000 of them in use, which works out as 320 inhabitants to one car. This figure is thought-provoking, especially when one remembers that in the United States there is one car for less than three inhabitants and that in France there is one car for every seven. There is a similar lack of proportion in output: fewer than 2,000,000 private cars were built in the U.S.S.R. in 1963, just about equal to French production in 1938! Nevertheless it is noteworthy that U.S.S.R. is the third largest producer of lorries, coming after the United States and Britain.

The first Soviet tourist car was placed on sale in 1927. It was made by the Russian "SPARTAK" factories and was called NAMI I.

Then a curious thing happened: Russia asked America to help her set up a modern automobile factory. Henry Ford promptly sent over a delegation of American technicians to supervise the erection of a new up-to-date factory and to get production started. For this occasion the old A-type Ford was brought out again and on the Soviet production lines it was given the name of GAZ - A.

Russian factories are customarily named after national political personalities. For a time the Gorki factories, which Ford had helped, were called ZIM. It was here that the Pobjeda (Victory) was first produced, and according to the Russians it was the first car in Europe with streamlined wings. In 1950 the large 8-seater ZIM was also launched. The old Ford factories are now building the Volga and Tchaïka cars (apparently in considerable numbers) while the Moscow factories are producing the solid little Moskvitch.

At present the range of specifically Soviet cars is as follows:

Skoda hard-top saloon, Felicia type, 4-cylinder 1,220 c.c. engine.

Above left: Tchaika convertible luxury cars, 8-cylinder V-type engine. Right: Ceremonial car, Zil III limousine type, 8-cylinder V-type engine developing 220 h.p.

ZAPOROJETS. The only car with a small engine capacity, 748 c.c., a four-seater with two doors, a 4-cylinder V-type rear engine, air-cooled. Before mass-production got seriously under way it was already announced that it would appear in a new form, with a more powerful engine (887 c.c. developing 28 h.p.).

VOLGA. A fairly large car of 2,500 c.c. capacity, with 4-cylinder engine, 75 h.p., similar to the British Humber. The engine block is in light metal.

ZIL III. A luxury car, similar to the Rolls-Royce in its gauge, height and weight. Radiator shell of the Plymouth type, outline similar to the Buick, engine capacity 5,980 c.c., 8 cylinders, 200 h.p.

TCHAÏKA M13. A luxury car of 5,500 c.c., eight cylinders and 195 h.p., comparable to the Ford Galaxy. It is equipped with twin headlamps.

MOSKVITCH 408. 4 seater, 1,360 c.c., 45 h. p., speed of 71 m.p.h. Similar to the Opel 1956 model. This car is produced on a large scale and is particularly sturdy. It also exists with independent 4-wheel drive.

Soviet technicians do not usually care to admit that the Russian car industry tends to copy foreign models. When they are questioned thoroughly they admit in the end that it is useless and ridiculous to "discover America a second time". And one of them has summed up the policy they adopt in these terms: "It is true that we take foreign cars and study them

thoroughly. We submit them to stringent tests in order to study their powers of endurance. Then we hand over the parts which have survived and can still be used to our manufacturers and we urge them to make Russian cars out of them.

"Why should we wear ourselves out repeating the expensive and long-drawn out research when we can find all the data in good existing cars?"

At the present time Czechoslovakia builds 60,000 cars per year, but it has undertaken a vast expansion programme which aims to bring annual production up to 400,000 cars in 1970.

SKODA are responsible for the greater part of Czech production, with their Octavia Super 1200, engine capacity 1,089 c.c., 43 h.p., and its reputation for sturdiness is known all over the world. This model also exists as a coupé and as an estate car.

The long-established *TATRA* factories have carried out pioneer work, notably in connection with the central column chassis, the rear engine, air-cooling, stream-lining and independent suspension. At present they are building the Tatra 603, engine capacity 2,472 c.c., with an air-cooled V-8 rear engine.

The fact that Czechoslovakian car factories cannot obtain supplies from specialised manufacturers, and are forced to do their own designing and manufacturing of accessories, may in part explain why production costs are still high, and output limited.

SAAB

DAF

HONDA

Cars from other parts of the world. Opposite page, above: The Saab, winner of the 1962 and 1963 Monte Carlo Rally, has a 3-cylinder, two-stroke engine of 841 c.c. Below: DAF (Holland) with 750 c.c. unit, 2-cylinders, fully-automatic Vario-matic belt-drive transmission. Above: Honda S. 600. Below: Volvo (Sweden) sports coupé P1800 type, 1,800 c.c. capacity, body designed by stylist Michelotti.

VOLVO

GENERAL MOTORS

Chevrolet, Pontiac, Oldsmobile, Buick, Cadillac, Vauxhall, Opel, Holden. This is the list of passenger cars produced by the mammoth organisation of General Motors, the largest automotive organisation in the World. Today, some fifty-five years after it was formed, General Motors not only turns out motor cars and commercial vehicles—it is deeply entrenched in the field of diesel-electric locomotives, tractors, aero-engines, refrigerators, and air-conditioning plant.

The formation of General Motors was one of the natural evolutionary stages of the motor car industry in its formative days. By the middle of the first decade of the Twentieth Century, car manufacturers in the United States were numbered in their hundreds. Many of these companies were founded on a shoestring, founded with hope—and a bright idea or two. The rapid development of the industry and its increasing competition meant that inevitably some of these smaller firms had to go to the wall.

As production methods became more professional and parts were in some degree standardised it was evident that a combination of manufacturing units, sharing technical knowledge, could survive more easily than single small businesses.

In 1908 the companies of Buick, Oldsmobile, Oakland (Pontiac), and Cadillac formed the nucleus from which General Motors grew. William C. Durant of Buick was the prime mover in this ambitious scheme for survival.

At the same time Henry Ford put his own philosophy into operation in the form of the immensely popular Model T. Durant, on the other hand, took the view that the industry would be better served by making a series of different models to suit the requirements of all types of motorists.

Durant had in the early part of 1908 tried to form a merger with Ford, but was unsuccessful, due to Henry Ford's demand for a price of $3,000,000—ready cash. In those days bankers looked down their noses at a loan of such magnitude, particularly to a new and untried industry.

Within two years General Motors had a dozen names to its credit. Many were small companies, soon to fade out of the motoring scene. They had bought several part-making companies, some useful, others white elephants. Another offer was made for the rapidly growing Ford empire, but now Henry Ford asked $8,000,000 for his business—too much for the uncertain finances of General Motors.

At this time Charles Nash was made president of the Buick Company, then a somewhat shaky concern. His energy and foresight pulled it out of the rut—and he was soon president of General Motors itself.

Thereafter General Motors began to move forward in top gear. Mass production required standardisation if cars were to be assembled without difficulty, so more supplying companies were bought up by the increasingly powerful General Motors. New develop-

Above: One of the world's luxury cars, this Cadillac is fitted with a 7-litre V.8. engine and develops 340 h.p. Its top speed is 125 m.p.h. Below: Chevrolet coupé Rondine designed by Pinin Farina, based on the Corvette Sports model equipped with a 5.3-litre engine developing 304 h.p.; its maximum speed is 138 m.p.h.

Oldsmobile, F85 "Cutlass" sports coupé. Opposite page: a Ghia-bodied Chrysler.

ments and inventions (the automatic starter was one) were made standard in all General Motors products.

After the first World War the American motor industry moved from infancy into strident youth. General Motors bought the Fisher Body Company, known and respected since pioneer days. This division of G. M. still manufactures the bodyworks and trim for the range. Later the corporation took the plunge into the non-automotive world and launched the Frigidaire company.

A reshuffle in the organisation during the Twenties swung the policy to growth from within rather than expansion by purchasing other companies. The psychology of selling was investigated in detail. For instance the Chevrolet was priced at about two hundred dollars above the Ford Model T (they were both designed to appeal to the same market) but for the extra outlay customers had a spare tyre, self starter, better upholstery and so on.

It became an established policy at General Motors to manufacture cars and commercial vehicles of all types as long as there was a demand sufficient to make mass production economical. Diversity was the keynote. For instance Chevrolet alone make fifteen different car models *every year*. Cadillac produce eleven, Pontiac fourteen.

General Motors now has organisations in Germany, Australia, Britain and Canada. In the United States G. M. control 90 per cent of the motor industry, operating some 130 plants, and employing well over half a million people.

Until comparatively recently the lines of most American cars were rather opulent, presenting the notorious 'shark mouth' carnivorous look to oncoming traffic. Today, following the lead given by Italy in the person of Pinin Farina a few years ago, General Motors cars have the 'scolloped' economic appearance that the motorists of today associate with fast European cars. Chrome is rapidly disappearing (the Corvair Monza is a good example of this admirable trend) and design is becoming more functional.

General Motors is an organisation of the people. It has nearly a million shareholders, most of whom are private individuals. How the 355 original investors must be chuckling now at the refusal of the banks to lend them the necessary cash to expand.

CHRYSLER

The Chrysler has always had an influence on the style of American cars, including both engine design and coachwork.

Do you remember the "Flight Sweep" style, consisting of fins above the rear wings? They later appeared on every rival car, more or less exaggerated.

Apart from the contemporary range of prestige cars in the "300" series, Chrysler have now entered another field, in which they already seem to have made marked progress.

Chrysler have become one of the principal suppliers of the National Aeronautics and Space Administration. They were responsible for the Redstone and Jupiter rockets, the success of which led eventually to the Mercury project. Chrysler were also the firm commissioned to make "Saturn", the engine with a thrust of 1,650,000 pounds which will be used in the ambitious space-explorations of the future, starting with trips to the moon. Although the first launching of Saturn in October, 1961 was described by the N.A.S.A. as a total failure, it caused no harm to the reputation of Chrysler.

This emphasis on research, coupled with their experience with jet engines, naturally led Chrysler to replace the piston engine by the turbine.

As early as 1956 the Chrysler turbine-driven car crossed the United States. This turbine, the "Crea", is fairly similar to the big turbines used in aeroplanes, and has certain very positive advantages over piston-powered engines: it has one-fifth less the number of parts (only one sparking-plug, for instance), its performance is satisfactory, and, an important point where atmospheric pollution is becoming a serious problem, there is no carbon monoxide in the exhaust.

While these projects are being studied for the future, Chrysler are producing a range of models complete enough to appeal to the tastes of Americans of all classes—from the luxury Imperial, with coachwork by Ghia, to the Valiant "compact car". In addition to the Plymouths and Dodges, which have a good reputation, the Lancer G. T. came out in 1962, with a definite "continental" look about it, and there was also a so-called "sports" model, the Plymouth Fury.

A 1911 model still lacked front doors.

By 1912, the tourer had grown front doors.

"Flivver" still had gaslights in 1914.

"Lizzie" entered high society: a 1915 town car.

This early sedan boasted centre doors, carriage lamps.

An electrically lighted, vertically styled, 1917 model.

FORD

Bedizened with brass in 1909.

Brass radiators lasted until 1915.

A classy Ford "Tudor" of 1923.

Of all the automobiles ever built, none did more to change the world than Henry Ford's Tin Lizzie.

Between 1908 and 1927 almost fifteen and a half million Model T Fords rattled their way off the assembly lines. On one busy day, October 31, 1925, an amazing 9,109 flivvers were built. Between 1917 and 1927 Ford made half the cars produced in the United States.

Like a million other farm boys of the Eighties, Henry Ford was mad about machinery. At first he tinkered with clocks and watches, but by the early Nineties, when he had a job with the Detroit Edison Company, he was desperately involved with an automobile. In 1896 he finally got it running.

This brakeless, reverseless, two-cylinder buckboard wasn't much of a machine compared to the fairly sophisticated cars already running in Europe, but it was good enough to get some friends of Ford's to advance him a little money to go on experimenting. By 1899 he had built a much better machine, left his job with the electric light company and had become superintendent of the Detroit Automobile Company.

Ford already had his mind on a cheap car almost anyone could afford, but he wasn't the boss, and the Detroit Automobile Company went under while trying to sell the few dull and expensive machines it succeeded in building.

Now, to make his name known, Ford began to build racing cars. With spectacular success he beat the great Alexander Winton's 70 h.p. machine and almost immediately new money became available to start the Ford Motor Company, first as a partnership with Alexander Malcolmson, a Detroit coal dealer, in 1902, and then as a corporation in 1903. In the five years or so until he hit the jackpot with the Model T, Ford brought out a series of fairly successful light cars and at the insistence of his partners, one elaborate flop, the Model K. This was not at all the sort of machine Henry wanted to manufacture. It was big, it had a fuel-hungry six-cylinder engine, and it was expensive. Even at the high price of $2,800, the company lost money on it. Further, it had a too-flimsy planetary transmission, which was most likely Ford's fault (he loved planetaries and later put one in the Model T).

By 1906, Ford was building the Model N and was approaching his ideal of "The Universal Car", as he called it. This Model N was the direct ancestor of the T—it even looked like a T in the shape of its radiator and its transverse front spring.

But although thousands of N's and its de luxe versions, the Models R and S, were sold at quite low prices (the N cost a mere $600), they had not acquired that stamp of pure genius which was to make "Ford" the best known car name in the world.

On October 1, 1908, the most maligned and the most praised, the most reliable and the most cantankerous, the ugliest and the most functional of all cars was born—the Model T.

Yet for all its simplicity, the Model T was full of innovations: Its 2.9-litre, 22-h.p., four-cylinder engine was cast in one piece, but it had a detachable cylinder head in a day when such a convenience was unheard of. Although the very earliest European machines' heads had been made separately because of casting problems, most manufacturers fought shy of having to make a water-tight, gas-tight joint at such a crucial point in their engines.

T drivers became expert at driving backwards, for even in low gear, chronically worn bands sometimes made smallish hills unclimbable. Undaunted, drivers went up backwards. But there was another reason for being a virtuoso in reverse. The fuel tank was under the front seat and fed the carburettor by gravity. With a near-empty tank on a hill the petrol

The Ford G.T. is similar to the track version which smashed lap records at Le Mans in 1964 and 1965. Although detuned for road use, it still produces 335 b.h.p. at 6,250 r.p.m., giving a maximum speed of 164 m.p.h.

was unable to climb up to the carburettor. Going up backwards raised the tank above the carburettor.

With all its little foibles, the T was nearly unbreakable, mostly because it was made of superlative materials, better than many of the more expensive machines of its day.

As the farmers realised that here, at last, was a cheap, reliable machine to lift them out of the mud, to set them free from the horse, and to end their isolation, production zoomed and prices went down.

In 1909, when the first T's reached their owners, the price was $850. By 1912, it was $600; by 1918, $450. In 1924 it reached its all time low of $290. Just before it went out of production in 1926 it cost $380. But by now it had electric starting and lighting and detachable wire wheels with balloon tyres.

Of course, it was mass production that made these incredibly low prices possible. And although Ford had certainly not invented mass production, he was the first to use it on such a colossal scale. In August, 1913, it took twelve-and-a-half man-hours to build a chassis. But as the technique of the assembly line was perfected the time dropped. By December 1913, it was two hours and thirty-eight minutes, by January 1914, one hour and thirty-three minutes. After that the factory remained silent on how few man-hours it took to whip out a Tin Lizzie.

Although the Model T gave way to the Model A in 1927, it still lives on. For it is the most popular (especially the brass-radiatored, wooden-dashboard examples of pre-1915) of all the machines treasured by antique car collectors.

STUDEBAKER

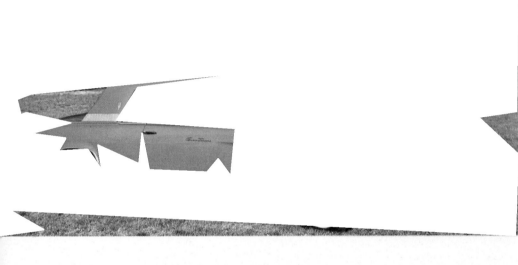

Left: "Gran Turismo" Studebaker coupé. Above: The Studebaker Avanti.

Clement Studebaker began to build horse-drawn carriages in a forge in 1852. Soon he teamed up with his three brothers and in 1860 they founded the Studebaker Brothers Manufacturing Company which built its first car in 1902, a kind of electric runabout.

Between 1920 and 1930 three Studebaker models —using piston-engines and petrol—became fairly well known: the Standard Six, the Special Six, and the Big Six. In 1929 and 1930 there were two eight-cylinder models, the "President" and the "Director".

The firm jogged along without any great distinction until 1947; it was then that Studebaker built the famous "shell car". The front was so similar to the rear that nobody could ever be sure whether the car was starting up or falling to pieces.

After this aesthetic fiasco the venerable firm of Studebaker (which had amalgamated with Packard in 1956) acquired a reputation for *avant-garde* design in the so-called "Continental" style, inspired by the Italian designers. Packard, moreover, quickly disappeared from both the organisation and the title of the Studebaker-Packard Corporation, which became simply Studebaker once more.

In 1959 Studebaker helped to launch the term "compact" in the American car industry, and all the big manufacturers afterwards took up the idea.

It's true that Rambler were making a small car, but it was really the dumpy "Lark" model (with 6 or 8 cylinders) which launched the word "compact", later to be adopted by the entire trade. At the same time the "Hawk" series, with coachwork designed by Raymond Loewy (a Frenchman by origin) kept up Studebaker's reputation for streamlined styles.

In 1963 Studebaker worked on a car which offered serious competition to the Ford "Thunderbird", then the most popular sports and family car in the United States. The Studebaker project was called "Avanti", and was the first Gran Turismo American car, in the classic Italian style, stripped of ornate fins and other chromium decorations, equipped with front-wheel disc-brakes and, according to the company, capable of 168 m.p.h.

Unfortunately, the disappearance in December 1963 of Studebaker as a United States manufacturer, makes the future of this model very precarious. Studebaker-Canada seem unwilling to manufacture it.

THE GOLDEN
AGE OF RACING

Preceding page: Graham Hill (B.R.M.) leads at the British Grand Prix, Silverstone in 1965. This page, above: Stirling Moss, in a W196 Formula 1 Mercedes, 2,500 c.c., 1955. Below: Jim Clark in a Formula 1 Lotus at Monaco, 1961. Page 273, above: World Champion Jim Clark on his way to win the British Grand Prix 1963, in his 1500 c.c. Lotus. Below: Chris Amon fights his Lola through Stowe corner at Silverstone in the 1963 British Grand Prix.

The 1966 season brought in the 3-litre Formula 1, after five years of the 1½-litre formula, and the comeback of the rear engine. Credit for this is due to British manufacturers, for they were the first to use it with positive results that convinced the most sceptical critics. Rear engines were by no means new; earlier examples were its first use by Rumpler on the Benz in 1923, and Ferdinand Porsche's work which led to the splendid achievement of the Auto-Union V-16's and V-12's between 1934 and 1939. This design allows a reduction in the total weight of the vehicle and allows it to rest more securely on the wheels that take the drive. It means that the front section can be lowered and the car can make a deeper cleavage through the air.

The Formula I of 1961 was the outcome of fifty years of technical data adapted from the basic needs of various established formulas. For the first time in the history of motor-racing, manufacturers competed with each other on an equal footing, the result of technical adaptations on all sides which led to quick results and the achievement of the highest specific power. Progress has been sensational and it's worthwhile going back a little to analyse the transformation that has occurred.

Racing cars were first made in 1906; the vehicles were limited to a weight of 2,200 pounds, but there was no limit to the engine capacity. In 1907 maximum petrol consumption was fixed, and then in 1908 the bore was limited. In 1912 the establishment of

formule libre led to gigantic engines of 11,000 to 16,000 c.c. and at the same time a formula was established for "light cars", allowing a minimum weight of 1,760 pounds with a fixed engine capacity. For the last fifty years this formula has supplied the basis of all technical developments.

In 1913 the maximum petrol consumption was reduced; from 1914 onwards the maximum engine capacity varied: in 1921 it was fixed at 4,500 - 3,000 c.c., from 1922 to 1925 it was 2,000 c.c. and in 1926-7 it came down to 1,500 c.c.

Then came a period of great confusion, when weight and consumption varied, leading to a period of great flexibility, 1931-33. A return to the formula limiting the maximum weight to 1,650 pounds, led to the appearance of the most fantastic cars; this was partly stopped in 1938 by the introduction of a formula limiting engine capacity to 3,000 c.c. when supercharged, or 4,500 c.c. at normal atmospheric pressure.

The principle was retained after the war from 1947 to 1953, but cars with superchargers were changed from 1,500 c.c. to the classic 4,500 c.c. at normal pressure.

Alongside this Formula I a Formula II developed, limiting cars to 2 litres and to 500 c.c. for those with supercharger. This formula discouraged the adoption of supercharger systems, and 2-litre cars were so successful that they quickly supplanted the Formula I cars and in 1952 the latter were abandoned.

John Surtees, driving a Formula 1 Ferrari, leads round one of the fast bends at the Silverstone circuit.

A new formula was introduced in 1954 which was to last six years; it merely limited capacity to 2,500 c.c. and thanks to advanced technical development it led to the formula used today — 1,500 c.c., non-supercharged, on vehicles with a minimum weight of 990 pounds.

All these conflicting regulations were bound to lead to uneven quality and lack of proportion in the appearance of cars. They led to confusion in the correlation of data necessary to technical development and unequal distribution of available funds. Nowadays it is possible to work out the basis of a highly-developed formula that is fair to everyone.

The victories of yesteryear were due to outstanding discoveries or technical achievements, and the marques which incorporated them were certain of victory. One simple example was the adoption of four-wheel brakes, which took a long time to come into general use.

In 1923 the volumetric supercharger was seen at a Grand Prix for the first time, ensuring victory for the marque concerned and allowing specific power to be increased to a staggering extent, though with varying degrees of success. Delage anticipated modern techniques and brought out the first racing V-12

which proved invincible. In the same year the Benz Rumpler incorporated the first hints of functional streamlining; this soon formed the basis of a whole technique which has now reached its peak on the race-tracks.

Racing today no longer looks to alchemy as a means of finding mysterious fuels. Fittings and accessories are available to everyone, and they are combined in extremely intelligent adaptations. There are only differences of a few horse-power between the B.R.M., the Cooper, the Lotus, the Porsche and the Ferrari, with their V-type engines set at an angle of 60, 90 or 120 degrees (the Porsche had a "flat 8" engine), their 6 or 8 cylinders and double row of camshafts per cylinder-head. All the chassis are multi-tubular, with slight intersection. The De Dion rear axle has been generally abandoned, suspension is entirely independent, based on double transmission or long forks, either transversal or longitudinal or sometimes in both directions. Disc-brakes have been adopted by every make, and there are no longer any fears about the general sturdiness of the cars.

In future a mark's success will depend mainly on the driver though motor history will be made with new technical developments.

274

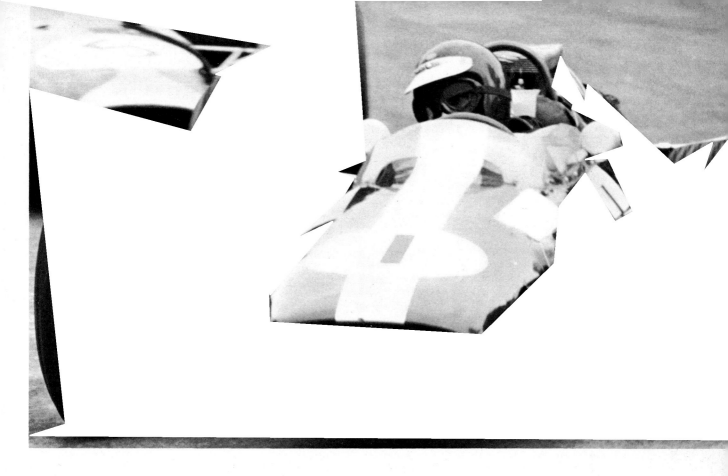

Above: Jim Clark in a F1 Lotus winds through Druids Bend, a fast hairpin, at Brands Hatch. Centre: Graham Hill in a B.R.M. Formula 1. Below: British driver Jackie Stewart in a B.R.M. at Station Bend on the Monaco Grand Prix course.

The Motor Manufacturers' World Championship is hard to define accurately and is full of subtle distinctions, for it is open to cars of all types, yet one category seems to be doomed.

In fact when racing-car engines are fitted to production cars in everyday use it becomes expensive and uneconomic to build a limited series to the specifications defined by the International Sports-Car Committee; Enzo Ferrari regarded this kind of car as "a one-seater disguised as a two-seater for no real reason".

And yet we saw a strange reversal of the situation in Italy, the country which was the outstanding producer of "Gran Turismo" cars and therefore had the best chance of winning championships.

The changed attitude of the organisers who promote races for Gran Turismo cars is more obvious – they want to preserve the powerful attractions of the race-track, with its noise and exciting atmosphere, for this is what the public has always craved.

Since material considerations prevail over the final development of an outworn formula, the Motor Manufacturers' World Championship will be open to "sheep and goats", that is, to cars of different engine capacity in the Gran Turismo class, in which sports cars can also participate. The latter will obviously romp home with the laurels.

So the pseudo-one-seater still has some good days in store on the tracks of Le Mans, the Nürburgring, the Targa Florio and Sebring. This state of affairs is due to the development of a formula, which though perfectly suitable for amateurs in 1923, hardly relates to racing cars in production today.

A victory at Le Mans can only serve the interests of a factory, for without factory support amateur racing would be impossible. This means that the manufacturer only emphasises the weaknesses of amateur racing, for everyone looks first and foremost after his own interests.

The outcome will be factory-like cars with highly developed equipment to make certain of the most valuable successes, for on these depend commercial expansion, even survival.

Le Mans now contributes less and less towards the

Opposite page: Porsche Carrera G.T.S. type 904. This new Gran Turismo first appeared in 1963. Equipped with a 2-litre engine and 4 overhead camshafts and developing 200 h.p. at 7,000 r.p.m., its top speed is somewhere in the vicinity of 165 m.p.h. The body is of reinforced plastic. Above: The start of a G.T. race at Brands Hatch in Kent, England. Right: A Sunbeam Alpine at Le Mans.

perfection of accessories or engines of recognised quality found in normal production; on the other hand, a hard fight at Le Mans can contribute in a sporadic way to the devolopment of revolutionary components, and the adoption of disc brakes was one of the more important proofs of this during the last few years.

The high-powered factories of Jaguars, Mercedes and Ferraris systematically crowded out production cars driven by amateurs, which were thrown into a world that was no longer theirs, constituting a permanent danger because any type of car can take part in the races and things may get out of hand. (The tragic events at Le Mans in 1955 proved this in a dramatic way, an example of the permanent sword of Damocles hanging over motor-racing.)

Perhaps after many roundabout attempts we shall finally set up one race open to all types of cars, like the Indianapolis 500 miles race, the "show" with the most prizes; it is much frowned on in Europe, but organisers, the Federation and manufacturers in the throes of vast economic problems, have already begun to discuss proposals for something on the same lines.

So there is no point in stopping to look at mass-produced sports cars, well produced at that, which are let loose on the race-track but only likely to win any prizes when real racing-cars with the same engine capacity drop out of the race in large numbers or have accidents.

Today Ferraris are on top in the world of G. T. competition. With wins at Le Mans in 1958, 1960, 1961, 1962 and 1963 they have virtually swept the field in latter years, allowing only the race of 1959 to go to another marque, Aston Martin.

The 1963 marathon race on the French circuit went to Enzo Ferrari's latest car, the very fast 250P (Prototype category), a semi-open rear-engined model powered by a 3-litre V12 unit. Even during practice the car put up the amazing time of 3 minutes 45.7 seconds, beating Phil Hill's record by over 11 seconds. The race itself was completely dominated by the red Maranello cars which took the first six places in the twenty-four-hour event.

Now it seems that we will see heavier American participation in this type of racing, and most welcome, too. And if the future brings official works entries from Jaguar and Aston Martin once more we may find that here too, as in the Formula One field, Italy will no longer find victory quite easy.

277

Above: A 250 G.T. Ferrari
passes the stands at Le
Mans. Centre: Morgan Plus
Four, mass-produced model
that is a special favourite.
Below: A.C. 6-cylinder roadster.

Top right: Alfa Romeo Giulietta SZ Le Mans, 1,300 c.c. Lower right: Aston Martin DB4R Gran Turismo.
Left: The Consten-Armagnac DB-Panhard at Le Mans, 1959. Below: Jaguar E type coupé, driven by Peter Sargent.

Right: Jim Clark, World Driving Champion since 1965. Below, left to right: Phil Hill, Bruce McLaren, Jack Brabham, Dan Gurney, John Surtees, Graham Hill.

THE DRIVERS

Right: The one and only Stirling Moss. Following pages: This 57C is one of the last Bugattis, 1940. Its coachwork is by Gangloff and it can travel at up to 110 m.p.h., thanks to its 175 h.p. engine, at 5,500 c.c. capacity.

One often hears it said that Fangio, or Caracciola, or Nuvolari, or another of the accepted great maestros of the track, was the greatest driver the world has seen. Many erudite discussions have taken place about the relative merits of the armchair style of Clark, Hill and other drivers of today, and the hunched, aggressive attitudes of Hawthorn or Gonzales, during the Fifties.

It's all rather a waste of time. Comparisons can be drawn only between contemporary drivers. Who knows what Nuvolari might have done to the delicate and diminutive Lotus if he had had the chance to get into its cockpit? One feels that he would growl, pick it up, and shake it like a rat, in his teeth! On the other hand he would certainly have put up the fastest lap before he tore it to pieces.

And who can fairly compare the driving abilities of Nazarro in his giant Fiat with its chain drive to the technique of Graham Hill in the low sleek B.R.M.? One can say only that great courage is still needed, superb skill is still the only way to keep alive, stamina and fitness are still supremely important.

Today's drivers must still have that cool nerve and an eye that can judge distance and speed with slide-rule efficiency. They must — perhaps even more than their predecessors — possess the stern quality of self-discipline on the circuit.

Now that the advancement in technical knowledge on the part of the racing car manufacturers has produced near-parity of performance, the ability — and the understanding of machinery — of each

driver has become more and more significant. A little while back the best drivers were given the best cars — drove for the best équipe — and were as sure of victory as the preparation of the cars allowed. Today all cars are meticulously prepared, their performance is within a shade of each other – and driving ability is at a premium...

Over the years this hazardous sport has taken its tragic toll of names: the list of drivers on the grid at the French Grand Prix of 1953 (one of the greatest motor races ever seen) comes to mind. The entry at Rheims that summer's day was a colourful list of the world's *crème de la crème* of international *pilotes*.

On the line were the Maseratis of Fangio, Gonzales, Marimon, Bonetto and de Graffenried. Ferraris were driven by Ascari, Villoresi, Hawthorn, Farina and Rosier. Moss was in his Cooper-Alta; Macklin, Collins and Giraud-Cabantuos had an H.W.M. apiece. The line-up was completed by Salvadori, Wharton, Gerard, Claes, Schell and Bayol.

That French classic was thirteen years ago. Today just one of that great list is still driving in top class racing: Roy Salvadori.

Wharton, Schell, Marimon, Collins, Ascari, Bonetto, Hawthorn, Rosier and Claes are dead.

Why then do they risk their lives in this sport, you say? The answer is another question: why do men climb mountains, why do they fly, why do they ski? Because it is in the nature of men to pit themselves against whatever can be challenged. And it all adds to the sum of human knowledge...

BUGATTI TYPE 57 C

FERRARI

Preceding pages: A ferocious, frontal aspect of the 250-GT Ferrari, with V-12, 3 litre, three-carburettor engine. Right: Small luxury saloon built by G. Bertone on a 1,000 c.c. 4-cylinder engine chassis, designed by Enzo Ferrari. The comfort and performance of this little car are quite exceptional, and it is planned to put it into production. Opposite page, top: Ferrari sports model, 2,400 c.c. Centre: 2.4 Ferrari; rear-engined. Below: 1961 Formula I Ferrari, rear engine V6 1,500 c.c.

A sports car, ideally, should be a de-tuned racing machine rather than a warmed-over touring car whose engine is either a puny mechanism tuned to within an inch of its life or a gross and lorry-like oaf of a "motor" out of an American passenger car.

A sports car should have a built-in feeling of excitement. It should be as taut and nervous as a racehorse. It must certainly be quick off the mark and very fast. Further, its mechanism should be good to look at, its bodywork decently finished and functionally sober in design.

The one maker in the world who builds cars that most closely approach this exciting ideal is the Commendatore Enzo Ferrari—the modern version of Ettore Bugatti—who builds his cars in a tiny factory in Maranello, near Modena, in the north of Italy.

Ferrari's three hundred or so workmen build a multiplicity of machines: Grand Prix cars, sports racing cars, Gran Turismo cars and even a "cooking" model.

For example, the 250-GT Berlinetta is the hottest practical machine you can drive on the public highway and then, by merely slapping a number on its flank, take racing—with a fine chance of winning.

The man who designed this car, Enzo Ferrari (b. 1898) is no engineer, in the formal sense. When he was a boy his father owned a small garage in Modena, and like many young Italians he was obsessed with cars and racing drivers. First he got a job with Alfa Romeo as a mechanic. By 1923 he was a racing driver. Those were the spectacular days of the P2

Alfas and the 3-litre RLSS 22/90's and of drivers like Campari, Sivocci, and Antonio Ascari. Ferrari, not quite of the racing calibre of these giants, didn't drive the P2's much, but did very well in hill climbs and sports-car races and minor Grands Prix.

However, as Ferrari became involved with the organisational and construction problems of the Alfa Romeo racing team, he raced less often. When Alfa decided to give up its racing department, the famous "Scuderia Ferrari" was formed to handle Alfa Romeo's racing cars.

During the Thirties, the giant vans of the Scuderia Ferrari, with the prancing horse shield on their flanks and potent racing cars within, ranged from Monza in Italy to Mineola, Long Island; from the Nürburgring to Tripoli.

At first the Alfas, driven by such legendary heroes as Nuvolari, Farina, and Varzi, had things all their own way and all but swept into limbo the Bugattis that had been the kings of the Grand Prix circuits. But by the mid-Thirties, the Mercedes-Benz's and Auto-Unions of the Third Reich were giving the Alfas a hard time, and in the last years before the war, Ferrari's Alfa Romeos were completely overshadowed by the Germans.

In 1938, a new management at Alfa Romeo, in a hopeless effort to make a comeback, formed a company-run Scuderia called "Alfa Corse" and Enzo Ferrari was free to go his own way.

Thus, in 1940, Ferrari entered two cars with 1½-litre, eight-cylinder engines in that odd, shortened,

wartime Mille Miglia (the Italian 1,000-mile race) which was won by a German BMW. These machines built in Ferrari's shop in Modena, where he had prepared the racing Alfas of the Scuderia Ferrari, were not destined to be the progenitors of what we now know as Ferraris. The first real Ferrari took to the road in 1947. This was the 1½-litre Type 125, designed by Gioachino Colombo who had been chief designer for Alfa Romeo. It had the first of the V-type, twelve-cylinder engines which were to become a Ferrari feature and which are now the only V-12's produced anywhere. With its extreme "over-square" cylinder dimensions, its light reciprocating masses, and very short con-rods, it was hoped that 10,000 r.p.m. would be possible. Columbo was disappointed when only 7,500 could be reached.

However, variations of this very successful twelve have been made in sizes up to 5 litres and developing as much as 450 h.p. There is no doubt that these engines have been among the most successful ever built.

A Ferrari at around £5,000 is still the most exciting and fastest sports car you can buy, and wealthy sporting gentlemen from Hollywood to the Riviera, from Buenos Aires to Biarritz, feel positively naked without one.

But what does the Commendatore, Enzo Ferrari himself, drive from the factory at Maranello to his offices at Modena?

He drives a 1,200 c.c. Fiat. Ferraris are just too rich for his blood.

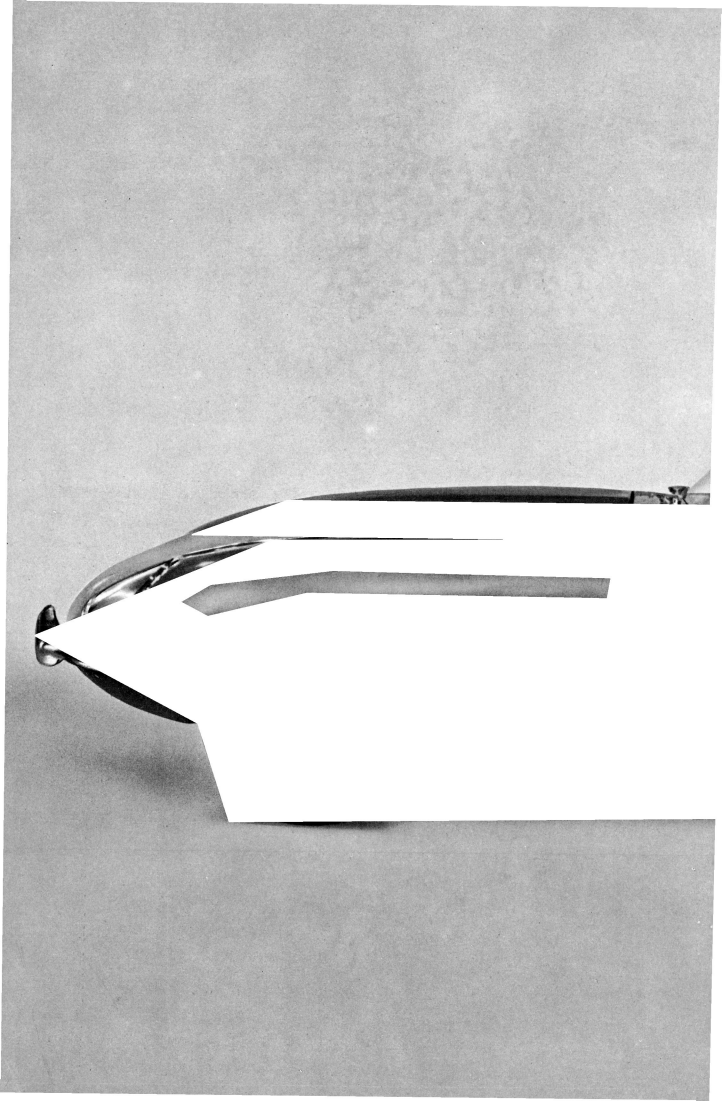

JAGUAR

The world-renowned Jaguar started out in a modest way as a sidecar for motor-cycles. In 1923, a twenty-one-year-old youth named William Lyons (now Sir William), noting the burgeoning sales of sidecars, went into the business of building, at a low price, a sleeker, racier looking "bathtub" than anyone else in England. He gave this tiny enterprise, which consisted of himself, a partner, and five workmen, the resounding and comprehensive name of "The Swallow Side Car and Coach Building Company".

Business boomed. Before long, "Swallow" was building special de-luxe bodies for many of the popular small cars: the Standard-Swallow, the Austin-Swallow, the Hornet-Swallow. Lyons was doing well, but he wasn't satisfied. He wanted to turn out a car that would be uniquely his own. To that end, Lyons made a deal with the Standard Motor Company whereby it would supply him with specially designed, underslung chassis upon which he could build his dream cars.

The cars (the SS-I and the SS-II) Lyons unveiled at the London Show in 1931 were certainly dream cars, the kind of machines imaginative schoolboys might doodle in their notebooks. They were excruciatingly rakish: Much of their length was taken up by a many-louvred bonnet; they had very low passenger compartments whose inmates peered out at the world through slit-like windows; they had wire wheels, cycle-type mudguards, and looked as if they might do 150 miles an hour.

Unfortunately, their performance hardly measured up to their appearance. The larger of the pair, the SS-I, which was available with either a 2-litre or 2½-litre L-head engine, could barely exceed 70 m.p.h., even with the bigger engine. The smaller SS-II had a 1-litre engine and was, if possible, even less sparkling.

But this didn't prevent the SS's from selling like mad. For despite their exciting looking and quite well finished coachwork, they were amazingly cheap. The SS-I cost a mere £375.

Rapidly, the SS got better. A new, well designed, six-cylinder, 2½-litre, push-rod, overhead-valve engine with a sturdy, seven-bearing crankshaft was developed and two versions of a potent sports car, in quick succession, were added to the line of much-improved saloons and sporty-looking open tourers.

The sports cars were the SS-90 and the SS-100. (The numbers referred to their approximate top speeds). The SS-90 appeared before the overhead-valve engine was in production and, surprisingly, was capable of reaching its advertised speed with a much-tuned, two-carburettor version of the old L-head engine. The SS-100 had the new 2½-litre overhead-

Preceding pages: Monocoque, stressed shell, steel body-work eliminated the conventional chassis in the E-Type Jaguar introduced in 1961. This car uses the well-tried thirteen-year-old twin-overhead-camshaft X K engine. With a capacity of 3.8 litres and three carburettors, it is said to develop 265 b.h.p. The factory claims it is capable of 150 m.p.h. Dunlop bridge-type disc brakes are fitted to the wheel hubs forward, but are inboard at the rear. It has a wheelbase of only eight feet and is but 48 inches high. The pre-war SS-100 (opposite page) was the bargain-priced sports car of its day. It cost only £550 in 3½-litre, push-rod-engined form and provided exhilarating performance, reaching 60 m.p.h. from a standing start in under 11 seconds. It was said to be able to approach 100 m.p.h. Left: The X K 140 Jaguar.

valve engine, and later a 3½-litre version which put out 120 b.h.p.

The SS-100 looked exactly like the popular ideal of a sports car in the mid-Thirties, with extravagantly sweeping mudguards, a long hood, giant, staring headlights, a squarely chopped-off stern, and cutaway doors. Its 104-inch-wheelbase chassis was quite ordinary, with half-elliptic springs at its four corners. But it was light and thereby gave wonderful performance for its price (£475 for the 2½-litre, £550 for the 3½-litre). Vintage sports car collectors will pay more than that for an SS-100 today.

By the mid-Thirties the SS was much more Lyons than Standard. The whole line—saloons, tourers, and sports cars—had a new name added to its initials: Jaguar. The cars were known as SS Jaguars until 1937.

The first car produced by Lyons after the war was the Mark IV Jaguar. The company had a new name, too: Jaguar Cars Ltd.

The Mark IV (1946) and Mark V (1948) were still developments of pre-war machines. In 1948, however, Sir William unveiled a new car and engine which broke entirely with the past and were destined to make the Jaguar one of the world's great cars.

It's hard to realise that the XK-120 goes back as far as 1948. We take its descendants, which are still basically similar, almost for granted, but when the XK-120 appeared it seemed fantastic, almost unbelievable, that a nicely made sports car, with a 3½-litre, twin-overhead-camshaft engine of 160 b.h.p. (at 5,400 r.p.m.) could be bought for less than £1,500.

Twin-overhead-camshaft engines with hemispheri-cal combustion chambers were nothing new in racing cars, Alfa Romeos, Bugattis, or even in the 3-litre Sunbeam, among others. But it was a startling innovation—even with chain-driven camshafts instead of gears—in what was, after all, a low-priced, mass-produced car.

The designers, W. M. Heynes and the famed Harry Weslake, had started with a clean sheet of draft paper to build what was considered impossible: a tough, almost indestructible, high-speed racing type of engine at a low price. Weslake, the great expert on the respiratory problems of engines, was mainly responsible for the light aluminium cylinder head with its nickel/cast-iron valve-seat inserts and its patented port shapes.

The XK-120 had a 102-inch chassis with independent front suspension through torsion bars. Surprisingly, it was quite heavy—about 3,200 pounds. In spite of this, it had excellent acceleration. Going from 0 to 60 took slightly less than twelve seconds, 0 to 100 twenty-eight seconds.

Although the XK-120 had not been designed for racing it not only scored well in amateur competition, but factory teams started winning races and rallies which until then had been the private preserve of great continental marques.

Since the first XK-120 appeared in 1949, it has steadily been developed and improved. Its basic engine has been modified for use in hot racing machines, in luxurious saloons (Marks VII to IX), in new generations of sports cars. Its chassis has gone through continual metamorphoses, through tubular frames, up to the monocoque structure of the "E" type.

291

ASTON MARTIN

Should some fairy godfather offer me my pick of the world's cars as a present. I would certainly look long and hard at the DB6-GT Aston Martin Volante convertible before making up my greedy little mind.

Lionel Martin had an agency with a man named Robert Bamford for the sale of Singer cars in those confused, halcyon days before World War I, when car dealers so often were racing drivers and car designers as well as businessmen.

At first, Martin and Bamford raced specially tuned Singers and even offered these reworked machines for sale. But Martin was dissatisfied and decided that they ought to turn out a high-quality sports car under their own marque.

The new machine was to be assembled from components built to their design by outside suppliers. Only the engine was already in existence: a 1,389 c.c., four-cylinder, L-head, 1,400 Coventry-Simplex of excellent design and workmanship. Martin couldn't wait to try it out and dropped it into a small 1908, Bugatti-designed, Isotta-Fraschini racing chassis.

This strange, albeit high-quality, hybrid was called an Aston Martin (combining the name of Martin, who was much more involved with it than Bamford, and part of the name of Aston-Clinton Hill, where the special Singers had done well in competition).

It wasn't until 1921, after the War, that an actual prototype of the new Aston Martin appeared, and even then changes were made before any cars got into private owners' hands.

The first L-head Aston Martins, true to the Bugatti-ish ideals of Lionel Martin, had first-class road holding, excellent two-wheel brakes (although slightly later models were among the first to have four-wheel brakes) and precise, quick steering by Marles. Marles, by the way, have long built superb steering gear for sports cars, but Martin had the steering boxes disassembled and even more accurately refitted to his standards. The chassis was underslung at the rear, with semi-elliptic springs all around (although a few earlier examples had three-quarter elliptics aft).

By now the four-cylinder engine was of 1,487 c.c. to allow it to race in the 1,500 c.c. class. It had a non-detachable head, a single carburettor, and a hefty three-bearing crankshaft. A feature to delight people who love interesting mechanical gadgetry was a trick oil filter sunk into one of the engine bearer arms. On the opposite front bearer arm was an oil filler

whose lid, when raised, automatically opened an overflow tap in the engine to prevent overfilling. A multi-plate Hele-Shaw clutch (whose metal plates were pressed into concentric V's, something like the diaphragm of an aneroid barometer), a four-speed gearbox, much like a Bugatti, in appearance and finish (but with constant-mesh gears incorporating a device for locking them into the gear selected), and a torque tube transmitted the power back to a fully floating rear axle. Although capable of only some 75 m.p.h. in standard form, racing versions were surprisingly fast for their day, one of them pushing the 1,500 c.c. hour record up to 86.21 m.p.h. with Kensington Moir at the wheel.

About the only thing one can hold against the Aston Martin people of that period was the ineffably cute names they gave their racing cars—"Bunny", "Sweet Pea", "Razor Blade"—some of which, by the way, had experimental twin-overhead-camshaft engines.

In spite of a comparatively low chassis price and the financial support of that famous and wealthy sporting motorist, Count Louis Zborowski, Bamford and Martin had their teething troubles. By 1926, a mere fifty cars had been sold. But before the name Aston Martin disappeared altogether a new company was formed.

During the early Twenties a young, Italian-born engineer named Augusto Cesare Bertelli, in company with a man named W. S. Renwick, was experimenting with a new type of engine and built a car in which to run it on the road. They called this prototype machine an R & B.

When Bamford and Martin folded up in 1926, Bertelli and Renwick, along with Martin, the Baron Charnwood, and a man named Benson, launched a new firm called Aston-Martin Motors Ltd., in Feltham, a London suburb.

Among the great sports cars of our day was the superb British Aston Martin DB4 and its more potent twin, the DB4-GT. The DB4-GT's engine develops 302 h.p., the less powerful DB4, 240. Yet, it was this "street" Aston which performed the incredible feat of accelerating from a standstill to 100 m.p.h. and then braking to a stop — all within 27 seconds. With a normal rear-axle ratio of 3.54:1, the DB4-GT is capable of 138 m.p.h. If you want "real" speed you can order it with a 2.92:1 axle and, according to the factory, reach 170 m.p.h.

Bertelli's first Aston, which came out in 1927, was an almost entirely new machine, but he retained one important feature of the old cars—their superlative quality. In their heyday (and even now, if you can find one), the Bertelli Astons were among the world's most desirable sporting conveyances.

The unusual feature of Bertelli's new engine was its cylinder head, shaped like the inside of a pitched roof; the sparking-plug was at the peak, but the valves, instead of being placed one on each side of the plug, were both placed on the same side of the peak. A single, chain-driven overhead camshaft actuated the valves through rockers. It was possible to decarbonise without disturbing the timing by unhooking the camshaft sprocket and hanging it in a little, specially made aperture in the head.

Only a very few Astons actually reached private owners until 1930, when the "International" close-coupled four-seaters were introduced. Capable of barely 80 m.p.h., these machines certainly looked much faster. In fact, their look alone was enough to make any sports-car lover dissolve with desire.

During those dreary and depressed Thirties, other models of the Aston Martin were bravely brought forth. In 1932, after Bertelli and a co-driver named Driscoll won the Biennial Cup at Le Mans, it was inevitable that a "Le Mans" model should be introduced. In 1933, the Mark II appeared with a more highly tuned engine, supposedly capable of developing 75 b.h.p., quite high for a 1,500 c.c. engine in those days. Now, too, the separate gearbox disappeared, as well as the torque-tube worm drive, which gave way to Hotchkiss drive.

After the Le Mans model came the "Ulster", a much more potent machine capable of the magic 100 m.p.h. Sadly, however, the Aston was beginning to lose something. There were now more stampings and fewer hand-finished castings in it. It was losing its precise, handbuilt charm.

In 1936, a 2-litre Aston came out, without cycle wings and sump lubrication. This four-cylinder 15-98 was fitted with a synchromesh gearbox, a clue to the feeling that the old Aston was perhaps too "tough"

During the Thirties, Aston Martin produced a series of "he-man" 1,500 c.c. sports cars. The "Ulster" was one of the more potent of these and could reach the magic 100 m.p.h. This example left the factory in 1934 and is said to have been in action at Le Mans in the 1935 race. Right-hand page, above: 1962 Lagonda "Rapide" saloon. Below: Aston Martin Volante convertible, a 2+2 seater, which has the same specifications as the Aston Martin DB6.

a car for the new generation of drivers.

For the hardier, old-school driver, a new "speed model" was offered which *did* have a dry sump and a crash-type gearbox; 100 h.p. was available at 5,000 r.p.m. in this machine.

Just prior to World War II, an experimental car called the "Atom" (really!) was built, using the 2-litre engine. This machine had an integral body-chassis and was the forerunner of the Astons of today.

In 1947, David Brown, head of the huge tractor and gear factories bearing his name, bought out Aston Martin. He also bought the ancient firm that produced the Lagonda. In 1950, the new company dropped the Aston 2-litre engine and decided to use the twin-overhead-camshaft 2.6-litre engine that W. O. Bentley had designed for the Lagonda.

The new Aston which evolved was known as the DB2 (DB for David Brown). It had a six-cylinder (2,580 c.c.) engine which developed 105 b.h.p. at 5,000 r.p.m.; a "Vantage" engine with a higher compression head developed 120 h.p. The valves were operated by chain-driven camshafts in the cast-iron cylinder head, which had hemispherical combustion chambers. The crankshaft of this power plant was supported on four large ring-type main bearings which were assembled on the shaft before being slid endwise into the rigid crankcase.

These DB2's were fast and would go from 0 to 60 in twelve seconds, but they were only a beginning. In the years since 1950, Aston Martins have been among the world's most successful sports-racing cars.

The current Aston Martin—the DB6—now has a 4-litre engine with aluminium blocks and heads. It still has twin-overhead camshafts, but the trick crankshaft is gone. It is among the great sports cars of our time.

MASERATI

My first contact with this elegant and beautiful *marque* shattered me. I had the experience in England when I discovered the unusual 16-cylinder model with parallel twin engines. They consisted of two groups of 8-cylinder double overhead camshaft engines with twin ignition, both fitted with a supercharger and a Solex carburettor. This delightful machine developed 300 h.p. at 5,500 r.p.m. and the foolhardy driver was assured of a speed of 155 m.p.h. Needless to say no such speed was attained or even approached by its choosy driver, and the car gave him so much ignition trouble that he became bad-tempered.

My second experience was when I purchased an old 4-cylinder 16-valve 4 C.L.T. Plate with supercharger. There was nothing aggressive about it, except for the record of its achievements, and its true quality lay in its unstable and touchy character. To this day I have never understood its changes of mood nor the variations in its behaviour which were expressed, in contradiction to all forecasts, in a lamentable series of back-firing.

I was convinced that the fuel being used was unworthy of the car and one day I prepared a truly infernal mixture which was a kind of liquid T.N.T. After carefully filling up the car with my explosive fuel I went to Montlhéry without giving anyone my name, determined to make the car spit fire.

I almost killed myself on the first lap, for I was literally thrown off the seat by a sudden jerking movement in the rear axle, caused by a displacement of the gearbox. And to finish the story I went into the ditch while taking a very easy corner, for the gear-lever came off in my hand.

My last Maserati was a magnificent 6-cylinder, twin overhead camshaft, 2-litre model, which had been given splendid tourer coachwork by Ghia. I wanted to pay a visit to one of my friends who used to speed up the hatching of his ducks by playing sonatas every two hours on an out-of-tune piano. I was not destined to be present at this interesting scientific discovery, for my left rear wheel came off and overtook me on the road.

After recounting these fascinating experiences let's see what happens at Modena, where these highly individual cars are made. These opening remarks are not meant to give the impression that the Maserati brothers, assisted by those eminent technicians Alfieri

and Bertocchi, pass most of their time in carrying out amusing practical jokes.

Let's go back first of all to the A6 GC5, which had a 6-cylinder engine, a single overhead camshaft and chain drive. The chassis was tubular, there was fully independent suspension with helical springs, transversal springs and, on the rigid rear axle, with semi-elliptic springs controlled by suspended arms. This was the car which gave Alberto Ascari the opportunity of winning the first victory of his racing career. This fact is worth remembering.

Then came the one-seater A6 GCM, designed to go with a single overhead camshaft engine, but it developed quickly and became a twin overhead-camshaft engine with bore and stroke of 78×81 mm. and capacity of 1,978 c.c. developing 130 h.p. at 6,000 r.p.m., the compression ratio being 11.5 to 1.

The engine was re-designed with a bore and stroke of 75×75 mm., leading to a capacity of 1,938 c.c. with a piston surface area of 265 square centimetres. It was equipped with three twin Weber carburettors and the compression was raised to 13.75 to 1, making it necessary to use a special fuel consisting of methyl alcohol, benzol and acetone. This 2-litre car developed 180 h.p. at 7,300 r.p.m.

This was the car driven by Gonzales during his outstanding performance at the Monza Grand Prix in 1952, while Bonetto, driving the same car, also regularly exceeded the speed made by Ascari in his Ferrari, although the latter finally won the race (at 109.8 m.p.h.) thanks to the sober reliability of his 2-litre model.

Near the end of 1952 Giovachino Colombo again transformed the engine completely, giving it a bore and stroke of 76.2×72 mm. and making the surface area of the pistons 273.5 square centimetres. Although the compression ratio was reduced to 12 to 1 this did not prevent the h.p. rating from being 200 h.p. at 8,000 r.p.m., thanks to a new fuel consisting of a complex mixture of benzol, alcohol, acetone, paraffin and water. The brakes were modified and were made of light alloy wound with steel and fitted with radial vanes which acted as a centrifugal ventilator.

This car proved difficult to drive. Fangio ran off the track while driving this model at more than 130 m.p.h. during the Italian Grand Prix test runs. 1954 saw the appearance of the new 2-litre 500 model

Preceding pages: Maserati V8 small saloon, 5,000 c.c., with fuel injection. Right: Maserati saloon, 3,500 c.c., 8-cylinder model, 1961, coach-work by Touring.

consisting of a 6-cylinder twin overhead-camshaft engine with bore and stroke of 84×72 mm., still based on the Formula II A6 GCM. It was equipped with a De Dion rear axle and a 4-speed gearbox mounted transversely on the chassis behind the differential. The suspension and the front wheel drive as well as the brakes were borrowed from the F II model. The cylinder-head underwent changes after the Pau Grand Prix, using larger valves which allowed an increase of power to 260 h.p. at 8,000 r.p.m. In spite of the wheelbase measuring over 7 feet the car weighed only 1,386 pounds unloaded, which ensured them a speed equal to that of the Ferraris, but a short career at each Grand Prix, unless they were prepared with extreme care. The amazing duel between Hawthorn (Ferrari) and Fangio (Maserati) at the French Grand Prix of 1954 was an unforgettable exception.

It should be recalled that as far back as 1954 a 6-cylinder injector-feed model was tried out at Modena without being entered for the Grand Prix. This was an experimental engine, entirely works-built, and it included many ingenious discoveries.

1955 saw the appearance of the celebrated 150/6/1500 which Jean Behra was to make famous at the Nürburgring. This was a 4-cylinder twin overhead-camshaft model with bore and stroke of 72×81 mm. and a total cylinder capacity of 1,484 c.c.; it developed 130 h.p. at 7,500 r.p.m. Jean Behra's victory brought many buyers for this little sports car, which was never to repeat its resounding triumph at the "Ring". The 6-cylinder 300S sports model appeared in 1956. Among other successes this 3-litre model won the 1000 kilometre race at Nürburgring with a team consisting of Behra, Moss, Taruffi and Schell. At the Mille Miglia a new 6-cylinder 3,500 c.c. appeared for the first time, as well as the extraordinary quadruple overhead-camshaft V-8 4,500 c.c. model which was to make news as the 450S.

Apart from the experimental V-12 model which was launched in the 1,000 kilometre race at the Nürburgring in 1957 the same sporting season was marked by the extraordinary high-powered model 450S. The V-8 cylinder engine had a capacity of 4,477 c.c. with bore and stroke of 93.8×81 mm. and a compression ratio of 9.6 to 1 developing 425 h.p. at 7,200 r.p.m.

Its inlet valves had a diameter of 50 mm. and the outlet valves one of 43 mm. They were set at angles of 33 and 35 degrees to the exhausts, and their return springs, which were treated to withstand a pressure of 187 pounds, were of the hairpin type, while the intermediate rocker arms were mounted on ball-bearing rollers. The tubular-type chassis had front suspension by double wishbone and coil springs while rear suspension was de Dion, radius rods and transverse leaf springs. The wheelbase measured about 7 feet 6 inches on a forward track of 4 feet 2 inches and rear track of about 4 feet. The total length was about 14 feet, the width 5 feet 3½ inches and the height to the top of the windscreen was just over 3 feet. This was a remarkable car and had a total weight (unloaded) of 1,836 pounds.

A book would be needed to recount all its details, its wonderful double train of gears allowing two ranges of five speeds and so on. The magnificently constructed brake-drums had the same diameter as the wheel-rim interior but it was found in the end that they were unreliable and that they made driving difficult.

The most handsome of these cars is definitely the 450S Zagato Coupé, based on a streamlined design by the English designer F. Costin. This dazzling model put up a mediocre performance at Le Mans in 1957. Apart from the weakness of its transmission the temperature in the cockpit was as hot as a furnace. This was a pity, but the 5000 Gran Turismo model of the present day is its decidedly worthy descendant.

It would be unfair to end the description of this productive season without mentioning the appearance of the Maserati V-12 F I which developed 310 h.p. at the fantastic figure of 9,700 r.p.m. The engine had a bore and stroke of 68.5×56 mm. and was driven by a quadruple overhead camshaft engine with its two groups of 6-cylinders set an angle of 60 degrees to each other. No ignition device could be found for it and the engine was started by 24 sparking-plugs fed by a battery and 24 separate induction coils. The same experiment was also made on a 450S, using 16 coils. This splendid car was tried out at Monaco with no success and was found unsuitable for the race-track because of its low number of revolutions per minute and low horse-power. Each time it appeared the results were disappointingly poor.

This too was the era of the renowned 250F Maserati, probably the most famed of all post-war racing cars, and certainly held to be of the most refined and beautiful design.

The 250F was a direct descendant from the 1954 2-litre car and had altered very little in appearance since that date. But the 1957 car was lighter and easier to handle – and it was considerably faster.

In 1957 Fangio made a successful bid for the World Championship in a 250F. This victorious year marked the "official" withdrawal of the Maserati works team from Grand Prix racing, although they continued to supply works-prepared cars to private teams for several seasons.

During 1958 Maseratis made only sporadic appearances at international sporting events. However, the firm produced a shorter Formula I model for private owners. The engine was still 6-cylinder with double overhead-camshaft, but had a capacity of 2,473 c.c. and a bore and stroke of 80×81 mm. which, with a compression ratio of 11 to 1, developed 266 h.p. at 7,500 r.p.m. The five-speed gearbox was mounted transversally at the rear.

We had to wait for the 1960 season to see the Maserati again—in sports car form—more original than ever and fitted with an incomparable number of technical devices.

The 61 type had a 4-cylinder engine with bore and stroke of 100×92 mm. mounted at an angle of 45 degrees and developing 250 h.p., with a capacity of 2,890 c.c.

This model was christened "Bird-cage" or "Spaghetti" because of the wire-like appearance of its body. It won the 1,000 kilometre race at the Nürburgring in a dashing manner.

The individual nature of this car constituted a landmark in the history of motor-racing and the development of technique. Its *avant-garde* characteristics, together with its unusual appearance, the windscreen broadening out towards the engine, the huge lateral ventilators, the high, truncated rear and the projecting coachwork of the wings – all contributed to make it attractive and unforgettable.

But Maserati production is not limited only to fast "track" cars intended to give spectators a thrill. Today's 3.5-litre model, for instance, was inspired by competition and the experience that had been gained on the circuit, and it is the living example of enlightened commercial development and discipline.

Right: Tubular-chassised Chevrolet Corvette SS appeared briefly at Sebring in 1957, before American manufacturers shied away from racing. Its chassis frame was not unlike that of the 300 SL Mercedes-Benz. It had a de Dion rear suspension and inboard rear brakes, plus a Halibrand quick-change differential. Its aluminium-headed, fuel-injected engine developed 310 b.h.p. from a 0:1 compression ratio. At Sebring it was troubled by overheating due to difficulties with its remote-mounted radiator header tank, which turned out to have been improperly constructed.

RACING IN THE UNITED STATES: THE "SHOW"

Every 30th May, the cops, baking in the Indiana sunshine, driven to a frenzy by the shouting, whistling and motor-cycle exhaust, sort out the flood of Cadillacs, Chevrolets, de Sotos, Tybirds, Jaguars, Aston-Martins and Ferraris, on their way to the brick speedway of Indianapolis.

The local drugstores are crowded out and already short of Coca-Cola and hot-dogs, in spite of last year's bitter experience. The staff are exhausted and don't know which way to turn. The petrol-pumps are pouring out Shell, Esso, Texaco, and Amoco, practically non-stop. The hotels are turning people away, attics are being let at the price of two rooms, while two rooms cost as much as a month in a villa at Palm Beach. In the midst of the noise and bustle, you can hear the staccato sounds of sports car engines, the Kurtiss, Offenhauser, Drake, Estes, Zuck, and every kind of "special" car with units ranging from fortissimo to pianissimo.

The air becomes thick with the oxide, dust and electricity which emanates from 250,000 people, for tomorrow is the traditional Indianapolis 500 miles race.

Beneath the blazing sun, cars fitted with vacuum cleaners remove the last scraps of dust from the sacred surface of the track, completing the work of the vans with their hoses and sweepers. Mingling with the shrill whistle-blasts can be heard improvised trumpet fanfares and wild snatches of jazz. Plump drum-majorettes, wearing short skirts that show most of their thighs, perform dazzling feats of martial gymnastics, while sticks festooned with ribbons are tossed up in the air and the sky is gay with multicoloured balloons. Hundreds of loud-speakers pour out floods of figures, records and forecasts. On the stands hundreds of "books" are furtively but effectively made, despite the vigilance of the police with their brilliant metal badges.

Left: The team of three Cunningham C2-type cars which participated in Le Mans, 1951. The engines were Chryslers V8, 5,424 c.c., modified by Briggs Cunningham. Above: An Indianapolis racing car during the 1962 competition at the Indianapolis circuit.

On the track, the mechanics in their brightly coloured fireproof overalls, are busy with the electric starters, while the lights down the track flash like sinister giant eyes.

The drivers sit in their cars chewing gum or cigars, while crowds of officials mill round them, yelling and gesticulating.

The racket reaches a climax, the very ground rumbles, windows are rattled loose, spectators are deafened, and still the crowd pours in in its thousands.

The cars go by in parade, following the drop-head coupé carrying the officials — this is later awarded to the winner — and the vast crowd roars, so loudly that it can be heard far away in the valley, as the drivers, at the mercy of their 600 h.p. cars, venture out to do battle.

Moments later the cars slip into second gear (they only have two) and speed up to 150 m.p.h., then up to 175 m.p.h. They hurtle round the inside of the bends, while centrifugal force sends them careering over at high speed towards the cement wall on the outside of the track.

The excitement in the stands is at fever-pitch. Trained observers follow the cars through powerful fieldglasses to check on abnormal wear to the tyres and to request stops. Whenever a car screams to a standstill it is raised from the ground by hydraulic jacks and in a matter of seconds the four wheels are unscrewed with bronze spanners and replaced by new ones with gold lettering on the tyres.

"Perchmen" sitting on high stands hold out sticks carrying anything the drivers may need – Coca-Cola or a wet sponge – while the car is rapidly filled up with petrol and oil, and fire-extinguishers held at the ready.

In the distance a fantastic cloud of dust forms as a car takes a corner too quickly and turns over and over in a series of terrifying somersaults; wheels are torn off, get in the way of other cars and cause terrible collisions. The impact sends the cars spinning lethally across the track. Fire breaks out with blinding suddenness. Ambulances and fire-engines rush over the "green" at fantastic speed with all their sirens wailing, while the signal-lights indicate that drivers must limit their top speeds to 100 m.p.h. or be disqualified.

As soon as the track is cleared the race goes on at a more frantic speed than ever until Jimmy Briand crosses the finishing-line. The race-track director rushes up to him in a frenzy of excitement, and he is momentarily lost from sight in the folds of the chequered flag.

The crowd greets him with thunderous applause; the flash-light bulbs click, and hundreds of glassy-eyed cameras record the long kiss bestowed on him by a glamorous, bosomy girl. He looks dazed, his eyes are wild and his limbs still trembling as he lifts aloft the huge cup, covered with inscriptions and portraits of previous winners. He will receive 80,000 dollars and for a whole year he will enjoy free food, drink, cigarettes and shoes. His brand-new bungalow will burst to the seams with gifts ranging from furniture, lawn-mowers, mixers and television sets to stocks of chewing-gum and insecticides.

In his huge, luxury lumber-room he will dream of the 500 miles race in the years to come.

The 500 miles race is not the only event of its kind in the United States. Thanks to the initiative of foreign car importers, and under the leadership of Alex Ulmann, the "12 Hours of Sebring" has been set up as a test counting towards the World Car Manufacturers' Championship. Unfortunately, the location and temporary nature of the track mean that this essentially continental-type race attracts only a limited number of spectators. The same is true of the Riverside Grand Prix.

The special world of the "hot rods" deserves a mention. These extraordinary machines have very narrow chassis with motor-cycle wheels in front and groups of two or four engines at the sides. They include a riot of novelties varying from the unusual to the utterly fantastic.

You need a fortune to build these machines, for everything about them is taken to extremes and their performances are spectacular. It isn't easy to make a 400-metre flying start and reach a speed of about 186 m.p.h. in a few seconds.

Motor racing in the United States is still in its early stages, but the popularity of the sport continues to grow every year.

A typical example of what the "hot rods" of the Fifties have become. One or more V8 engines with detachable cylinder-heads have since replaced the classic Ford or Mercury engines with lateral valves.

THE
FUTURE

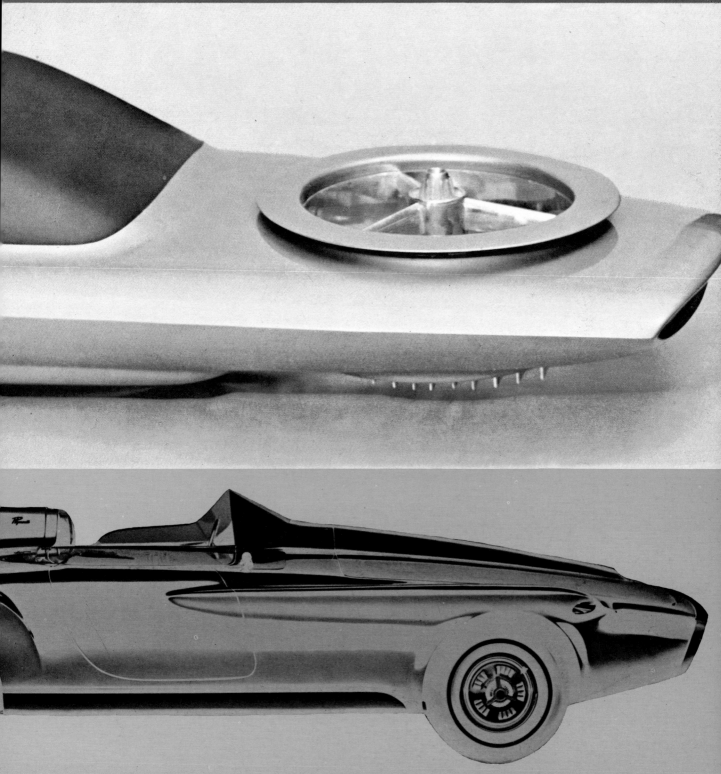

The Rover Company's four gas turbine cars demonstrate their speed at Silverstone, 1963.

Ask a Detroit automobile executive about the kind of car his company might build in the next two years, or even five years, and his mouth clamps tightly shut, perspiration appears on his brow, he takes a furtive look over his shoulder.

For, although every manufacturer's new model looks like the spitting image of every other manufacturer's new model, the bigwigs of Detroit are always darkly reticent about their plans for the future. The near future, that is. They'll talk readily and happily about the cars of twenty years hence.

The big companies all spend great wads of money on the huge, beautifully designed research laboratories in which they are designing the distant future's passenger-carrying vehicles. You'll notice we didn't say cars, because the scientists thinking up these machines seem to be trying to make them as un-car-like as possible.

One outfit is trying to eliminate wheels, others are ready to abandon the piston-powered petrol engine. Still another laboratory wants to eliminate the road. Most laudable of all, perhaps, is one company's efforts to get rid of the driver, or at least take the steering wheel away from him.

Before examining Detroit's chromium-encrusted crystal ball, however, let's try to foretell the characteristics of the car of just a few years hence.

The passenger car of tomorrow will almost certainly borrow heavily from the sports car of today. The channel-framed chassis is almost done for right now. The unitised-body chassis has taken its place,

at least in the cheaper cars. For the more expensive machine, the tubular space frame covered with an aluminium skin is almost certainly in the offing.

Since the early Twenties, aluminium engines have been common in Europe. Hispano-Suiza and A.C., for example, had aluminium blocks with ferrous cylinder liners some forty years ago. Recently, Buick and Oldsmobile, and even staid Rolls-Royce, have gone over to light alloy engines. Within a very few years the cast-iron engine will be as rare as the horsecollar.

The disc brake will become universal in a very few years, even on the cheapest Detroit car.

Will the engine stay up in front in most cars? Yes, but there will be an increase in the number of rear-engined designs, as engines grow lighter in relation to the power they produce. Owing to the use of aluminium alloys it will become more practical to use more powerful engines in the rear without making cars unmanageably tail-heavy.

Transmissions, both automatic and manual, will also move towards the back, and what Detroit calls a "trans-axle" (gearbox and differential in one unit) will be commonplace. Nor is this anything new. Stutz, Packard, and A.C. used rear axles incorporating gearboxes generations ago; Lancia and the Pontiac Tempest use such an arrangement today.

Inspired by the spectacular success of the tiny rear-powered British Formula I machines, like the Cooper and the Lotus, Ferrari and Maserati have built racing sports cars with rear engines in tubu-

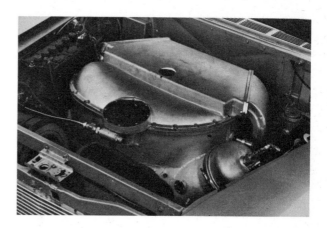

Preceding pages: Cars in Detroit's crystal ball are General Motors' turbine-driven Firebird III, Ford's "Volante" – an inoperable model of a fan-flown "Aero-car" – and Plymouth's conception of a sports car – the XNR. Chrysler's gas-turbine engine (below) has been successfully tested in a Plymouth. The Rover-B.R.M. gas turbine car created great interest at Le Mans in 1963 and 1965 when it was one of the few cars to complete the 24 hour event.

lar space frames. Sports two-seaters with similar chassis-engine arrangements, but with a bit of weather protection and a modicum of luggage space are almost a certainty in the near future.

But what about the distant future? What about gas turbines, for example?

Ever since the last war and the development of the jet engine, fantastic amounts of money have been poured into experimentation with the jet engine's near relative, the gas turbine, not only by Detroit's big three, but also by Rover, Renault and Fiat.

You can't blame them, for the gas turbine has many advantages:

1. It is light and small for the power it produces. Chrysler's latest turbine weighs a mere 450 pounds (a conventional V-8 weighs about 800) and delivers 140 h.p. to the drive shaft, giving a performance comparable to a 200 b.h.p. piston engine. Yet it measures only $27 \times 27 \times 25$ inches.

2. It is much simpler, having about a fifth as many moving parts as a piston engine.

3. It needs no radiator or liquid cooling system.

4. Its electrical system is simpler. No ignition system is needed, apart from one sparking-plug for starting.

5. A turbine is vibration free.

6. It starts better in winter and needs no warm-up.

7. A turbine will run on almost anything from whisky to whale oil.

The gas-turbine car for Everyman is almost, but not quite, here. The problems of early turbines—high

307

Fuel cells installed in Allis-Chalmers tractor (top) provide enough electricity to power 20 h.p., D.C. electric motor, which develops 3,000 pounds of drawbar pull. The German NSU-Wankel engine (above) is believed, in some quarters, to be the next step in automotive power. Unlike either piston engines or gas turbines, the combustion cycle takes place in constantly moving, banana-shaped chambers which grow larger and smaller as an eccentrically mounted, "trochoid" rotor revolves in its casing. Water is pumped through concentric outer casing for cooling purposes. The engine runs with turbine-like smoothness due to absence of reciprocating parts. An experimental engine weighing 35 pounds, developed 40 b.h.p. at 8,000 r.p.m. and was said to be capable of 15,000 r.p.m. with a considerable increase in power. Experiments mounting four engines on a single shaft are in progress. Curtiss-Wright holds American manufacturing licence. Right: Experimental Fiat with turbine; the layout is based on that of the V-8 small sports saloon: the special design was the work of the engineer Rapi. A rear turbine of 200 h.p. turning at 30/60,000 r.p.m. allowed the car to reach a hypothetical speed of 161 m.p.h. The car had its first demonstration on April 23rd 1954.

fuel consumption, especially at low speeds and part loads, lack of engine braking capacity, and slow speed response to pressure on the accelerator—have just about been mastered. In mass production a turbine can eventually be built more cheaply than a reciprocating engine of equal power.

As far back as 1956 a turbine-engined Chrysler made a successful 3,020-mile trip across the Continent. In 1959, a Plymouth Saloon averaged 19.39 miles per gallon at an average speed of 38.3 m.p.h. for 576 miles. In 1956, George J. Huebner, Jr., executive engineer in charge of Chrysler research, predicted that the turbo-car would be a reality in ten years' time.

Why then the delay? As Mr. Huebner pointed out to me recently, the turbine isn't just a new kind of engine to be slapped under the hood of next year's Plymouth as it moves down the assembly line. It is an entirely new kind of power, as different from the reciprocating petrol engine as the gas engine was from the slow-turning steam engine sixty years ago. It will eventually require an entirely new concept of automotive design, new methods of production, a retraining of workers and service personnel, even a new technique of driving.

Nor are the big manufacturers about to jettison the billions they have invested in plants for producing the perfectly usable—and continually improving— piston-engined cars of today.

The electric car, because of its silence and simplicity, always has fascinated automotive dreamers. But, as we have seen, the electric of the past was far too slow and much too limited in range. "If only someone would invent an ultra-light, powerful, quickly rechargeable battery," they say. No one has, and it doesn't look as if anyone will in the near future. But an electrically driven car, powered by an entirely different kind of battery, may be coming.

This battery is the fuel cell. Unlike the storage battery, it is not merely a crude reservoir for the electricity with which it is supplied, but actually *produces* current. A fuel cell utilises the phenomenon whereby oxygen and hydrogen form water when combining. In the fuel cell these two gases are fed through metal tubes into a caustic solution. As they combine, they make not just H_2O, but also a small, one-and-a-half volt electric current. The cells can be tiny—an experimental Allis Chalmers tractor recently had its hood stuffed with no less than 1,008 of them; about 1,500 volts worth—but they delivered enough power for the tractor to plough up a golf course in a demonstration.

The cells can deliver their current directly to a small electric motor at each wheel hub, eliminating in one fell swoop drive shafts, transmissions, clutches — even the kind of brakes we have been used to, since the motors can be instantly reversible.

Thus far, however, most fuel cells have been used in space projects for powering the gadgetry in satellites and such. So you'll have to wait.

You'd think that the people who put America on wheels with the Model T Ford would have some special respect for wheels. Far from it, Ford for some years now has been doing its best to figure out a means of doing in the poor old wheel. Ford calls its wheelless wonder a Levacar: levitation car. It is quite unlike vehicles supported by reaction to air jets, such as the British Hovercraft and its American counterparts built by Curtiss-Wright. Those are, I hope, flying machines. This book is, I think, about cars.

Instead of wheels, the Levacar is supported on discs several feet in diameter and flush with the flat bottom of the vehicle. These discs, called Levapods, are perforated with holes through which compressed air is forced downward. This raises them very slightly above the road surface on a thin cushion of air. It is this frictionless cushion, only a small fraction of an inch deep, upon which the Levacar rides.

The Levapods do not propel the car. They only provide the air cushion. The car itself can be propelled horizontally by means of ducted fans, jets, propellers. The Ford people talk about 300 to 500 m.p.h. speeds. The power required to make the compressed air is very slight and can be produced by a small auxiliary to the main horizontal power source.

To demonstrate the amazing lack of friction when riding on a thin cushion of air, the Ford researchers built a lovely little device called the Levascooter, which looks like a kid's scooter without wheels. It makes just enough air to raise itself a few thousandths of an inch off the floor. Its forward movement is provided by your strong right leg—if you can get on the blasted thing. For it slides around the floor as if it were on ice. A pavement outdoors would be too rough for the scooter, just as present-day highways would be too rough for a car-sized Levacar. Therefore, the current idea at Ford is to run bus-sized Levacars on smooth, monorail tracks, embraced top and sides by frictionless Levapods. But, again, these are railways, not motor cars.

For some time now, General Motors has inclined towards the belief that you should not be trusted with a steering wheel in your hands. You may remember that during the past few years they have turned out various turbine-powered, super-dream-cars that actually could run. These are the Firebirds I, II, and III. The steering-wheel thing started with a publicity film on Firebird II, which showed an advertising man's dream of the all-American family, all shiny teeth and ruddy good looks, setting off on a trip. All of a sudden Pop folds up the steering handles (it wasn't a wheel, even far back in 1956) and turns on

a radio transmitter. In clipped tones, he tells a man in a tower something about going into "auto-control", meaning that this special Buick, or whatever it was, would from then on head for Cincinnati, or wherever, with nobody steering. The car would get there by following an electric wire sunk in the road. After a few "Rogers" and "Overs", Pop relaxes with a drink and the car sets off into the sunset and eternal happiness.

Although I believed it implicitly at the time, Firebird II couldn't *really* follow its nose along an electric cable buried in the road. But a couple of engineers at G.M.—Joe Bidwell and Roy Cataldo—thought they could actually make this no-hands pipe-dream work. By 1958 they had a car with two electronic probes under the front licence plate sniffing its way along a magnetic cable buried in a piece of highway. The probes sent signals back to an electronic analog computer in the glove compartment. The computer then translated the signals and "commanded" the power-steering system to turn right or left.

Since then, G.M. has refined this system. Bidwell and Cataldo's first machine could only steer. It couldn't put on the brakes if the car got close to an obstacle ahead. Nor could it gradually reduce engine speed as it approached a car travelling in the same lane. Now, by means of a multiple wire cable buried in the road, a block system like a railway's, and a small control-box in the trunk, G.M.'s "Auto-Control" system can do all of these things. They haven't built a full-sized road like this yet, as far as I know, but I have seen a scale model work. Perfectly horrifying.

G.M. has another device that still lets you control your car, but it's not a steering wheel. This thing looks like the short and stubby gear lever surmounted by a ball that is beloved by pukka sports-car drivers. After you start the engine and set the transmission in "drive", you control the car entirely by manipulating this ball-on-a-stick. Push it ahead and the car accelerates in a straight line forward. Pull it back and the engine slows down while the brakes go on. Move it to the left and the car turns left. Move it right and you turn right. (I forget how you reverse). The limits of movement are short; about two inches. Oddly, you still have the "feel" of steering and braking; it's easy to get used to. This "unicontrol" stick has no mechanical connection to the engine, brakes, or steering. Its movements control rheostats which signal computers which, in turn, signal the various hydraulic mechanisms doing the work. Control is steady, regardless of your speed. A quick movement of the stick at high speed won't send you into a wild skid.

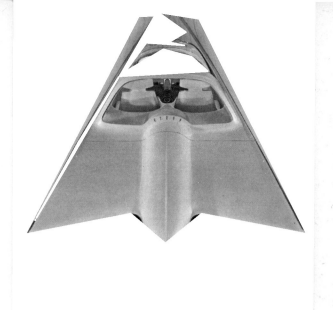

One of the engineers at the technical centre told me about a Chevrolet saloon they had fitted with "unicontrol". He drove it into a service station to fill the tank. The attendant was fascinated. He looked the car over thoroughly, ooh-ing and ah-ing, because it was a brand-new model not yet in the showrooms. He never even noticed that it had no steering wheel.

But don't tear your steering wheel and column out by the roots. Not yet. G.M. has no intention of building cars without steering wheels for quite a while. Maybe never.

A friend of mine, a low, beatnik-type fellow, who, I suspect, hates cars, told me the other day of a fine new method of automatic propulsion he had thought up. "As you know," he said, "we are, all of us, just an agglomeration of magnetic particles that make up the atoms which compose us."

Knowing nothing of the nuclear sciences, I agreed.

"Since we're all just a lot of magnetic impulses," he went on "why couldn't you just break a fellow down into his electronic components and put him on tape? Then all you have to do is send the stuff on the tape, by radio, to wherever the guy wants to go. There they reconstitute him. Or if he isn't in a hurry, you could even post the tape."

"That's a *really* compact idea," I said, "I'll take it right over to American Motors."

Non operative, two-wheeled Ford "Gyron" (top) is a typical example of styling department doodling. General Motors Unicontrol (above), fitted to experimental, turbine-engined Firebird III, eliminates the steering wheel, the brake pedal, and the accelerator. Moved forward, it speeds up the car in a straight line; backward, it throttles the engine and applies the brakes. Moved at an angle, it steers the car. Control actuates electrical devices that signal hydraulic mechanisms which steer and brake the car. Left: Prototype Pinin Farina (1966), showing research into style and mechanism. This aerodynamic coupé, built around an Alfa Romeo 1600, will probably never be sold to the public, although its function will have been fulfilled if its line and novelty is carried over into a future production model.

Let's take another look at our crystal ball. Isn't it inevitable that sooner or later cars will use atomic energy?

The turbines of certain ships and submarines are already propelled by nuclear power, and when they take on a "full load" they can go several times round the world without refuelling.

Obviously the volume and weight of such a source of energy still take up a great deal of room and for the time being atomic power has been a practical proposition only for sea transport. During the last few years, however, serious consideration has been given in both the U.S.A. and Russia to using atomic power for aircraft.

The trouble with atomic piles is not only their size and weight but also the danger of radiation, especially when accidents occur. These are unfortunately only too frequent. But none of these problems is insoluble. In fact atomic piles weighing only a few pounds have already been built in the U.S. and they can generate an electric current for several years,

although admittedly the current is still fairly weak. These piles, known as "SNAP", supply several man-made satellites with power, while others, which are larger, produce heat and electricity to isolated stations in the Antarctic.

Were these atomic piles to be used in cars they would have to be covered with a layer of a substance which would prevent radiation and protect them against shock. Neither their weight nor their size would be excessive, though the cost of their construction might be.

In time, it may be centuries or only decades, these devices will become necessary, for world supplies of petroleum are not inexhaustible. Sooner or later man will have harnessed atomic energy to provide his peaceful day-to-day needs, including transport.

The American physicist R.M. Langer has forecast that the motor car of tomorrow will be driven by a steam-turbine engine powered by a strip of radioactive uranium U 235 no bigger than a pencil. This source of energy will remain active much longer than

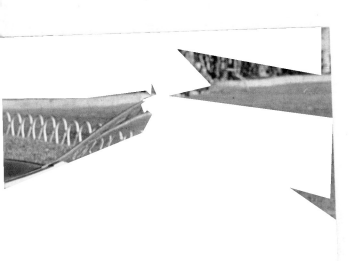

Above: Research prototype for line and comfort, worked out by Pinin Farina on the Fiat 600. Tests showed interesting fuel economies (1961-62). Left: Project of American "dragster" streamline design worked out by Ghia (1961).

the car itself and can therefore be reinstalled in new models as and when necessary.

Nothing could be simpler than the engine itself: steam under pressure, heated by the uranium, will drive turbines fixed on the same rotating axis. Speed, therefore, will depend entirely on the amount and pressure of the steam, and the accelerator will open a valve controlling the amount of water made available for turning into steam.

The motor car of the 21st century will not necessarily have to carry its small atomic pile with it, but may possibly use atomic energy which it will have to take in from time to time at atomic service stations. You might say that this is science-fiction. But the Wright brothers would have said the same about the jet engines of today, and Marconi might also have said it of the pocket transistor radio.

We finished with the history of cars proper a few pages ago. Since we've already been wondering whether the cars of tomorrow will have wheels, steering-wheels or pistons, we may speculate as to whether there will be cars or whether there will also be...

But we must stop here and patiently await the course of events. Our great grandchildren will take it all in their stride.

315

PICTURE ACKNOWLEDGEMENTS

ACTION AUTOMOBILE TOURISTIQUE: 192-193.

ALBERT MECHAM COLLECTION OF THE LONG ISLAND AUTOMOTIVE MUSEUM: 46-47, 70 (lower).

ALBERT SQUILLACE: end-paper, page 3, 217 (second and third rows).

ALLIS-CHALMERS MFG. CO.: 308 (upper).

ALPINE: 244 (centre right).

A. MAGGIO: 184 (upper).

ANTIQUE AUTOMOBILE: 100 (upper), 101 (lower).

ASTON MARTIN LAGONDA LTD: 218.

AUSTIN: 247.

AUTOSPORT: 230, 235 (upper and lower), 236 (lower).

AUTO-UNION: 186 (lower).

BERNARD JOURDES: 124-125, 127, 158-159, 172-173, 203 (lower). 238-239, 242, 244 (lower and centre left), 252, 253, 254, 282-283,

B.M.C. CROWLEY: 207 (centre and lower), 246.

BRITISH CROWN COPYRIGHT, SCIENCE MUSEUM, LONDON: 19 (lower).

BRITISH FORD: 246 (lower).

BRITISH PETROLEUM CO.: 272 (upper), 287 (lower).

BRITISH TRAVEL ASSOCIATION: 111 (lower), 197 (upper) 208 (lower left), 237.

BROWN BROTHERS: 90.

CAMERASCOPE: 295 (lower).

CAR AND DRIVER: 205 (lower), 294.

CHARLES DOLLFUS: 14-15, 17 (upper right, centre left, lower right), 18, 20 (upper left), 22, 23 (lower right), 28-29 (right), 34 (lower), 36 (lower right), 43 (lower right), 78, 87 (three pictures lower right), 108, 109 (lower).

CHEVROLET-CORVETTE: 263.

CHRYSLER CORPORATION: 304 (lower left), 304-305 (lower right), 307 (upper), 311 (lower).

CITROEN: 241.

DAF: 260 (lower).

DAIMLER-BENZ: 32-33, 33 (lower right), 94, 126.

EMILIO RONCHINI: 27 (upper right), 57, 67 (lower), 146-147, 154 (lower), 165 (lower), 256-257, 265, 286-287, 296-297, 299 (upper), 309, 313.

FACEL-VEGA: 243.

FIAT PHOTO: 174, 220 (lower left).

FORD MOTOR CO.: 190, 246, 266-267, 268, 304-305 (centre).

FRANCIS MORTARINI: 135 (lower), 175.

FUMAGALLI, MILAN: 187 (lower).

GENERAL MOTORS CORPORATION: 301, 304-305 (upper), 311 (upper).

GIORGIO BELLIA: 225.

GHIA: 312-313 (lower).

GUNTHER MOLTER: 308 (lower).

HENRY FORD MUSEUM: 102.

HOFFMAN MOTORS COPORATION: 220 (centre).

HONDA MOTOR CORPORATION: 261.

HUTIN: 24 (upper).

INDIANAPOLIS MOTOR SPEEDWAY CORPORATION: 178-179 (upper), 302.

IRVING DOLIN: 136, 223 (centre).

JACQUES ROUSSEAU: 31, 35 (lower), 38 (upper), 49, 52, 56, 69 (lower), 70 (upper), 74 (upper), 91, 95, 101 (upper), 107, 122, 135 (centre), 142, 156-157, 163, 167 (lower), 170, 179 (lower), 181 (lower), 182, 186 (upper), 189 (upper), 196, 200, 204, 205 (upper left), 209, 244 (upper), 302.

JAGUAR CARS LTD: 198-199 (lower), 245, 249 (lower), 288-289, 290.

KIRKPATRICK COLLECTION OF THE LONG ISLAND AUTOMOTIVE MUSEUM: 183 (lower).

LONG ISLAND AUTOMOTIVE MUSEUM: 37 (lower), 40-41, 48 (lower), 55, 58 (upper and lower), 65 (upper right), 68-69 (upper), 68 (lower left), 74-75 (lower), 100, 134-135 (upper), 208 (upper), 210 (centre), 212 (upper), 227 (centre), 228 (upper and lower), 231.

LOUIS KLEMENTASKI: 205 (upper right), 206 (lower), 210 (upper).
LUIGI GHINETTI MOTORS, INC.: 199 (upper).
MARCUS W. TAYLOR: 215 (upper).
MAURICE PERIMOND: 62, 66-67 (upper), 104-105, 111 (upper), 112-113, 137, 144-145, 161, 162 (upper), 165 (upper), 181 (centre), 185, 198 (upper), 232, 233 (lower), 236 (upper), 241, 260 (upper), 264, 269, 278 (upper and centre), 279 (upper left and lower).
MENCH PUBLISHING CO., RIDGEFIELD, CONN.: 202 (lower).
MERCEDES-BENZ: 130, 250 (upper).
MICHEL DUPLAIX: 138-139, 162 (lower), 167 (lower), 211 (centre), 278 (lower), 279 (two pictures upper right).
M. L. ROSENTHAL: 280 (four pictures), 298.
MONDADORI: 280 (upper), 281.
MONTAGU MOTOR MUSEUM: 160.
MUSEE DE LA VOITURE ET DU TOURISME, COMPIEGNE: 76-77, 80-81.
MUSEO DELL'AUTOMOBILE CARLO BISCARETTI DI RUFFIA OF TURIN: 27, 57, 67 (lower), 146, 165 (lower), 173.
OPEL: 253 (centre).
OWEN ORGANISATION: 275 centre.
PANHARD ET LEVASSOR: 243.
PATRICK BENJAFIELD: 151 (lower).
PETER ROBERTS: 142 (lower), 190, 219, 223 (lower and upper), 233, 234, 235 (upper), 270-271, 273 (upper and lower), 274, 275 (centre, lower and upper), 277 (upper), 280 (upper right), 306, 307 (centre).
PEUGEOT: 241
PHOTO HOLMES LEBEL: 303.
PHOTOGRAPHIE DU CONSERVATOIRE NATIONAL DES ARTS ET METIERS: 17 (upper left), 25, 33 (lower right), 34 (lower right), 36 (lower left).
PININ FARINA: 310-311 (lower).
PORSCHE: 252, 276.
PORSCHE OF AMERICA: 213 (centre).
RADIO TIMES HULTON PICTURE LIBRARY: 17 (centre right), 20-21 (centre), 21, 23 (lower), 28 (left), 39, 42-43 (lower left), 53 (upper), 63, 64-65 (upper), 71, 79, 82 (upper), 87 (upper), 98-99.
RALLYE MOTORS, INC.: 217 (top row).
RALPH STEIN: 18-19, 30 (lower left), 35 (upper), 54 (lower right), 74 (upper), 187 (upper), 208-209 (centre), 208 (lower right), 211 (lower), 214 (upper), 227 (upper left and lower).
REGIE NATIONALE DES USINES RENAULT: 242 (upper), 307 (lower).
R. M. GROSSMAN, INC.: 215 (lower).
ROAD & TRACK: 118 (lower), 184 (upper), 188-189, 190 (upper left and centre), 191, 197 (lower), 201, 206-207, 210 (lower), 212, 212-213 (lower), 213 (upper and centre), 214 (lower), 216.
ROBERT S. GRIER: 123.
ROLLS-ROYCE: 115, 118 (upper), 119, 151 (upper), 248, 249 (upper).
ROOTES MOTORS: 220 (lower right).
SIMCA: 242 (lower).
SKODA: 258.
SMITHSONIAN INSTITUTION: 26, 27 (upper left), 30 (upper), 38 (lower), 43 (upper left and right), 53 (lower), 60, 110.
STANDARD-TRIUMPH MOTOR CO., INC.: 203 (upper).
STUDEBAKER: 269.
SUNDAY TIMES: Photographed by Graham Finlayson 310-311.
TAUNUS: 252 (upper).
TECHNISCHES MUSEUM FÜR INDUSTRIE UND GEWERBE: 30 (upper left).
TEMPLE PRESS: 280 (upper).
THE AUTOCAR, LONDON: 50 (lower), 64 (upper left), 72, 82 (centre and lower), 83, 86 (upper right), 96.
THE MOTOR: 162 (centre), 183 (upper), 206 (upper).
THOMAS H. BURNSIDE: cover and title page, endpaper page 2, 37 (upper), 44-45, 48 (upper), 50 (upper), 51, 54 (upper), 59, 73, 84-85, 88-89, 92-93, 109, 116-117, 120, 128-129, 132-133, 140-141, 148-149, 152-153, 168-169, 176-177, 180, 194-195, 217 (lower left), 220-221 (upper left), 221 (upper right and lower), 224-225, 232 (upper right), 284-285, 293, endpaper pages 322 and 323.
TONY BIRT (FOR HAMBRO AUTOMOTIVE CORP.): 202 (upper).
UNDERWOOD & UNDERWOOD: 106.
U.S.S.R.: 259.
VAUXHALL: 246 (upper).
VOLKSWAGEN: 250 (lower), 253 (lower).
VOLVO: 261 (lower).
WARREN S. WEIANT: 227 (upper right).

BIBLIOGRAPHY

A PICTURE HISTORY OF MOTORING L.T.C. Rolt, London, 1956.

A RECORD OF MOTOR RACING Gerald Rose, London, 1909.

ASTON MARTIN Compiled by Dudley Coram, London, 1958.

BUGATTI — A BIOGRAPHY W. F. Bradley, London, 1948.

CHRONIK DER MERCEDES-BENZ FAHRZEUGE UND MOTOREN Stuttgart-Bad Canstatt, 1956.

COMBUSTION ON WHEELS David L. Cohn, Boston, 1944.

DUESENBERG J. C. Elbert, Arcadia, California, 1951.

ELEMENTS D'AUTOMOBILE L. Baudry de Saunier, Paris, 1906.

FILL 'ER UP! Bellamy Partridge, New York, 1952.

FROM VETERAN TO VINTAGE Karslake and Pomeroy, London, 1956.

GRAND PRIX Barré Lyndon, 1935.

HISTOIRE DE LA LOCOMOTION TERRESTRE L'Illustration, Paris, 1936.

HORSELESS CARRIAGE DAYS Hiram Percy Maxim, New York, 1937.

LA LOCOMOTION Octave Uzanne, Paris, 1900.

LA VOITURE DE DEMAIN Jean Grand-Carteret, Paris, 1898.

LES 24 HEURES DU MANS Roger Labric, Le Mans, 1949.

MAINTAINING THE BREED J. W. Thornley, London, 1956.

MONTE CARLO RALLY Russell Lowry, London, undated.

MOTORS AND MOTOR RACING Badminton Library, London, 1902.

MOTOR VEHICLES AND MOTORS W. Worby Beaumont, London, 1902.

RACING HISTORY OF THE BENTLEY Darell Berthon, London, 1956.

RACING VOITURETTES Kent Karslake, London, 1950.

RALLYING TO MONTE CARLO Mike Cooper, London, 1956.

TECHNICAL FACTS OF THE VINTAGE BENTLEY Bentley Drivers Club, London, 1956.

TEN YEARS OF MOTORS AND MOTOR RACING Charles Jarrott, London, 1906.

THE ANTIQUE AUTOMOBILE St. John Nixon, London, 1956.

THE BENTLEYS AT LE MANS J. D. Benjafield, London, 1948.

THE BUGATTI BOOK Compiled by Eaglesfield and Hampton, 3rd edition, London, 1958.

THE COMPLETE MOTORIST A. B. Filson Young, London, 1906.

THE FERRARI Hans Tanner, Boston, 1960.

THE GRAND PRIX CAR Laurence Pomeroy, London, 1949.

THE MAGIC OF A NAME Harold Nockolds, London, 1949.

THE RACING CAR Clutton, Posthumus, Jenkinson, London, 1956.

"W. O." — THE AUTOBIOGRAPHY OF W. O. BENTLEY London, 1958.

AUTHOR CREDITS

The editors are indebted to the following authors for original contributions to this book:

M. Jacques Rousseau: **Minerva, Isotta-Fraschini, Daimler.**

M. Francis Mortarini: **The Era of the Great Classics, The New Golden Age of Racing, Fiat, Maserati, Racing in the United States.**

Mm. Rousseau and Mortarini: **Lancia.**

Mr Peter Roberts: **More Americans, Great Britain, General Motors, The Drivers.**

M. Francis Léopold: **France, Western Germany, Eastern Europe.**

Mm. Mortarini and Léopold: **Italy.**

M. Alexandre Dorozynski: **Chrysler, Studebaker.**